The Reach of a Chef

The Reach of a Chef

— BEYOND THE KITCHEN —

✾

Michael Ruhlman

VIKING

VIKING

Published by the Penguin Group

Penguin Group (USA) Inc., 375 Hudson Street, New York, New York 10014, U.S.A. • Penguin Group (Canada), 90 Eglinton Avenue East, Suite 700, Toronto, Ontario, Canada M4P 2Y3 (a division of Pearson Penguin Canada Inc.) • Penguin Books Ltd, 80 Strand, London WC2R 0RL, England • Penguin Ireland, 25 St. Stephen's Green, Dublin 2, Ireland (a division of Penguin Books Ltd) • Penguin Books Australia Ltd, 250 Camberwell Road, Camberwell, Victoria 3124, Australia (a division of Pearson Australia Group Pty Ltd) • Penguin Books India Pvt Ltd, 11 Community Centre, Panchsheel Park, New Delhi–110 017, India • Penguin Group (NZ), Cnr Airborne and Rosedale Roads, Albany, Auckland 1310, New Zealand (a division of Pearson New Zealand Ltd) • Penguin Books (South Africa) (Pty) Ltd, 24 Sturdee Avenue, Rosebank, Johannesburg 2196, South Africa

Penguin Books Ltd, Registered Offices: 80 Strand, London WC2R 0RL, England

First Published in 2006 by Viking Penguin, a member of Penguin Group (USA) Inc.

10 9 8 7 6 5 4 3 2 1

Copyright © Michael Ruhlman, 2006
All rights reserved

LIBRARY OF CONGRESS CATALOGING-IN-PUBLICATION DATA
Ruhlman, Michael, 1963–
    The reach of a chef : beyond the kitchen / Michael Ruhlman.
        p.   cm.
    ISBN 0-670-03763-X
    1.Cooks—United States—Biography.   I. Title.
    TX649.R8 A3 2006
    641.5092—dc22   2005057908

Printed in the United States of America
Designed by Carla Bolte • Set in Berkeley with Centaur

FOR DONNA, ADDISON, AND JAMES

who extend *my* reach in ways I could never have foreseen

CONTENTS

❧

Part One: The Chef Has Lost His Shoes

Part Two: CIA Revisited

Part Three: The American Chef

Part Four: The Power of the Branded Chef

Part Five: The Chefs at 10 Columbus Circle

PART ONE

※

The Chef Has Lost His Shoes

❦

CHAPTER I

"It's Not the French Laundry, Per Se . . ."

I entered the Per Se kitchen through the back door at seven P.M., more than an hour after service had begun on what ought to have been a normal Thursday night, to find chaos. Per Se is Thomas Keller's ultra-luxurious and fantastically expensive Manhattan restaurant, one of the country's temples of haute cuisine, a hushed world of urbane refinement and grace on the fourth floor of the Time Warner Center overlooking Columbus Circle. Normally during service it's like a watchmaker's shop. Tonight it's a circus.

It had been six years earlier that Keller sat on the back deck of my home in suburban Cleveland, beneath a towering black locust tree on a perfect July evening. He had then but a single restaurant, not four. He had no books, no lines of porcelain or silver, no signature-engraved knives for sale. He may have been, at that moment, cresting the apex of his professional career, the artist-monk of the French Laundry, financially successful, lionized in the press, admired by colleagues. His Napa Valley restaurant had one year earlier been called "the most exciting" restaurant in America by *The New York Times*. It became so popular that reservations were almost impossible to come by.

He'd gotten here by the relentless pursuit of perfection. He had always sought perfection, but he was careful to clarify for me on that summer evening that perfection is not an end, but rather a direction. "Perfection doesn't exist," he'd said, "because once you reach it, it's not perfect anymore. It means something else."

He was in a calm place mentally, relaxed, away from the day-to-day responsibilities of running and cooking for the French Laundry, summer birds and humming insects a backdrop for his thoughtful voice, words that would conclude his story in a book I titled *The Soul of a Chef*.

We had been talking about cooking and how a person takes a single, fundamental lesson from youth—say, from one's mom on how to clean a bathroom so that it shined—and translated that into everything one would do later in life. We spoke, that is, of how standards are created and of how Keller's standards had become him: that to extricate his standards from his personality would be to end him altogether, so that he would cease to be recognizable as Thomas Keller.

Keller had, since that suburban-pastoral moment of peace and reflection, brought those standards to bear on a bistro, elevating French classics to a four-star level. Then he opened another, this one in Vegas, the food Gomorrah of America. Working with his designers and the prominent porcelain manufacturer Raynaud and silversmith Christofle, he helped design and put his name to lines of fine dining products. If he was going to be a brand, he said, he wanted that brand to be like Hermès. His cookbooks were so lavish that they were sometimes criticized for being *too* fine (and too big) to actually use. Like everything Keller put his hand to, they seemed sprinkled with magic dust and sold in big numbers.

And here he was, in the fall of 2004, at the helm of his most ambitious project yet. He had returned to New York, the city from which he'd departed in defeat in 1991, and he intended to succeed big with Per Se. He was now one of the most famous chefs in the world, after all. He had the magic dust. His Manhattan shrine to haute cuisine would have a kitchen bigger than the dining room. The dining room would have a huge wood-burning hearth and a sweeping northeastern view of Central Park. It had cost a staggering amount of money for a restaurant, and some in the business thought he'd never be able to pay it back, given the profit margins of a four-star Manhattan restaurant—Keller *hoped* it would be four-star, that is. He couldn't abide just three stars. But that was not up to him, but rather to a *New York Times* reporter named Frank Bruni.

Wary of the press that had given six-star Michelin chef Alain Ducasse such a powerful thrashing for his perceived arrogance and his expensive menu, Keller wooed the media, going so far as to close down the French Laundry to demonstrate how absolutely committed he was to this new Manhattan restaurant.

In Manhattan on other chef business then, in November 2004, I decided to stop in at Per Se. It would be my last chance to see Keller before I sat down to write. *Could he be any higher?* I wondered. His entire oeuvre— he had an oeuvre now!—had drawn raves and financial success, as well as, tonight, a crew from *60 Minutes Wednesday.* I'd stopped by the restaurant to check out the scene, but I was surprised by the unusual energy the show's commotion had stirred in the place. I felt it the moment I entered. I moved through the back corridor past the bakery, past the small enclosed patisserie station, past the offices, and turned right to the corridor leading to the kitchens, now with tables squeezed in along the wall where people in street clothes were eating dinner. I had to slide sideways between their chair backs and reach-in coolers as I said hello to producer Steven Reiner, some crew members, and the correspondent Lara Logan, looking movie-star perfect even with food in her mouth. They were having family meal but receiving white-tablecloth service per Keller's instructions. I turned left past a glassware station and a stock/ prep room—the walls throughout are tiled white with blue tile trim; the kitchen has the mazelike feel of a fantastically clean Parisian Metro station—then past a kitchen that is huge not only by Manhattan standards but by the standards of American restaurants generally. It's not even the main kitchen, but rather the private-functions kitchen, where chef de cuisine Joshua Schwartz and his brigade were cranking out dinner for a big party in the private room through the doors opposite this kitchen.

I then reached the primary Per Se dining-room kitchen and the bizarre carnival of busyness and unfamiliar people—camera and sound crews miking a server at the pass, where all plates arrive and are finished before being floated away to the dining room. Per Se chef de cuisine Jonathan Benno had also been miked for the *60 Minutes Wednesday* Keller profile, in between calling out "Ordering four tastings, two by two. . . . Fire agnolotti. . . . Fire beef." Servers stepped over dangling cords to and from the pass. I turned to see Jeff Cerciello, executive chef of Bouchon, Keller's Yountville bistro, in a dark gray sweater, a black traveling bag over his shoulder, looking a little disoriented himself, head fogged with a cold. Because of the strangeness of the commotion, I didn't immediately realize that it was unusual for Jeffrey to be here. He was feeling it too, I could tell, because he squinted and said, "What are *you* doing here?"

Laura Cunningham, who is a standardbearer in the casual elegant service she has created at both the French Laundry and Per Se, is severely refined, unsmiling, and apparently tense given the craziness of the evening. She'd had to ask a diner if he would mind being miked for the show; he'd agreed, but it would alter the mood of the meal, needless to say. Men in jeans and pullover shirts carrying cameras on their shoulders tried to be inconspicuous in the otherwise library-quiet room filled with men and women dressed for an occasion that would cost about three hundred dollars apiece, buffed Riedel glassware, Christofle silver, and a fire crackling in a hearth encased in glass, the whole scene offset against handsome dark walls of Australian walnut.

In the kitchen, Thomas Keller, dressed in a crisp, clean chef's coat, walked back and forth near, but not at, the pass in his busy new kitchen. Something was wrong, but I couldn't place it. At first I thought maybe it's all this craziness—there's simply too much chaos and noise in the kitchen—this doesn't happen here; it felt like a mess. Maybe this was what was bothering him, why he looked off center. But then, no, there was more to it—he didn't look right physically.

Then I recognized the strangeness. He was a couple of inches shorter than normal. Keller is tall and lanky, about six-two with trim dark hair and dark eyes—and now he shuffled rather than walked, sliding instead of striding on the tiled kitchen floor. He was in stocking feet in the middle of this crazy service, and he was obviously self-conscious about it. He passed me, saying hello, adding, "I can't find my shoes."

It already felt like a carnival here, but this was an especially disorienting detail. Keller is a maniac for details and impeccable organization. This is a man, for example, who, after he takes his own laundry out of the dryer at home, shelves all the towels in a hotel threefold. He used to wear cowboy boots but no longer. At home in Yountville, a dozen pairs of cowboy boots line a high shelf leading into his bedroom, a miniature museum display of a period of his life. In the kitchen he wears clogs, the traditional kitchen footwear of chefs and cooks (and also, not insignificantly, of surgeons), primarily for the comfort they give to those who work long hours on their feet. He used to wear showy white clogs, but he long ago switched to the more conservative black leather ones, with a light pale-wood sole, an elegant, clean shoe—at least until today. He couldn't *find* them, and it was driving him to distraction. Chef can't find his shoes. He'd been wearing black dress shoes all day long, and they were killing his feet. Adding to the strangeness was the reality that he could comfortably do so—walk around in socks. The floors of most restaurant kitchens are covered with fat black mats that let the slop fall through and also give the cooks traction on spills. Such is Keller's mania for cleanliness that his sheer black dress stockings were completely comfortable here. The tile was cool and pristine. The cooks worked on soft carpeted mats, which were shaken out before service. But it was still not right; he was unnerved and couldn't quite concentrate because of it.

As if to get away from the commotion, Keller stepped into Josh's private-party kitchen, which was plating several rows of a single course, banquet style. I followed him. A window looks from this kitchen into the Per Se kitchen, and Keller fell back against the ledge here.

I said the first thing that came to mind: "How is your mental health?"

Keller shook his head, looked at his toes, looked at me, and said without irony or humor, "I'm losing my balance."

CHAPTER 2

⇥·⇤

The Morphing Chef

It's hard to find a more dramatic example of The Successful Chef in America than Thomas Keller, one who has apparently never compromised his vision, who has built one success after another without fundamentally changing the cook he is. Untrained, Keller took over the kitchen of the Palm Beach Yacht Club in 1974, a little box of a place his mother managed on the Intracoastal Waterway in West Palm Beach, Florida, and there he began his self-styled apprenticeship. Twenty years later, unemployed and virtually penniless, he bought the French Laundry. And a mere ten years after that, he had become one of the most famous chefs in the world—and also one of the most respected.

But he's not alone in the food world. When he began, the names of chefs were unknown; now, like baseball stars, they have their own cards and are famous for specialties within the industry. Keller may be the most successful emblem of *the four-star chef still in his kitchen*. Wolfgang Puck, beginning in the early 1980s, was the leader in expansion and product development—nine fine-dining restaurants and scores of high-end fast-food joints (called "fast casuals"), a line of pans, pizzas, soups. Emeril Lagasse, who had single-handedly put the TV Food Network on the map, was the leading force in cooking as entertainment. Jean-Georges Vongerichten specialized in opening numerous and distinct high-end, high-concept restaurants serving innovative food in hip rooms.

The successes of these chefs, and others like them, had the cumulative effect of creating something of a gold-rush mentality in the chef world. Even chefs not yet in the ranks of celebrity or even nationally known had their noses in the air—they sensed opportunity all around them; they could smell the lucre but didn't quite know its source. The country was fertile, in the midst of a food revolution, and they were its figureheads. How and where to grow? For a chef who'd created a famous flagship restaurant there were any number of ways to move forward, but it was still the Wild West—the frontier for the modern American chef was largely uncharted territory. And the chef was out of balance.

I'd arrived at culinary school in 1996, more or less at the end of perhaps the finest stage in the evolution of the chef—the chef still in the cultural role of artist-monk, its most romantic form. I was a journalist and intended to write a third-person narrative of cooking school and what it really meant to be a chef. I quickly saw that you couldn't know what this work was all about unless you became one of them, and so I did, learning to cook, starting with Skill Development I (mincing an onion and peeling a carrot) and ending on the hot line at one of the school's restaurants and ultimately working briefly as a cook in the industry. I'd learned not only chef skills but chef language; I knew my way around a kitchen, and so was particularly suited to watching and writing about this world. And the world had changed since I'd entered it. The kitchen door had opened on a grand, exciting, and mysterious vista. Some chefs had already left the kitchen for the land of milk and honey, and most of the rest craned their necks to see what was out there.

What were "chefs"? What had become of them? Even one of their best had realized he was out of balance, wasn't sure anymore who he was or what he was supposed to be doing. It was a brand-new role.

There were signs of what the new American chef was becoming, or might become, in Puck, Lagasse, Vongerichten, Keller, and even chefs lesser known outside their markets, such as Joachim Splichal, of the Patina and Pinot restaurants, who in a decade created a series of successful establishments and sold this business to a big company for a boatload of cash. But there was no known long-term model.

For better or for worse, chefs were stepping out of their monk's robes, slipping off their clogs, and donning pairs of hand-stitched John Lobb loafers. They were moving into the realm of commercial branding. America loves the notion of the chef as artist, the creative genius working magic in his or her kitchen. That same chef, however, is considerably less compelling when he or she becomes a commercial for raisins or espresso or pots and pans. So what will happen to our perception of the chef? The chef is in transition. The chef is looking for his shoes. But with the phenomenal popularity of this once blue-collar labor and the potential dollars to be generated by it—whether in pots and pans, salsa, baby food, spice rubs and sauces, or in television shows, books, and rollout restaurants—chef branding, with its product lines, multiple name-recognized restaurants, and entertainment venues, has lured the chef out of the kitchen.

❧❦

The esteem accorded well-known chefs had another effect outside the industry: The new recognition ignored the dues paid, glossing over the work that got them there, of how hard and how long they struggled, the ongoing grinding toil of the devoted and talented chefs in the early phase of their careers. Which is why we now get perplexed articles in the *Wall Street Journal* headlined "Reality Bites: Would-Be Chefs Vie for Stardom," an article noting a 40 percent increase in enrollment in culinary programs to 53,000 students over the past four years, attending "in the hopes of becoming the next Emeril, Mario Batali or Bobby Flay," and the resulting disgruntlement when that doesn't happen or even come close. The story not only lays bare the typical career circumstances of a recent graduate—with eighty-hour workweeks and a salary in the low five figures—but interviews culinary school graduates surprised and miffed at eighty-hour weeks and a salary in the low five figures.

They're mad because this is a part of the industry they didn't see when they signed on—it simply isn't much on view. They see Batali and Flay and Lagasse doing shows, having their faces and names on books, entertaining bestseller-worthy crowds at their signings and demos, and opening fleets of hot, A-list restaurants. They see Thomas Keller, the apotheosis of the American Chef, in magazines and on network television, but not the labor of his four hundred employees, the staff that allows Keller to be who he is and to remain there. They don't see Emeril Lagasse's twelve-hundred-plus workers or the legions who drive Wolfgang Puck's empire.

Those chefs are the models of the future. But where had the artist gone, the figure the American restaurant-going public most adored? What did it mean to be a chef? What happened to chefs *cooking?* Had the profession spun out of control? Had we, the audience? What was going on here? Had we built it up too high, being a chef? Are we in danger of burning out on chefs, of suddenly turning on them, shouting that they have no clothes on, and dumping them in favor of the latest pop idol or sports giant?

Perhaps, on the other hand, our chef-mania, our grossly out-of-touch understanding of the work, is a good thing, a way for America to at last get a grip on its own relationship with food. Since the end of World War II, this country has been out of sync with the natural order of sustenance and nourishment, embracing processed foods, revering canned goods, "instant" breakfasts, and frozen dinners, then elevating fast food to a way of life with such force that its impact has become global, then simultaneously abhorring animal fat for health and dietary reasons, while still becoming the fattest community on earth, then turning around to proselytize on diets composed entirely of salt-rich protein and animal fat, and banishing *bread* of all things—the staff of life was now the evildoer, and just when bakers in this country had figured out how to make it well. We completely upended the food pyramid we'd always accepted as undeniable and good common sense. Ours is a country that for years held out a silver cross at eggs. Eggs are bad for you! *Eggs!* The most natural food on earth, a symbol of life and fertility, a compact package of proteins, fats, and carbohydrates whose versatility in the kitchen, pleasure at the table, and economy at the store is unmatched by any other food. We learned to hate the egg! Do you need any further proof that something is seriously wrong with this country that teaches people to avoid eggs? Only when they became a good strategy for slimming down did we reverse ourselves on the egg quandary.

But in addition to inept thinking about the egg, we've also managed to debase our eggs on a massive scale, to contaminate them so that they may actually make you sick if you don't cook them till they're hard, and downright dangerous for the very young and the very old. We've done the same to our animals, too, by pumping them full of chemicals and feeding them crap they wouldn't naturally choose in generations of evolution. Our major commercial hog producers are breeding the fat out of hogs to try to please the knuckleheaded consumer, who doesn't know anymore what's good for him or not—*how could he? he's been taught to fear the egg!*—degrading a once-fine animal beyond recognition, and yet we think nothing of supersizing our french fries and burgers and Cokes. We're breeding chickens without feathers. Most people scarcely know anymore what their food looks like when it's alive. They get grossed out at a proper pig roast. They wouldn't know what to do if they saw an asparagus growing wild—*you can't eat that, it's gotta come in a bundle with a rubber band around it.* If food doesn't come in a package or a box or wrapped in plastic, we aren't comfortable with it, don't trust it. *It might hurt us. Gotta be processed. Gotta have an expiration date.* It's sometimes hard to remember that what comes out of our boxes and packages first comes out of the earth.

Chefs, thanks to their celebrity, now have the clout and the passion, as well as the knowledge, to point us back to the things that matter—to sustainable farming, to raising animals naturally in fresh air, rather than inside cement barracks pumped full of antibiotics. We're slowly, too slowly, recognizing the scary results of chemical-laced livestock in over-crowded spaces—not merely inferior beef and tasteless chicken, or un-pleasant bacteria such as *Salmonella* and *Listeria,* but also the evolution of truly deadly bacteria such as *E. coli* O157:H7.

Alice Waters, of Chez Panisse, began working with farmers thirty years ago and asked us all to understand better where our food comes from because it matters. This former *schoolteacher* had the authority to do this because she ran a popular restaurant. A generation later, chefs are a powerful force in the way we raise hogs, cattle, and chicken be-cause Americans are spending their dollars at these chefs' restaurants and buying their cookbooks—capitalism at its best—and reading about their beliefs and philosophies, in addition to trying to actually cook their food, and believing what these chefs believe. Which is, as Keller has said, "If I have a better product, I can be a better chef than you." Or to put it in more sweeping but no less accurate terms for the rest of us: We better take care of the earth or we're gonna have shitty food, and having shitty food is no fun.

⊰⊱

For all chefs' potential in society, though, much of the country has gone a little batty over them, according chefs a power and an intelligence few of them actually possess. This is a country, after all, that barely distin-guishes an Olive Garden from an Olives, or an Outback Steakhouse from a Jean-Georges steak house; or even recognizes that all steak houses are a kind of fast-food restaurant dealing in heat-and-serve protein, no mat-ter how fancy the side dishes. Nevertheless, what chefs do individually and collectively is important and potentially powerful, everything from running excellent restaurants to supporting good farmers and growers to raising money for countless causes. They've been especially productive, more so perhaps than any other industry in the world of commerce.

One of the biggest organizations, the antihunger, antipoverty non-profit Share Our Strength, for instance, marshals chefs to help raise about $20 million a year, according to its founder and executive director, Bill Shore. Shore guesses that nationally, the totals that chefs raise for charities are closer to $100 million annually.

In this profession that has undergone rapid advancement and enjoyed a sudden elevation in esteem, the role of the chef has become increasingly specialized. For these reasons and the seemingly endless range of potential work, chefs often don't understand their role anymore or who they should be as a chef. I'd set out again to explore the nature of this work and the ways it was changing, both for the chefs, in all their varying capacities and the decisions they face in this new food world, and for the people for whom they do the work—us, the cooking-struck, chef-adoring, restaurant-crazy consumers.

CHAPTER 3

❧

Shadow Urge

On the other hand, it could be *me*—maybe I needed to understand the work better, to get to the source of my own enduring fascination with it. Maybe it's just me who's chef-struck. Maybe I've had my head in ovens too long. Or maybe not long enough—maybe I'm not fully baked and that's why I keep returning to the brutal-elegant contradiction of the restaurant kitchen and the work of the professional cook.

❧

I had first entered the mysterious world of the chef and the professional kitchen via the gauntlet of a "Skills" kitchen at the Culinary Institute of America, run by Chef Michael Pardus. I was thirty-two. I'd been a hobby cook since fourth grade when, an only child bored after school, I decided to bake a pie. I'd just seen Julia Child do it on TV. She'd made an apple pie seem easy and fun. It was the middle of a Cleveland winter, 1973, and I don't think we had a fresh fruit in the house, but I located a can of pears in syrup back in a cupboard and so moved forward with my canned-pear pie. (I'd love to know a ballpark figure of how many people Julia inspired. I'm sure we'd circle the globe if we all lay down head to foot. Not even counting the people she inspired who went on to do their *own* teaching and inspiring, surely an exponential figure.)

The pie itself was not worth eating as I recall (serious crust problems owing to the soaked fruit), but I'd loved making it, and so would continue cooking, just as I would writing, which I had also begun to do at this same age. The writing was no more worth reading than the pie was worth eating, but I'd liked the process of writing as much as I'd enjoyed the process of cooking, enough to keep on doing both. I've always suspected that for me, the act of cooking and the act of writing are linked, that the desire to cook and the compulsion to write arise out of the same spot in my unconscious, as two different manifestations of the same innate urge.

In my case, the food got better before the writing did. Cooking was a lot easier than writing, no question. Cooking, moreover, had a distinct advantage over writing. Cooking mistakes could usually be eaten. Written mistakes had to be thrown out, and most everything I wrote early on and for a harrowingly long time was a mistake. Nevertheless, providence saw to it that despite at first possessing more culinary than literary acumen, I would earn my living by writing rather than by cooking, with the single and instructive exception of a four-month stint as a clock-punching grill cook. (I acquitted myself acceptably on the line—ever the B student—no great shakes, but not a travesty either, at least dependable during a Saturday-night crunch.)

My last full-time white-collar job ended in 1993. I'd been an editor and a writer at a local magazine in Cleveland and had, rather cleverly, I thought, invented a monthly column that would not only serve the magazine but feed what was by then my incessant hunger for information about food and cooking. I would call up a chef, invite myself into his or her kitchen, and get a private lesson. The chef would get a picture and a profile in a magazine. I was more or less indiscriminate about where I went—chefs weren't particularly well known, even by the time I'd quit to write my first book about an all-boys high school. But I'd been struck when reporting those columns by one thing especially: at least half the chefs I'd interviewed and worked with had gone to the Culinary Institute of America, in Hyde Park, New York. I'd never heard of it till I'd started my column, but enough chefs had named it as the place where they'd gotten their initial training that it made an impression on me.

Having finished my first book in the summer of 1995 and needing a subject for the second, I figured I'd simply expand my erstwhile magazine column to book scale. With an arrogance unique to journalists, I wrote to the CIA's president, Ferdinand Metz, and invited myself in to write a book about young chefs and learning to cook at this, the first and most prominent cooking school in the country. When I didn't hear back, I phoned. Metz's assistant informed me that my letter had been passed on to the school's executive vice president, Tim Ryan. It was July and I was ready to go. I called Ryan's office. When I reached Ryan's assistant, I was told that Mr. Ryan did have my letter and that he could meet with me in the middle of October.

October? That was three months away. My clock's ticking—I had to do things like rent our house, find an affordable dwelling up there, five hundred miles away, and I had cashed the advance check.

When I described my urgency, the assistant assured me this was really his first availability. I would have to wait patiently, learning what I could in the meantime.

October at last rolled around, and I trekked out to Hyde Park with my wife and infant daughter. I met Ryan in his office on the third floor of Roth Hall, the CIA's main building, a classic brick structure that was once a Jesuit seminary. Ryan was straightforward and plainspoken, though he maintained a corporate coldness that intimidated me. Friendly to a degree, open and honest, yes; warm and fuzzy, no. After a meeting, a tour of the school, and lunch at American Bounty, the institute's restaurant showplace, Ryan said he was "favorably inclined" about my idea, but he'd have to think about it. Then he left. I was encouraged to have some dessert.

Ryan "thought about it" for three more months before acting on his initial inclination. I'd honestly thought they'd leap at the opportunity to host me. In truth, they were wary of letting a stranger into their school. For all they knew, I was just some schmo trying to scam a free education. It's a point that could be better argued now than at the time, because then a culinary education is not what I wanted, but in the end it's what I got. Changed my life, in fact.

⇥⇤

I'd hatched this plot to write about learning to cook at the CIA at an auspicious moment in the cultural life of the chef. Indeed, I was amazed no one had already done what I was about to do, and I knew there wasn't a moment to lose. The same week I'd written to the school with my nifty idea, I'd been alerted to a segment on the *Today* show in which a couple were being interviewed about their new book called *Becoming a Chef,* a kind of survey of the profession up to that time. The husband-wife team Andrew Dornenburg and Karen Page, he a chef and she a Harvard-educated businesswoman, had interviewed scores of chefs and put together a potpourri of chef lore, restaurant history, profession pontifications, recountable memories, and how-to advice that cumulatively painted a portrait of the chef in America at the exact moment of launch into the stratosphere of celebrity. One of the book's strongest features was its documenting the new restaurants and chefs beginning to change the way America ate—naming not only such landmarks as Lutèce and Spago and Charlie Trotter's but regional restaurants as well, Norman's in Miami, Mustards Grill in the Napa Valley, and Coyote Cafe in Santa Fe. The authors also placed these chefs and restaurants in a broader historical context of the new American food scene. The book was published as a sporty trade paperback, and its content and design were so popular that *Becoming a Chef* spawned several more books by the authors (and a few less-worthy imitations). The authors have made a mini-industry out of their work and continue to document the scene, most recently with a more traditional cookbook, *The New American Chef,* exploring international influences on our country's already dynamic food scene.

Becoming a Chef is the best of their books, perhaps because it was the first to provide a truly broad, comprehensive, balanced view of the life and work of the professional chef in the words of the chefs, all of it organized and written *by* a chef. Dornenburg and Page had correctly sensed that America had an incipient interest in the work of the professional chef and were really the first to start feeding what has proved to be an astonishingly voracious and still-unsated appetite for information about food and cooking and the men and women who do it for money—the real information, not the stylized fluff available in food magazines, which had been the only material available for decades.

I sensed it, too, but could do little other than tap my fingers while waiting, waiting for Mr. Ryan's favorable inclination to take effect.

At last it did. I entered K-8—a large rectangular teaching kitchen in the heart of this old elegant seminary on the verdant banks of the Hudson River—looking to seventeen fellow enrollees and one chef-instructor like something resembling a culinary student. My intent had been no more complex than to get in with my notebooks, get out with a story and maybe a few cooking tips, write a book, and move on to the next subject. How was I to know that learning to make a veal stock would change my life, that sauce Robert (*ro-BAIR,* one of the oldest derivative sauces, veal demi spiked with mustard) could be as mind altering to me as several tabs of Timothy Leary's finest, that the true measure of a man was not determined by slaying the dragon and capturing the Holy Grail but, rather, by the proper cooking of a green bean. *Yea, verily!* The meaning of life could be found in an onion, and the battle of a busy restaurant service could deliver you to an altered state of being—equal parts grace and shame—in fact, to a kind of parallel existence without any relativity regarding the speed of light, for me a new universe. I would become a cook. I liked this place and I wanted to stay.

❧

I wrote that book on learning to be a chef at the CIA. Then, through a fluke that can happen only if you live in Cleveland (or perhaps as some sort of divine reward for living there), I was invited, via Cleveland food pro Susie Heller, to the French Laundry, in Yountville, California, where Chef Keller, the recent winner of the Outstanding Chef Award from the James Beard Foundation, was planning a cookbook. Keller said he wanted his book to be different. He said he wanted it to be filled with stories in addition to recipes. So I looked for and wrote as many stories as I could find out there in and around Yountville, and as far away as Maine and Hawaii.

The thing that most impressed me then about Keller, who was quickly rising to be one of the most famous and revered chefs in the world, was not the fact that he was becoming this because of miraculous innovations in cooking technique, but rather because he was a maniac about properly cooking green beans—in fact, demanded that his brigade go to absurdly difficult lengths to cook them. He didn't dismiss the stuff I'd learned at the CIA as child's play or outdated or overrated, as many chefs did; rather, he embraced the fundamentals of cooking like a mad dog, said the CIA didn't go far enough. On the inside he was ferocious in his determination—one had to be in order to do the work he was attempting—and on the outside he was all quietness and grace (except to his cooks, no doubt, to whom he was a lot like most chefs, a pain-in-the-ass bastard who could fire you at any moment, only, as he was Keller, more so).

Keller's literary agent called me after *The French Laundry Cookbook* and my two chef books had come out to say that her client Eric Ripert had a quirky idea that she thought I might be interested in. Eric, whom I knew to be the chef of Le Bernardin, often called Manhattan's seafood Mecca, had been for several years running the city's best restaurant according to the *Zagat Survey,* the people's-choice forum. I knew little about Ripert himself, though, other than that he was relatively young to be leading one of New York's few four-star restaurants, that he was very French, and that, whenever I'd seen him invited to cook on TV, he was a very elegant and articulate guy, handsome besides, and with a heavy accent American chicks really dig.

We met outside Pastis in the Meatpacking District in Manhattan at noon on a spring Sunday. He strode along the crowded street wearing goldish green gogglelike shades that made him look like a bug. He wore jeans and sneakers and was still rushing on the adrenaline of the all-night techno binge that often followed a Saturday night's service at the restaurant. He was ravenously hungry, and after eating a lardon salad, he devoured a rare burger with a raw yolk on top and a heap of fries.

"Michael, I want to do a book about cooking and art," he explained. "I want to visit places that will inspire us. I am bringing a painter, photographers. If I can afford it I want to bring a musician. I want you to write, write whatever you wish. We explore art through food and cooking."

It was the strangest cookbook idea I'd heard of, and I knew it would be all but impossible to pull off and that for me, as the writer, the one in charge of creating an intellectual framework for the book and articulating the often ineffable whims and intuitive musings of the chef, this one was going to be a lot of work for me for very little money. Eric was so ebullient and energetic, though, and so in love with the idea that I couldn't help but join him. That, plus the opportunity to work with another chef of this caliber and experience (he'd worked for several years as the poissonnier under Joël Robuchon); moreover, the locales he'd be taking us all to—Sag Harbor, Napa, Puerto Rico, and rural Vermont—made the idea especially appealing.

Not long after finishing this book with Eric and company, and in between other longer nonfiction projects on the subjects of wooden boats and heart surgeons, I would return to work with Keller again, traveling in France, to Limoges, to write about his porcelain project, and on to Lyons and Paris, and then back to the Napa Valley, to write about bistros and bistro food.

How could I fail by now to wonder at my circumstance? Eating Eric's stuffed saddle of lamb, an ode to his mentor, Jean-Louis Palladin, while looking out over the verdant Napa Valley, or lunching on slabs of foie gras with grilled toast and roasted chicken at Chez l'Ami Louis, 32, rue du Vertbois, in Paris's Third Arrondissement—maybe the best bistro in the world—as *research* for the Keller bistro book: All of it was in the name of work! What incredible luck! What a gift! All the result of taking good notes in a skills kitchen at the CIA, of watching Julia and making pie with canned pears—and giving in to the shadow urge to write about it.

✦

A main reason for my good fortune, of course, had to do with changes in our culture and its relationship with food, with chefs, with cooking. *Food Arts* magazine called it a "Food Revolution" and devoted regular articles to exploring its range and reach, and pretty soon everyone was calling it the food revolution. *Gourmet* magazine, under the formidable Ruth Reichl, had committed itself to exploring the people who were growing our food or producing it by hand, focusing on the local, environmentally minded cheese maker or dairy or hog rancher or apple farmer, and profiling the chefs who were using their products. Consumers now had easy access online to farm-raised pork, Pacific oysters, Maine lobsters, and fresh foie gras that was the same stuff used at the finest restaurants in the country.

Another formidable marker of chef popularity has been the extraordinary success of cable TV's Food Network. Beginning in 1993, the network had extended its reach into 87 million homes, its prime-time shows watched by a half million people each day. In 2004 the network generated $225 million in advertising revenue and produced 800 hours of programming, numbers not likely to decrease, despite intellectuals' and serious foodies' complaints of FN's dumbing down cooking. The network has only recently gotten into ancillary marketing—partnering Rachael Ray with the company that makes the knives she uses on her program, all three splitting the profits of sales reaped by her endorsement and her show—but such efforts may soon generate as much money as advertising.

In the not-for-profit world of public broadcasting, stations have almost doubled to more than seventy the number of cooking shows they broadcast across the country over the past few years. Food programming is the most popular kind of show PBS produces, its reach far enough to tap my shoulder and ask me to join one.

And, of course, the chef made it onto network reality TV in 2003 in the form of Rocco DiSpirito, on NBC, a show called *The Restaurant.* The show documented the partnership of DiSpirito and restaurateur Jeffrey Chodorow and the ensuing train wreck that ended in lawsuits, court orders, and two closed restaurants. "It was an embarrassment to the industry," said one insider. But the sexy chef and the New York City restaurant world had proven ready for prime-time network television— more was on its way.

And yet for all this television, for all this interest in chefs, for all the cookbooks pumped out each year—3,591 were published in 2005, more than ever before according to Andrew Grabois, senior director of publisher relations at R. R. Bowker, publisher of *Books in Print,* an annual database for books published in North America—for all the popularity of chef-driven restaurants and their outposts, for all the chef-brand pots and pans and sauces, I don't think the *chef's work* is understood much better now than it was twenty years ago. Perhaps a little bit better, as the number of culinary students rises, a figure that surely contains more people who might not have chosen culinary school during a time when chefs were less glamorized, but not a lot. Some TV describes how difficult and unglamorous the work is. Gordon Ramsay's *Ramsay's Kitchen Nightmares* out of England does it well, and his American show, *Hell's Kitchen,* doesn't, but that's more a problem with America than with Ramsay. Anthony Bourdain's *Kitchen Confidential* was the first book to describe the New York City restaurant kitchen from the vantage of the line cook, to get the culture and the voice right. The book was embraced by cooks and noncooks throughout the world, became a bestseller, and inspired a food-adventure-travel TV show, planting Bourdain in the ranks of international celebrity. (The guy actually gets mobbed in *Asia,* says he can't even leave his hotel room.) He doesn't cook in the restaurant anymore and doesn't want to—twenty-eight years of hellish, backbreaking slog was plenty for him. He's content to option his book to

Darren Star, the creator and executive consultant of *Sex and the City,* for a FOX sitcom. Is it true or glamorized? A little of both, like Hollywood, only on television's smaller scale.

The Hollywood version can be seen in the film *Spanglish,* in which Adam Sandler plays a chef of Thomas Keller–like talent and success. Ironically, it's all about family life, the one thing a chef of that caliber almost never has. It's an illusion but one we like; we're comfortable with it. It's why Bourdain still suits up and returns to the kitchen—for show, for photo shoots and filming—because we like the illusion that the chef actually cooks. The legions who watch Emeril with awestruck wonder want to believe that he's making this same food in his restaurant all the time. The chef-struck diner still wants to believe that the famous chef at the name-brand restaurant is back in the kitchen *personally* preparing his food and fussing over its presentation like a foppish milliner. Somehow, we *need* this fantasy. If there's going to be magic, a sociologist told me, there's got to be a magician. And it can't be just anybody— everybody can't make magic, or it ceases to be magic. It's got to be the territory of the magician, of the select few versed in the dark secrets of the elders.

⋠⋗

The motive for all my pseudo-highbrow philosophizing, of course, is to conceal a simple selfish fact: I wanted to be back in kitchens. Part of me was still a cook. I missed kitchens—but why? What was I looking for? The work is hard and monotonous, and most of the time I wouldn't even be cooking, just watching, scribbling notes on my little pad and looking for something to do during the long hours. Thinking of it like this, it should be a relief to know that I'd never hang out in a kitchen again—ever the interloper, the eternal impostor dressed for work in an old CIA chef coat, ink stains at the pocket, and battered Dansko clogs— to peel ginkgo nuts in New York so that I might interrogate Ryan Becze, a young cook working for the sushi Buddha, Masa Takayama; to mince Amy Pickle's anchovies in Frisco's iconic Zuni Café because I've taken too much of her time in talk and it's the middle of service and she needs them for the Caesar and mincing those piles of anchovies is an onerous task I can take off her hands (and keep busy), onerous even for those who've built up a solid callus on the bottom joint of their index finger and don't have to wrap their knife hand in a towel to keep from bleeding into the salt-saturated, oil-soaked, soft-boned fish.

"You want to work a station tonight?" Grant Achatz, the former French Laundry sous-chef, asks me. I long for such a chance, of course. And so I take over for CIA extern Stephen Parkerson, dipping a battered shrimp into hot oil for the sixteenth course of a twenty-eight course "Tour de Force" tasting menu and slicing little disks of radishes and hearts of palm, alternating coins on a bed of rain forest plum gelatin with mint oil and microgreens, the garnish for a duck-and-foie course. But the shrimp concoction is not your standard tempura—the delicate Maine crustaceans are skewered onto a vanilla bean along with cured Meyer lemon and a chunk of cranberry sauce that has been gelled with agar so that it won't melt out, will stay solid even though it's piping hot within the deep-fried batter. None of these things, especially the delicate jelly and shrimp, want to stay on their fat vanilla bean skewer, a fact necessitating extreme delicacy in battering the construction and swimming it in the hot oil. Having gamely accepted the invitation into the battle of dinner service, I am soon praying to God that this little fish on a stick won't plop off into the fry oil, again, exactly when the rest of the courses are on their way out the door. *Who am I, what am I doing on this line?!* "You know what *T-F-L* stands for?" asks sous-chef David Carrier beside me, also a veteran of the French Laundry, as he slices beef and holds a glass over a smoldering stick of applewood to capture the smoke to send to the diner with the meat. I'm supposed to answer "The French Laundry" as I rest the crispy shrimp tempura into its funky steel holder, but don't take the bait. *"Too Fucking Long,"* Carrier says, referring to my fish on a stick.

What was I doing? How many nights did I intend to slot myself out of the way between an order printer and a dish shelf to record the endless drumbeats of "Ordering!" and "Fire!" and "Pickup!"; to watch the unfortunate server returning with four plates of duck, explaining that table fourteen doesn't eat meat ("They ordered a tasting menu—duck is *printed* on the menu—and they're telling us this *now?*" asks the chef, with intensity); to sympathize with the poor schmuck on sauté who can't see his way out of the weeds, admitting defeat, dispatching the line cook's SOS: "I need an all day on the pork, Chef!" (There's a look of terror in his eyes—he knows he's going down and he knows he's powerless to change it. Nothing worse in the world for a cook, nothing. *YOU'RE NOT GOOD ENOUGH!*)

But more often than not—I was in some of the best kitchens in the country—it was uneventful service: a lot of hot pans under control, clean hands plating food, damp rolls of white towels making crescent swipes around edges of plates, smart servers arriving with perfect timing as if by instinct, thumbs on the under-edge of plate rims, the elegance of service in a seamless glide, skills built on repetition, mind numbing, day after day, endless repetition of the very thing that is, in the moment, beautiful to watch—the euphoric timelessness, for those who are in it, of the dance.

I love the professional kitchen. It's one place in this world where I know there are answers—my answers at least—and answers for a lot of cooks I know. I make eager, compulsive forays into worlds I've never seen and return home to write about them. I love these ventures because they're new, but they're brief, and I rarely revisit the places or the people, no matter how much a part of me they've become. I covet the rank solitude of my office, where I try to make sense of the chaos and restore my soul. But out in the world I'm most at home in a kitchen and so have returned again and again, an impostor cook looking for Answers. Hard, shining surfaces, big machines, steel knives, craftsman's tools—the Silpat, the wooden spoon, the ring cutter, the pastry brush—sauté pans and flame, the sweet brown smell of stocks kept just at a tremble, the sound of mushrooms in crackling hot oil. Even without the food, it's a sensory heaven. But add food, an abundance of it, the overflowingness of food at a restaurant doing good business, and the place can be a glory to stand in, to work in. Tools are meaningless without the food. I love the food and I love the physical labor that brings the food and tools and heat and cold together for the great and forever meaningful goal to feed people and to make them happy. To earn your pay and feed yourself.

I love a kitchen's unspoken rules, the hidden crevices where treachery and stupidity fester, the camaraderie created by intense protracted physical labor, occasional grace, the inarticulate humanity of people who cook to earn their daily bread, the kitchen's peaceful glades—morning when few are there or late night, surrounded by cooks, service over and the kitchen clean—the private euphoria of service gone well and the private shame of the weeds, known less grandly in kitchen parlance as "getting your ass kicked."

Perhaps above all, though, what has propelled me back into the kitchen, what convinces me that Answers are there, is the fact that in a good kitchen you can't lie to yourself. It's a black-and-white world. A truth pervades the restaurant kitchen that is undeniable, impressive in its immediacy and clarity: Your food is ready or it's not, you're in control or you're a mess, you're in the dance or you're in the shit. It's plain to see.

That this is the critical fact of the professional kitchen became clear to me not in a kitchen but in an operating room, a place closely linked to the professional kitchen in its own, more standardized and professional ethos of cleanliness and orderliness. Both are temples of mise en place (everything in its place, a state of preparedness), of efficiency of movement, of cool decisiveness. My teacher was a young heart surgeon, a doctor in the harrowing business of opening babies' chests and fixing their hearts, FUBAR hearts incapable of pumping blood to the system or to the lungs, of sending blue blood to the brain and red blood to the lungs, hearts like Swiss cheese, hearts missing parts, hearts like sponges, opening the chests not of healthy kids who might more easily withstand such a violent assault to the body with power saws and steel clamps, but of babies already critically ill, babies clinging by a thread to life, their parents clinging to the skills of the surgeon by nothing more substantial, the surgeon hunkered over the child's open chest and stopped heart with the weight of a community squatting on his shoulders.

"It's clear," the surgeon told me with a kind of mad grin that described his world. "It's beautiful. Elegant. Brutal. There are not many jobs where you're forced to know exactly who you are. You can't lie to yourself here, because if you lie to yourself, it becomes very obvious. Somebody dies."

That elemental a world is more by far than I'm prepared to live in on a daily basis, but it helped me to understand the kitchen a little better, and my fascination with it.

Thomas Keller said as much to me one day before service at the French Laundry. This paragon of perfection, of elegance, when asked if he was anxious before service, replied no. "If I fuck up," he said, "I'm not going to kill anyone."

This is a major advantage that cooking has over heart surgery, as far as career choices go. But that's about it. Otherwise the work was more alike than not.

I loved to be in kitchens. I missed them. I loved to cook and to watch people cook. I loved to do the same things with food over and over and over. I never got tired of making a mayonnaise, or cutting chives with a really sharp knife, peeling an onion, or taking the germ out of a clove of garlic. I loved to learn about food and its behavior and think about it while I was cutting it and cooking it. And I loved to eat—loved it. When you're cooking you're kind of eating in your mind the whole time. I can't imagine the drudgery daily cooking would be if you didn't love to eat.

My strategy would be to visit new kitchens and new segments of the industry such as the Food Network and the incredible impact of televised cooking lessons. And I'd return to some old stories and old chefs to explore how their world had changed in the intervening years. It wasn't only Keller's life that had changed. In no instance did I find a situation that I'd written about previously unaltered; in fact, the changes were profound given how little time had passed. The restaurant kitchen had been an amazing world; it was even more so now. This was an exciting time to be writing about the work of the chef, but it wasn't all hopeful and salutary. Much of it was simply confusing, and some of it was sad.

The chef in America had undergone extraordinary convolutions even since I first learned what it meant to be a chef, a job now influenced by sweeping cultural changes—chef branding, the remarkable popularity of food TV, this country's dysfunctional relationship with food, the growing popularity and influence of restaurants as dining out evolved into a new kind of theater. I would try to describe not the soul of a chef but rather the reach of a chef: how the work has changed even during the past five years, let alone twenty years or longer, and what The Chef means in this huge, sprawling, food-neurotic country.

PART TWO

CIA Revisited

CHAPTER I

❧

Can't Go Home Again

"I'm not telling you fifth-of-gin-and-waitress-in-the-bathtub anymore," Michael Pardus said. "You're like the press." That was a change I hadn't anticipated before my return to hallowed ground. It meant I was not the person I used to be; he said, "You're like *the press*." (At least he was kind enough to say "like.") The kind of information I'd be able to dig up might be a little tougher to come by now and might be of a different nature than when I first began writing about this world, when no one in it knew who I was or what I was likely to do with the things that came out of their mouths.

I'd returned to the place where it all began for me. In the eight years since I'd left the campus to write that book, my skills teacher had become a friend. I could e-mail him about his thoughts on the finer points of poaching duck legs in fat (you don't want the fat to get much hotter than 190 degrees; we'd both had stringy, tough confit and were sure that too-hot fat was the reason) or advice on natural pickles (pickling vegetables using saltwater in a way that encouraged good, acid-producing bacteria to make the vegetables sour and also preserve them—he was a nut about this stuff). When he'd invited a Vietnamese chef from New

York City to do a dinner and presentation at the institute to raise money to bring a group of students to Vietnam, he asked my help in luring celebrity Anthony Bourdain—a Vietnamophile and, with his black leather and foul, hilarious mouth, a guaranteed crowd-pleasing ticket seller. Pardus suggested I come along as well, which, ever game for a food boondoggle, I was only too glad to do.

⇒·⇐

A word about Bourdain—for clarity, if such a state can ever be connected with the man . . .

My first encounter, in January 2001, with the skeletal six-foot-four-inch former chef—now celebrated author, popular television personality, globe-trotting gadabout, restaurant-kitchen pundit, and exuberant bon vivant (or perhaps *mal* vivant is more appropriate)—had proved harmless (as far as I could know). Stopping in Manhattan the night before I flew to Puerto Rico with Eric Ripert and crew, I went for a steak-frites at Bourdain's superb bistro Les Halles. We talked there, then caught a taxi to Siberia, the subway bar, where Eric met us, dressed in a black jacket, black wool cap, black backpack, and black jeans. He looked like someone you'd see scaling a Midtown building thirty-four flights up. Tony kept bringing beers from the bar, and the evening grows hazy for me at this point, and then goes black.

I awoke the next morning at 30,000 feet, seat belt buckled and blanket tucked, Eric having upgraded my coach ticket to first class, where he snoozed beside me. Bourdain had slipped something into my Heineken, evidently. (In his book *A Cook's Tour,* he conceals the details of that night beneath a veiled description of "senseless debauchery and indulgence," alas, so I'd never know what Eric's and Tony's chuckling about that night referred to.) But as I had my wallet, all my teeth, and apparently plenty of sleep, I closed my eyes and thought about San Juan.

Later that spring, Bourdain flew me, Ripert, and his chef buddy Scott Bryan out to the French Laundry to have dinner while his crew filmed the kitchen all day and then our marathon meal all night for an episode of his show, also called *A Cook's Tour.* The kitchen there served Bourdain, an unapologetic pack-a-day-plus smoker, a dish called Coffee and Cigarettes—a coffee tuile served with a custard infused with tobacco from a Monte Cristo cigar, which tasted and felt when it slid down your throat exactly like the first drag of a really good cigarette—an astonishing work of craftsmanship and good humor.

Bourdain was turning out to be a lot of fun, I thought, and the brief CIA jaunt had been more of the same—a talk with the students, a signing, an evening of Vietnamese street food by Michael Huynh, chef and co-owner of Bao 111 in New York City's East Village—until I returned home to find that Bourdain had posted on a popular Internet forum lunatic ravings of incredible intensity about some of my actions at the CIA.

What sparked his preposterous rant, an extended hallucination of our brief time on campus, who can say? Jealousy? While I still have a few remaining shreds of integrity, he's far more popular than I am and his books outsell mine by several miles—so jealousy is not likely. Insecurity? Perhaps. Sudden successes, especially sudden successes who happen also to be chefs, suffer from the impostor complex: he's terrified of being found out. Or perhaps he's simply twisted by nature. He's a great writer, I'll give him that, something of a freak of nature, in fact. He's got a hilarious mouth and is a gifted raconteur in the best scoundrel fashion. And I'm often lulled into complacent vulnerability by his large very dark brown eyes, which have a down-turned curve that gives them a sorrowful, soulful, almost feminine aspect. Regardless, I'd promised myself to be careful when he was in the vicinity.

And yet, for all my ambivalence about this Bourdain character, I owed him: I would never have made this trip to the CIA were it not for him, and it was a revelation for me.

❊

I had to come back to the CIA and see how the place had changed. The kitchens and the hallways here remained powerful, like a drug. And it was more than the fact that it had become a marker in my working life, a place that transformed me and sent me on a new and unexpected course. It was still the world I remembered, a place *seething* with chefs, a huge mad hive of manic culinarians personifying chefness before fleets of gonnabe chefs of every shape, size, color, and age. I started buzzing the second I got back.

It was spring in the Hudson Valley; the air was fresh. I walked with Pardus, my chef, the guy who started it all, maybe changed everything, by treating me not like a writer when I first arrived but rather like one of his lazy-ass students, and telling me I wasn't good enough but that it was OK, we were just different, that's all. The guy could really piss me off when he wanted to.

It was that very night, in fact, in winter 1996, after he'd said those words to me, that we went out after classes were over, ate fries and drank beer, and he told me his story, which included some youthful shenanigans involving a fifth of gin, a bathtub, and a waitress. It wasn't really germane to the "making of a chef," but it wasn't without its own message regarding the life of a chef, either, and so it went into the book.

When he indicated eight years later, rather frankly, that there would be no such stories forthcoming this time, it occurred to me exactly how different I was and that my work of gathering information was changed because of who I was. Most people in my home city of Cleveland have no idea who I am, but at the CIA I'm a personage, "the guy who wrote that book." This has its advantages, but not when I'm working.

I recalled as I strolled through the quad not only who I'd been when I first arrived but also who I'd been when I left, changed. I was different now from *that* person, too. I'd been out in the industry; I'd worked closely with and written about some of the best chefs in the country. My standards had only gone up. And I was nearly ten years older—a middle-aged man now—and most of these students seemed fresh out of high school, half my age.

The Culinary Institute itself had changed. It had always looked like a proper college campus, especially with the dorms and the new library that had gone up after its move from New Haven, Connecticut, in 1972. But now there was a state-of-the-art fitness facility—weight-training and cardio-vascular machines, swimming pool—a gorgeous stand-alone Italian restaurant and teaching center straight out of Emilia-Romagna, with terraces and herb gardens. And further changes were in the works—new housing for students in the bachelor's program, an underground parking lot in front of the building for visitors, a plan to replace the massive crumbling blacktop out back, a real eyesore, with grass and trees and a playing field.

The makeup of its student body had changed as well. Demographically, of course, but that was less significant than an evolved zeitgeist reflecting broader societal changes. The personality of the writhing organism of the CIA student body, a huge chunk of which had come of age during the Clinton presidency, had known only national peace and prosperity, had been raised by doting baby boomers who remained intensely involved in their kids' adult lives. All the lifestyle articles about parents being in continual communication with their kids in college via e-mail and cell phones and text messaging applied at the CIA. These students felt just as entitled as the ones down the road at Vassar and across the river at SUNY–New Paltz. Which meant that they complained just as much as the next—kids bitching about grades was nothing new in academia, but it seemed to me unseemly in cooking school. And not only did the kids complain here, their doting, involved parents did so, too, in noticeably higher numbers.

This school had another interesting demographic facet that academic colleges did not: a huge influx of career changers, roughly 15 to 20 percent of the student body. The work of the chef had come to seem so glamorous that white-collar professionals who were not happy in their work looked to culinary school and the exploding opportunities in the food world as an exciting new option for financial reward and personal fulfillment. So in addition to the twenty-year-old high school graduate who'd had two years' restaurant experience and was entering the CIA's four-year bachelor's program (a cooking school–business school hybrid), I met students who were former real estate agents, social workers, educators, cops, bankers, lawyers, and physicians. These career changers ranged in age from their midtwenties to their early fifties, and, importantly, those coming out of the corporate world brought their corporate behavior and corporate expectations with them.

Traditionally, kitchen culture has been, let's say, unfettered by social niceties, political correctness, and inconvenient laws prohibiting things like discrimination and sex-related intimidation. When I was first at the CIA, I'd heard a funny story about an instructor who, when approached by an inept student asking where he should hold his now-worthless pot pies, replied, "Why don't you stick them up your ass and hold them there?"

This was once acceptable repartee in a kitchen, but try saying that to a fifty-three-year-old female marketing executive well versed in laws concerning sexual harassment in the workplace. The chef-instructors now knew this and were even given special seminars and instruction in appropriate and inappropriate behavior. And the students knew it, too— until they left this place, they were the consumers and they were entitled. It's a brave new world out there—you can hear it anytime a cell phone goes off in a student's knife kit—and it made some chefs sad. I talked to Corky Clark about this, the madman who used to run the CIA's fish kitchen and delighted in burying his class in weeds and making them fight their way out. I liked and admired the man. They'd taken away his fish kitchen in a curriculum revamp (fish cookery would be integrated throughout); he lectured and butchered, but he no longer cooked. Things were different now, he said quietly—he didn't even want to talk about it, just shook his head and looked down. His expression broke my heart.

Part of the appeal of working in a kitchen had always been its draw as refuge for outcasts and misfits and, undeniably, immigrants needing to enter the weave of a city. Also, a kitchen was a place that worked when the rest of the world was relaxing, by nature set apart from mainstream society. You could see what was happening in America from the top of the profession, in kitchens like the French Laundry's and Charlie Trotter's, to the place that taught and generated the workers, the Culinary Institute of America. The professional kitchen was going mainstream. It was getting respectable, and the CIA insisted on bringing standards of white-collar professionalism to every one of its thirty-nine teaching kitchens—yet another of the changes rolling like a wave over America's culinary landscape.

※※

I'd always known the CIA was a place that rarely changed, and if it did, it did so slowly. Tim Ryan himself had said it to me years ago: "We're not trendy." And yet how could the most prominent and influential cooking school in the country be immune to the food revolution and the incredible changes reaching into every corner of the industry.

It couldn't, of course. I suspected the opposite might be true: that the changes at the CIA might reflect and make vivid the broader changes in the industry as a whole, especially now that Ryan had been named president. Ryan—an American baby boomer fond of using the adjective *cool,* who urged you to call him Tim and was easily accessible by e-mail—had replaced Ferdinand Metz (whom everyone, even Ryan, called *Mister* Metz), who represented the older Germanic order and European traditions and formality.

When I'd first come to the CIA to write about the institute and the work, I'd waited till the very end to meet President Metz, whom I came to admire greatly. Old European order or not, Metz, who had come to the States as a young cook at Manhattan's famed Le Pavillon and risen through the chef and corporate worlds to one of the industry's most prominent and influential positions, was considered a visionary in the field, one who'd brought the CIA strongly into the twenty-first century, shaping up a sloppy student body, building innovative restaurants, exploring nutritional and regional cuisines, and instituting forward-thinking educational initiatives no less significant than a four-year Bachelor of Professional Studies. But I was no longer a student, and so this time reversed my course, requesting first a discussion with the new president to see where he thought the chef stood in this new world and how the Culinary Institute itself had evolved along with the changing role of the chef in America.

CHAPTER 2

※·※

Doctor Ryan

I met Tim Ryan at his office on the second floor of Roth Hall, and we left immediately for lunch. At the bottom of the main staircase he stopped, bent his big frame down to pick up a foil-and-plastic rectangle, empty of its cold pills, and carried it till we passed a trash can. When I wrote about the boys' school, the headmaster was forever stooping to gather scraps as he walked through the school. When I was out at the French Laundry, Keller *and* his sous-chef at the time, Eric Ziebold, were regularly picking up cigarette butts in the gravel parking lot. I don't think I walked anywhere with Ryan during my time there when he didn't stop at least once, bend to pick something up, and throw it away. Picking stuff up was more important than most people recognized, and it had little to do with the actual scrap of paper or a cigarette butt.

We ate at the Colavita Center for Italian Food and Wine, which had supplanted American Bounty as the school's showpiece restaurant, to begin a conversation that went on for most of my stay there and traversed the most important topics of the food revolution as it related to the elevated status of the chef in American culture. The Culinary Institute graduated between one thousand and thirteen hundred students each year, influenced thousands throughout the country via its programs for working chefs, and was now heavily into media, producing extraordinary professional cooking texts as well as books for the home cook, instructional videos, and television shows. Perched atop this sixty-year-old institution, attending national and international chef and food conferences, tracking the industry he'd been a part of for nearly thirty years, Tim Ryan had a uniquely comprehensive view of the chef in America.

"If you went to where I was born and raised right now you might be shocked to see what those surroundings are like," Ryan told me. "And I think that is a very common story. I started out washing dishes—Nino's Restaurant in Pittsburgh. There are so many people who have started out that way, and it goes back to the service industry being the industry of opportunity at every level. You talk about Ray Kroc or Dave Thomas or Nick Valenti, who is president of Restaurant Associates, folks who had humble beginnings and got involved in this industry—that happens every day. This is really the industry of opportunity in a way that others aren't. People can aspire to be the next Joe Baum or Ray Kroc or whomever in a way that I don't think you can aspire to be the next Bill Gates."

Lawrence Timothy Ryan was born in 1958, and now, at age forty-seven, his dark hair, trimmed above the ears, had a distinguished gray cast. His round face and cool blue eyes were typical of his Irish heritage. He was solidly built—he ate only a small portion of his lunch (chicken) and no dessert, though saw to it that I'd have the panna cotta—and seemed to be keeping fit. I'd once seen a picture of him in whites, when he was a young chef-instructor, but now it was hard to imagine him in anything other than a suit, except perhaps dressed for the golf course, a place I knew he enjoyed being.

The grandchild of Irish immigrants who'd settled in Pittsburgh, Ryan is a classic American success story of the food business. His paternal grandparents had been so poor that his father, Lawrence Sr., born in 1916, was forced to leave home at thirteen and ride the rails toward California with his brother, looking for work during the Depression. After World

War II—Lawrence was an army sergeant stationed in Oregon—he returned to Pittsburgh and worked in a brewery, fathering two daughters in addition to Tim, who was the eldest. The family was poor, but "we didn't know it," Ryan said.

As a teenager, Ryan had vague notions of being a lawyer, but as the family had few resources, as his father had only a sixth-grade education, and as he didn't know any lawyers other than the ones he saw on TV, law didn't happen. His role model, instead, became Nino Sorci, a big charismatic chef-owner of the restaurant where Ryan had worked throughout his teens, and as far as the young Ryan could see, the richest man he knew personally. Moreover, Ryan loved the kitchen—"I was enchanted by the activity and the flames. . . . And even as a kid, I could work the line." Sometime toward the end of high school, Ryan walked several blocks from his home to the Carnegie Library to see what was available in the way of a culinary education. The only thing going then was the CIA, and he knew exactly—"with total clarity," Ryan recalls—what he was going to do. There was never a doubt.

Ryan enrolled in the Culinary Institute in 1975 and graduated two years later. His father had died of bone cancer while Ryan was in school, so rather than travel in Europe, work in New York City or on a cruise ship, as he'd originally foreseen, he instead returned home and found work as a chef at a place an hour outside Pittsburgh, three bus rides away, at the highly regarded Ben Gross Restaurant, then later as the chef of La Normande, which became one of the finest restaurants in the area and whose owners periodically sent him to Europe.

Metz, who was then an executive with Pittsburgh-based H. J. Heinz Company, dined at La Normande and got to know its young chef, encouraging him to participate in culinary competitions and occasionally judging his food. In 1982, not long after he was named president of the CIA, Metz—fresh from leading the United States to its first gold medal in hot foods at the Culinary Olympics—placed a call to the kitchen of La Normande in the middle of a busy service. A flabbergasted Ryan—he was just twenty-four—took the call. Metz wanted to know if Ryan would consider coming up to Hyde Park to open a new restaurant that would specialize in exploring American regional cuisine, one of the first in the country to make this its goal.

At the time, if you were serious about cooking, nouvelle cuisine and all things French ruled. "I didn't want to do chowder," Ryan says now. But he came for a visit and was inspired by Metz and the challenge of having an impact on students. It was later to be remarked at the school that Ryan was Metz's number one draft pick.

After opening the American Bounty Restaurant, Ryan would excel with impressive speed at everything he did—he passed the Certified Master Chef exam at age twenty-six, the youngest ever to do this, became captain of the champion U.S. Culinary Olympic team, also the youngest to do this, and was the youngest president of the American Culinary Federation. In the midst of his day job and extracurricular cheffing, he earned a bachelor's and an M.B.A. from the University of New Haven, then a Ph.D. in education from the University of Pennsylvania. Clearly, the guy was driven. He brought to every assignment the focus and tenacity of the chef. But the chef was now a doctor.

This was consistent with what I knew about being an excellent chef. It was not something you could turn on and off. If you were truly a chef, that was your core; it defined who you were and directed your every decision. Chefness was not a hat you put on when you got in to work. Perhaps this is why he refused to let his kids, when they were toddlers, win at Candy Land. His wife, Lynne, thought this was ridiculous, but Ryan defended the practice. It was not that he played to win at everything he did no matter whom the competition happened to be; it was, rather, that he wanted his kids to play to win, and when they did win, he wanted it to mean something. Also, he'd realized what he called the American Dream, a key facet of which was to be able to give your children more than you had as a child. But privilege, he wanted his kids to understand, did not mean you got things for free—you still had to earn everything. This meant that if you were one square away from King Kandy's Castle and you drew Plumpy—back you went, three years old or not.

He was a chef and a perfectionist. Lynne was a chef, too. A tall, attractive blonde from Alabama, she had been a nutritionist who didn't take to hospital work and so enrolled in the CIA, graduating in 1987. Ryan was already in the administration by then, and their paths never crossed. She met him a few years later at a chef convention when she was the corporate chef for BlueCross BlueShield. They endured a year's long-distance relationship, then married, fifteen years ago. Ryan refused to eat the first meal Lynne cooked for him when she finally moved up. Roast chicken. She hadn't trussed the bird. Lynne couldn't believe it: They were in the middle of upstate New York—where was she supposed to get butcher's string? She was pissed. When she told me about the event, now fifteen years in the past, she was still pissed. Ryan remained unapologetic. "I believe in trussing a chicken," he said, by way of explanation. And that was that.

Ryan was now the man in charge of the place at which he'd spent all but five years of his adult life. He retained the chilliness I'd always sensed from my first meeting in 1995. This bothered me because I couldn't see its source. It wasn't as if the guy were an asshole or some blowhard corporate dude. Ryan was a nice guy who went out of his way to welcome me. I hadn't graduated from the school, but he said he looked upon me as if I had. I got an appointment right away this time. And lunch. And all the time after I needed for further discussion. Nor did I feel as if he were hiding something, or not speaking frankly—he was unfailingly straightforward, and I usually agreed with what he said or at the very least understood his reasoning, which was clear and to the point. The guy knew food and cooking as well as or better than any chef I'd met, and he was smart and articulate.

Here's an e-mail, his response to my request for a follow-up interview by phone to answer a few outstanding questions, and it's typical of his tone generally:

Hi Michael,

Happy New Year!
It is always good to hear from you.
All is well here at the CIA.
I'll ask Rona, to set up some time for us to talk.
In the meantime, it would be helpful if you could e-mail
me the questions that you'd like to cover.

All the best,
Tim

And yet there was something that made him seem dangerous, as though you had to watch your step around him or he'd cut you—nothing personal. He played to win and never let that guard down. He was still a chef at his core—indeed, that chef core had likely made it possible for him to succeed outside the kitchen, in business, higher education, and administration. Anyone would have had to be ferocious to accomplish what he had by forty-three, his age when he replaced Metz. I'd seen this quality in great chefs and great surgeons. You had to be ruthless. Even when you played Candy Land or when your new wife served you a chicken that had not been trussed, you never let your guard down— ever. That was your standard, that was who you were. I wondered how much this had to do with how he grew up. Poor but not wanting for anything, he'd made his own way pretty much from age twelve. But his father, born into the Depression, was more or less forced from his family at that same age and spent his adult life as a poor laborer in a brewery. Perhaps part of Ryan's ferocity was rooted in the anxiety of the immigrants' shadow and a determination that harsh circumstances would never touch anyone in his family again—I don't know. Nor did he—he would say only that he never saw anything he did as an accomplishment but, rather, as part of the process of reaching some bigger ultimate goal.

We returned to the elegant, ornate boardroom at the top of the main stairway on the second floor behind leaded- and beveled-glass doors.

He gave me a PowerPoint slide show of the renovations about to begin, as well as some motivational and informational presentations the institute gives to faculty that underscores the changing nature of the workplace, everything from the new business environment to what does and what does not constitute sexual harassment. The conversation continued to swerve into the nature and meaning of chefs' sudden celebrity. He'd had to stop himself from talking about it at lunch because I was trying to save it for a more considered time when I could concentrate and take notes. But it was impossible not to talk about it—chef celebrity seemed to precede all topics.

Ultimately we sat down in his office at a round wood table, the very one where I'd grilled Mr. Metz and ended my obsessive quest eight years earlier for the proper color of roux for a classical brown sauce. It was a warm June day and the windows were open, the Hudson River visible in the distance.

Ryan prefaced our conversation about celebrity with what he considered to be related to but separate from celebrity. What can we say defines greatness? What does it mean to be a "great" chef today?

"You ask people 'Who are the greatest artists?'" he said. "They say Picasso or whatever, and I ask, 'Why do you say that? Because someone told you, just like they tell you Shakespeare is the greatest writer?' Who is 'they'? Critics and the like?"

Ryan listed the four criteria that define greatness in any artist:

- They are excellent craftsmen.
- They are innovators—they do something that no one has done before.
- They are "on trend," as he put it—their innovations are perceived to be of value; people buy their stuff; they aren't tragic and misunderstood, appreciated for their innovations after they're dead.
- They are influential—others begin to do what they started.

By these criteria, the first chef in America to achieve greatness in this modern sense was Alice Waters, at her Berkeley restaurant, Chez Panisse, which opened in 1971. André Soltner was the well-known chef at his Lutèce, which opened in 1961. He was a superlative craftsman, chef, and restaurateur, but can we say he was great by Ryan's modern definition? He was greatly admired, was a role model for young cooks, and was successful by any chef's standards of the time; indeed, he remains an icon of the solitary chef working in his kitchen and practicing his craft (classic French cuisine) with monklike devotion and extraordinary stamina and longevity. He was not innovative, however, and thus he could not be said to be hugely influential, regardless of how revered he was and remains.

But Waters didn't really develop fame until much later, after the influence of her Chez Panisse chefs began to reverberate throughout California and the country. The first true celebrity chef—and I'm referring only to restaurant chefs, not the early TV cooks and chefs, Julia Child and Jacques Pépin, James Beard and Graham Kerr, who had long been on the scene by now—may have been Paul Prudhomme, who opened K-Paul's Louisiana Kitchen in New Orleans in 1979. A talented chef, he brought the heavy seasonings of Cajun cuisine into the national consciousness, and his techniques—notably, blackened fish—were, for better or worse, widely imitated.

Three years later, Wolfgang Puck opened Spago in West Hollywood, then fired up the steamroller and carried his California cuisine—American nouvelle gone rustic, but still created with classic French technique and served on fine china in a dramatic setting—across America, first with restaurants and innovations, such as the open kitchen in a fine-dining restaurant and Asian fusion cuisine, then with his pizza and fast food.

After these three chefs, whose rise and monopoly span about a decade, comes a slew of groundbreakers, but few stand out to match these forerunners, chef-restaurateurs whose influence on the American dining scene remains apparent even today (less so with Prudhomme, though his spices helped pave the way for celebrity-chef products). Who followed? Larry Forgione, An American Place, 1983 (American regional cuisine). Charlie Trotter, who opened his eponymous Chicago restaurant in 1987 (big tasting menus, small portions), and also in Chicago that year, Rick Bayless, who debuted Frontera Grill (popularizing an authentic artisanal approach to an ethnic cuisine, in this case Mexican). Jean-Georges Vongerichten (innovative techniques and food in exciting rooms, Jojo and Vong) and Nobu Matsuhisa (fine-dining Japanese) in Manhattan. Thomas Keller in Yountville (numerous innovations in classic French technique, presentation, and conception).

That would be my list of the Great American Chefs to date—a list that would be fun to argue with anyone because no doubt legions would be up in arms about his or her omission: How can you leave out Madeleine Kamman, Jeremiah Tower, Jonathan Waxman, Barry Wine? My response: They don't hew to the four criteria. The shorter the list, the more meaningful it is.

But the guy who really started things for this modern era of the chef as cultural star, the man Tim Ryan calls "the Elvis Presley of the culinary world," the person who could be said to be the original great modern celebrity chef was French. Paul Bocuse.

"There have been celebrity chefs for a long time—La Varenne, Carême, and Escoffier was undoubtedly a celebrity chef," Ryan said, but it was the arrival of "Bocuse, starting in the seventies—that's when things started to heat up." Bocuse was really the first to play to the media and begin to elevate the chef's standing toward what it is today.

When Ryan was starting out, Bocuse was who everyone wanted to be. In America, the role model had been Soltner—the chef as monk. But that changed in the seventies. Young American chefs went to Europe and returned aspiring to be, Ryan said, "like Bocuse and his band"—the Troisgros brothers, Alain Chapel, François Bise, Louis Outhier, and Raymond Thuilier, all disciples of the legendary Fernand Point and La Pyramide.

"And then we have the beginnings of the American food revolution in the eighties—folks become a lot more media savvy—media certainly gains traction and wants to write about chefs. They used to be called 'star chefs' back in the eighties. That's when Wolfgang Puck started, and

Larry Forgione and Jasper White, Todd English, Dean Fearing, Jeremiah Tower, and you can go through the list—many of them still big names today, or bigger names today.

"Then comes television, and I think that notches it up, because you have twenty-four-hour cable television, and that makes a big difference.

"But by and large I think it's a good thing for the industry. The respect that chefs have as professionals is enhanced and higher than it ever has been before."

To support this claim he mentioned two names synonymous with American fortunes and high society who now attend the institute. Indeed, that becoming a cook was now acceptable in the American aristocracy said everything about what America thinks of its chefs.

"This is a wonderful profession and opportunity," Ryan said. "You can really do something great, and make a name for yourself, and maybe make another fortune if you already come from a fortune. It is socially not only acceptable but desirable."

But I wondered aloud at this. This fact is due to a romanticized version of the chef. How long will the scion of blue-blooded aristocracy last in his first kitchen where he does nothing but peel veg and turn artichokes. You don't just open a restaurant after graduation and expect booming business and TV show offers. It takes years of hard, hot work before you have the clout to move into the upper echelons of the profession—for those who make it at all into the upper echelons.

"Is this romanticized version of the chef harmful?" I asked Ryan.

"The answer to every question legitimately is, it depends. It's no different from wanting to be Tiger Woods and having an idealized version of that, or wanting to be Tom Cruise. Very few people end up making it to those rarefied levels. But part of being American is to be able to aspire to that. That any kid can be president, that may be a uniquely American perspective—I don't know. But is that ability to dream, to aspire to do great things, good for society? I have to believe it is."

"Why are so many people interested, some would even say obsessed, with this work, with 'The Chef'?" I asked.

"It sounds trite," Ryan answered, "but it's one of those things that everybody in the world has in common—everybody eats, and everybody has to cook or go out or whatever." In the fifties, the country had different priorities, he explained. We weren't focused on food. But society began to change—America began to change. "Without a highway system, the food-service industry really doesn't evolve in the way that it does—without a popularization of the automobile, you can't forget about that and modern transportation. But people can relate to food, and think they have some experience with it and try it out. I can admire Ernie Els or Phil Mickelson or Tiger Woods just by watching them on TV even if I'm not a golfer. But if I go out there and try to do it, and see how hard it really is, your appreciation and respect is enhanced, and since everybody eats and the majority of people cook, when you see a truly great practitioner you can appreciate it in a different way.

"I think we have some characters, too," he continued. "Chefs have personalities, there's no question about it. We tend not to be bland individuals. God bless all my friends in the accounting industry, but you tend not to want your accountant to be flamboyant and adventurous and risk-taking. But in an artist and in a chef those things are desirable. That's part of who they are. These people have personalities and are entertaining and they have talent. They're not just comedians or actors—they are practitioners of a craft."

The comedian remark made me think of Emeril, the biggest celebrity chef there was, but whom Amanda Hesser in *The New York Times* had called a "jester."

"You have to take a look at the big picture," Ryan said immediately upon my bringing this name up. "Is Emeril Lagasse good for the profession? The answer is yes."

This of course was a tacit way of saying he didn't like what Lagasse did on his show, an all but unanimous opinion among chefs.

"I don't know if you read *The New York Times* article," he said. "That was true."

Politically astute and in a position of authority, Ryan didn't want to say anything bad about Lagasse publicly, but I pressed. He was willing to talk off the record about his feelings and ultimately composed an opinion via e-mail that he felt comfortable with:

> Cooking on a television show is quite different from cooking in a restaurant. The food cannot be smelled or eaten—a fact that Emeril often highlights by teasing his audience to request "smell-a-vision" from their cable companies. Given the situation, Emeril does some things that he probably doesn't do in his restaurants. I also often hear chefs criticize Emeril's culinary techniques, but television is entertainment—it is not a training program or culinary school. In fact, television audiences often love it most when the talent messes something up and has to recover. That was certainly true of Julia Child, and beyond the realm of cooking shows—Johnny Carson was the master at turning a joke that bombed into something funny. Whatever the criticisms about Emeril, I think that net, net—he is a positive force. I like Emeril and respect him. I do wish that he could move away from throwing raw spices on his plates, but I don't think that his audience would allow that. It's one of his signature moves now. Anyway, it could be worse—he could be screaming profanities at someone, or acting unprofessional, and thankfully Emeril has never done that.

I sensed the remark about raw spices was a particular peeve of his—he'd mentioned it before—and it's one I appreciated. Emeril had become famous for throwing raw spices on food and shouting *"Bam!"* That was his trademark, the move he was most associated with, the technique that half a million households were being trained to do nightly. Be like Emeril, go out and buy your own bottle of Emeril's Essence and "kick it up a notch" by taking big pinches of raw spices, slamming them into the pan, and shouting at your food. For me, fun though it was, good TV though it was, this single act was symbolic of the worst of Emeril: His most famous message and lesson to millions was a bad one (not to mention a sales pitch for his line of spices). He was teaching a lot of people a lesson in mediocrity. How do you best use spices? You toast them for maximum effect. Do you *have* to toast the whole seeds and grind them fresh in order to use them? No. Can you just open Emeril's blend, which you've had in the cupboard for six months, and throw it into your food? Sure. Will it change the flavor? Yes. Should people know the difference between one way and another, the right way and the compromised way, at least be able to make a considered choice in their own kitchens? *I* think so. To me that's what cooking's all about. Cooking is not about shouting at your food, but also there's nothing wrong with shouting at your food. We take the good with the bad. And anyway, I'd feel too much like a foodie snob to say anything truly bad about Emeril. I'd hear about how great a guy he is—has a big charity fund. Kids with terminal illnesses have made a trip to this guy's show their top make-a-wish priority. He's a unique American celebrity, the first of his kind, an original.

❧

Ryan leaned back in his chair, relaxed and comfortable. Behind him spread the beautiful Hudson Valley, students in chefs' whites thronging below, the CIA nearing its sixtieth anniversary, stronger than ever in a culture that promised only to increase the opportunities and esteem for chefs. I just looked at him.

I said, "You must be having a blast."

"Yeah, I totally am," he said, smiling warmly—it seemed he was dropping his guard. "I think I'm at one of the great places of the world. And I would say, part of what has happened [in the chef world], the CIA is responsible for. Don't forget in 1946—"

He halted. The scent was powerful, and we'd both smelled it at the same time and thought the exact same thing. *Spices.* The aroma of coriander seeds and peppercorns being roasted somewhere below had wafted up and into the room. Ryan was delighted to have support material floating in through the window. "See! We're not throwing in raw spices— somebody's got 'em in a pan, toasting them!"

It smelled great, and I wondered how they'd be used—some sort of

Asian preparation, perhaps, or maybe someone had finished curing a beef brisket and was about to turn it into pastrami.

"In 1946," he resumed, "the image of a chef is pretty damn low. Anything good is European dominated, and Mrs. Roth, with the help of Mrs. Angell, formalized culinary education. The level the CIA was aspiring to achieve did not exist in the world. And so we started off with this uniquely modern approach."

Frances Roth, a lawyer by profession, founded the CIA, then called the New Haven Restaurant Institute, to give war veterans a skill useful in the food industry. She could scarcely have imagined that the American food industry would in four decades become a food revolution. The place opened with a class of fifty students. Today approximately fifty-five thousand people are enrolled in hundreds of culinary degree programs throughout the country. Ryan believed that not just the school but the level of professionalism this lawyer brought to the mission of the school was responsible for its growth and prominence, and the status of the chef in America.

"Without professionalization it doesn't happen—chefs are perceived as fry cooks and hash slingers," he said.

"When modern-day chefs do things that somebody—let's say there are some things that people see in Rocco's show that they don't like or in Emeril's show culinary-wise, or in Tony Bourdain's book, their fear is that we'll go back to those days when we were viewed as hash slingers. So there is some real fear of that. But I think the momentum professionally is too great."

"So where's it going?" I asked. "Are we at a crest?"

"I have to think that we're only beginning on this journey," he said, noting that he's been searching other businesses and industries for a model he might learn from, but as yet he hasn't found a profession that's "become so white-hot and done some wrong things and exploded."

He also notes that the world is different than it was when the CIA opened its doors. Ryan is well versed in business literature, often bringing up gurus Jim Collins and Tom Peters. It's not just a matter of getting the right people on the bus; you've got to get them in the right seat, he explained when talking about hiring his staff.

Business in the old economy, he says, is like a crew race on the Charles River: a competition on still water against a clear competitor, a rigorous, organized, concentrated effort expended over a known period. At the end there is a clear winner, and it is done.

Our current business world is white-water rafting: "You're hanging on for dear life," he said. "It's not linear. It's *directional* at best. You can't see obstacles, you can't see competitors. This white-water situation is permanent, so get a grip."

And it's that kind of world he wants CIA graduates prepared for when they leave. Students have to be more than cooks. The dynamic of history can be described as one of "increasing complexity." There was only one time in history when we went backward, he noted, and we named it the Dark Ages. Everyone entering the work world, culinary graduates no less than anyone, needed to account for this increasing complexity. To the kids who come in here saying I just want to learn how to cook, Ryan says, once you're out in the world "you don't get to *just* cook. You're going to be doing a whole lot of other things, so to prepare students to just cook, it's belittling to the profession.

"What do you think a chef is?" he concluded. "What does chef mean? It means *leader.*"

❧❦

Shortly after he became president, Ryan oversaw a major revamp of the curriculum, a tightly constructed rotating system that allowed, typically, ninety new students to arrive the Monday after ninety graduates departed, once every three weeks. It's called the progressive learning year, in which each class moves through the curriculum in blocks of fourteen teaching days, each block building on the last. It was a colossal headache to reorganize this old curriculum—switch classes around, get rid of some, lengthen others, give students longer periods in specific restaurants. Almost as soon as it was implemented, Ryan asked his lieutenant, Victor Gielisse, to start planning for an even bigger change.

He intends to revert the progressive learning year into a trimester system more like a traditional academic university, a curriculum that would maintain a common core for all but also allow students to pursue varied segments of the food revolution. By way of example, he noted that the great English universities, and those in the early years of the United States, had a core curriculum of the classics, and the graduates went on to be either politicians, lawyers, or ministers (doctors, remember, were closer to barbers in the work hierarchy at the time). Then the scientific explosion happened, and suddenly, given an unprecedented inpouring of new knowledge, the old model of education couldn't contain it or address it.

That situation now applied to the food world, an industry flooded with information from all over the world. It's not unlike the transformation of the worlds of medicine, law, or business. In the early years, doctors were generalists. More and more knowledge poured in, forcing doctors to grow increasingly specialized in order to make use of that information. Food professionals must make similarly narrowing choices, and Ryan wants to accommodate students' desires to explore the paths that appeal most to them. Law school and business school curricula have gone the same way. "Joe Wharton came and initiated a special business course at Penn and look at it now," Ryan said. The CIA is often called the Harvard of cooking schools, but maybe it more closely parallels the Wharton School.

And no wonder. When Ryan was a student, you came here to learn how to cook. When a recipe called for mushrooms, it meant white button mushrooms. Wines were white or red, and the good ones came from Europe. Fresh herbs beyond curly parsley were a rarity. And when you left, you got a job as a cook and maybe became a chef. That was about it.

In a class currently taught to CIA bachelor's students, Introduction to Interpersonal Communication—needless to say, not a class or even an idea when Ryan was a student—one assignment is to choose and explore a food-related career from a list of 250 options divided into 8 broad categories: Communications, Education, Management and Service, Nutrition and Sciences, Visual Arts and Design, Culinary Arts, Baking and Pastry Arts, Farming and Growing. Here's a sample of jobs within those categories:

Literary Agent
Restaurant Public Relations
Bacteriological Technologist
Industrial Hygienist
Catering Director
Military Foodservice Manager
Commercial Kitchen Designer
Food Stylist
Winemaker
Hydroponic Farmer

The field wasn't relegated to chef anymore, and the key to success after school seemed to be combining a broad-based education with a deep focus in one of those eight arenas.

"We're not a training institution—we're an institution of higher education," Ryan said. He wanted the graduates of this former trade school (don't call it a trade school today; "I made that mistake once," a chef confided in me, noting he'd not do that again around top brass) to progress from making money with their hands to making money with their heads. He gets resistance about this from some people within the CIA who want to train broiler cooks. "That's what you need on a Saturday night," he said. "But it's not what the industry needs for the long haul."

Ryan clearly had an ambition to make this institution not just a great one in the food industry but one of the great educational institutions period.

"I want this to be a place of inquiry and original thought," he concluded.

CHAPTER 3

A Kinder, Gentler Kitchen

"How you guys doin'?—Good." Chef Turgeon hadn't waited for an answer nor did he look at anyone as he spoke. He'd taught about fifty three-week blocks of Garde Manger, cold food and buffet preparation, the last class before students left for their externship, four months' working in the industry before returning for the second year of culinary school. He knew the seven A.M., glazed, just-shaking-the-head-clear nonresponse from just as many blocks of the American Bounty restaurant, the final teaching kitchen at the CIA, where he'd been my chef in 1996.

Dan Turgeon had fair hair, graying at the sideburns and now thinning beneath a toque that made him seem taller than his six feet, a long, narrow face, blue eyes, a stiff-straight posture that projected an instructorly disposition. His speech was monotone, but his words were commanding in their blunt, declarative nature.

"What you gather now, you don't gather later," he said to his eighteen students, grouped in threes in the windowless boxcar-shaped kitchen. "Get what you need, get it at your station. You want to stay in one place and cook for four hours. Lot of demos today. I'm gonna suck up about twenty-five minutes of your day. Questions?—All right, go." Turgeon perched on a stool at the computer terminal to check e-mail as the students scurried to dry storage, to the cooler, ducking into their lowboys, to collect their mise en place.

Turgeon had welcomed me back and, at my request, put me to work with one of the groups. I wore my old jacket, houndstooth-check pants, neckerchief, and paper toque. I'd asked to be in his class mainly because Turgeon had been such a terror to me when I was first here. I'd spent just seven days on the grill station at American Bounty, but the impact of the experience was such that it seemed as though I'd been there for months. Experiences that make a permanent mark on the way you think ought to take longer. I'd spent a matter of days with the guy, which I recall more or less as continual white-knuckle fear that I wouldn't be ready for service, and even now I hear his voice in my head, telling me to stop what I'm doing and clean my station, that it's a battle, every day, me against the clock. A shrink would tell me my seven days in Bounty have all the benchmarks of classical trauma. I was shell-shocked for life.

All of which is to try to explain why I had such affection for the guy. He'd been right about everything, and I wanted to see what he was up to.

Turgeon was my age, Chicago born, found a job as a kid bussing tables, moved quickly to where all the cool stuff was happening (the kitchen), and had been there ever since. He graduated from the CIA in 1985, the year I graduated from college, and surely accomplished a lot more as a cook and a chef, much of it in D.C. and Maryland, than I did at anything in the eleven years between our graduations and the day he threw me on grill. At the time he seemed years older than me. He still seemed older, I found, but he was a lot more pleasant to be around now.

Dan had been in garde manger for four and a half years, a leap back to the middle of the curriculum and students of a different level from those he was used to in Bounty, where he got a new kitchen staff every seven days—truly a unique situation in the restaurant business. Now he had students for fourteen days over a period of three weeks, teaching a very different kind of food, a branch of cooking that was of particular interest to me, personally, because of the craftsmanship required to make it great. This was not Saturday-night restaurant food, heavy on the mise, high on the heat. This was food that was eaten cold, or if it was served hot, nevertheless came off the buffet line. This was the arena of the *pâté en terrine* and *en croute,* the plated ap for a party of thirty, wedding receptions, buffet service for big groups.

In restaurants, the garde manger station is the salad station, but traditionally the garde manger was the keeper of the food, the scavenger, the leftover wizard. He or she ground meat trim and fat and salt and seasoning and cooked it, thereby extending the life and usefulness of what had been scraps. The garde manger chef was an expert in seasoning because this food was often eaten cold and therefore required especially forceful use of salt and spices. The garde manger had to be especially keen in making food look good, because cold food almost never had the visual appeal that hot food did. The garde manger had to be versed in preservation techniques, such as salting and drying, had to understand specialty items like foie gras and cheese, had to be an ace saucier, again because cold food needs the serious muscle of craft behind it.

Garde manger is ultimately about specific specialty techniques, rather than a type of food, techniques that include forcemeat (from *farcir*—"to stuff"—it refers to meat, fat, and seasonings ground and mixed in preparation for a pâté or a sausage, or even a ravioli or some blanched cabbage leaves), curing and smoking, and more generally the creation of hors d'oeuvres and canapés.

"I was really apprehensive about this," Turgeon said, "but it's turned out to be my favorite class."

❧

Classical garde manger has long shouldered the burdens of its past—big buffet tables heaped with cold food, cut fruit garnishes, and tallow sculptures. They featured one if not many *pâtés en croute,* which in thoughtless hands is a dry meat loaf surrounded by rubbery meat gelatin and soggy pastry crust. Even the CIA course guide acknowledges its ambivalent past: "From its opulent roots with great master chefs such as Carême (with his lavish but not always palatable buffet presentations), Garde Manger has changed to meet the more practical demands of today." Not just meeting practical demands, but embracing the new dynamism of American cuisine, I might add.

The garde manger class concluded with what's called a Grand Buffet, an event that sounds straight out of the age of Carême and takes up four of the class's fourteen days, three in preparation, and one day for setup and service. It's a big deal. Large serving tables beneath vast tablecloths are assembled in the center of the dining hall (a former chapel that retains its stained-glass Bible scenes) and special serving platters are brought in. All of it has to be trucked from the basement level, where the garde manger kitchens are, to the main floor. Baking and pastry classes, held in a different building, bring in all their buffet concoctions, from baguettes to pretzels, plated desserts to petits fours on mirrors. And half the school is invited to have lunch here on this day, the day of the Grand Buffet, or several hours later, their dinner, prepared by the P.M. garde manger students.

Turgeon has divided the class into six teams working three stations, each station serving a particular style of cuisine. Almost needless to say, there is a classic French station—France is where so much of the garde manger discipline originates. So Turgeon will oversee the slicing, presentation, and serving of dishes one expects to see at a Grand Buffet— roulade of foie gras and magret (the breast of the Moulard duck, raised for its foie gras—it's almost as rich as a thick strip steak) with a fruit compote and sliced toasted brioche; a salmon *pâté en croute;* a smoked chicken liver terrine.

For the Italian station, he's included a pork loin stuffed with sausage, which will be served with a Caesar salad and eggplant "croutons." He calls out "Demo!" and the class huddles around station six as he demonstrates rolling the loin, butterflied and pounded flat, around the sausage and tying it. It will be browned, then roasted. "Watch the sear on the pork," he tells the group, noting pork's low-fat content. "The industry has raised these pigs to be chickens—they oughta have feathers." Next he moves on to the table preparing the favas for the three-bean salad, served with the tuna confit. He peels a raw fava—it's kind of a pain, he says, but it makes a difference. This was new—I'd peeled thousands of favas for his American Bounty succotash, and I always cooked them, shocked them, then peeled them. When they've been cooked, they pop right out of the skin; raw, it's like peeling an egg. When I noted the change, Turgeon informs me, every now and then with the old method, a batch would turn brown; this way, they never turn brown. Then on to the tuna, which he wants cut very small. "Portion size is really critical," he says. "You don't want a lot of big stuff on the plate. Get in touch with your feminine side, don't be afraid of it. Think of this as Barbie food." Then he barreled forward, on to the foie gras roulade.

I felt lucky he'd put me with the group in charge of something a little less familiar and more exciting: the Southwestern station. This was what the school meant by embracing the more practical demands of today. There would be a terrine, of course, but on this station it would be a chile-chicken terrine—dark meat ground with fat and seasoned with shallot, jalapeño, garlic, and oregano. Its interior garnish (things left whole and folded into the meat-loaf mixture that make the pâté visually and texturally dynamic) included roasted poblanos in addition to ham and chicken breast. The team making it must research and devise a suitable accompaniment—it would be some sort of chunky salsa.

Turgeon had a bent toward this kind of food, with its vivid flavors. In Bounty the steak that came off my station got a dry rub of ancho and cayenne powders, cumin, mustard, paprika, salt, pepper, sugar, and dried oregano before being grilled, and was served with a barbecue sauce—with a base of roasted tomatoes and veal stock—that included more dried and ground peppers, coriander, molasses, honey, and was at the end spiked with cilantro and bourbon. Now, for his Grand Buffet menu he did an ancho-rubbed skirt steak, which would be served as a tortilla with lime-cilantro sour cream, roasted red pepper and achiote salsa, and a chipotle pico de gallo. That's delicious just to think about, just as delicious sounding even if you didn't know what all that stuff meant, and you'd have to be a really bad cook to screw something like that up.

He did a sweet corn–and–shrimp soup, a chowderlike concoction seasoned with jalapeño, cumin, coriander, and lime. There were pork empanadas and barbecued lamb tamales (which used a barbecue sauce similar to the one I'd made in Bounty; mercifully, this one included no brown sauce about which I had become bitter and resentful while working there) and wild mushroom–and–cheese quesadillas. Even the salads were exciting, especially the one featuring fingerling potatoes, chorizo, and roasted poblanos.

This was American regional cuisine from the Southwest, a breath away from Mexican cuisine. But it was also, now, amazingly, the stuff of a classically influenced Grand Buffet.

Turgeon would stride past the tables during setup in the main hall, looking serious as a Doberman. Directly behind these students, the other A.M. class set up its stations. Casting a glance at the instructor of this class, John Kowalski, CIA class of 1977, Turgeon, ever straight-faced and deadly serious, said, "Hey, those recipes you got out of *Martha Stewart Living* are looking pretty good."

Kowalski, busy with setup, grimaced but failed to come up with a return thrust. There's a healthy competition among instructors here, especially when their food is on display side by side.

Turgeon estimated this was about his fiftieth Grand Buffet—nothing compared with the four hundred or so Chef James Heywood did during his many years as a garde manger instructor, but it felt impressive nonetheless. For his students, every thirteenth day of every block went like this: 7:00 A.M. to 9:00 A.M., gather mise en place, post To Do sheets, glaze, slice, dress, and finish all food. From 9:00 to 9:20, take equipment upstairs. By 10:00 A.M., finalize mise en place, change jacket (this is public cheffing, after all—gotta look clean), and organize stations. From 10:00 to 10:30, take food upstairs. At 10:30, Turgeon would demo each "interactive" station (those stations slicing meat to order or heating and finishing soup). At 11:00, roughly 350 students filed in and had their pick of French, Southwestern, and Italian foods, or, on the other side, Kowalski's class's stations, American regional from the South and from the Hudson Valley, and a station devoted to fish. In an hour their work and three days of preparation was done, time to break down, clean up, scrub the kitchen, and set out stools for the day's evaluation and a Day 13 quiz. (Turgeon, who was doing doubles this week, would repeat each step exactly seven hours later with the P.M. class.) Tomorrow would be the students' last class before leaving for an externship, paid work in the field, for at least four months.

❧

My very first day there, Turgeon called to me: "Hey, Michael, c'mere." He wanted me to see an e-mail that related directly to something we'd been talking about.

When I'd been there earlier in the spring, I began asking most chefs I spoke with how the place was changing. There were various responses, of course, but a single issue was almost unanimously common: the students had begun to complain. Not about anything specific; they were just generally more quick to voice discontent—about homework assignments, grades, workloads, stress factors, how difficult this or that instructor was being. If they didn't complain to their instructor, then they complained to the dean in charge of that instructor's team, and if not to the dean, then to their parents, who then called the school.

When I asked Ryan about this, he said, yes, both students and parents complained with increasing frequency. He said he hoped he wouldn't be like that when his kids were in school, but then shrugged as if to say, *How can you know?* Indeed, perhaps it was a change in the culture at large, related to parents' deepening involvement in their kids' lives as well as to a culture increasingly attuned to diversity in the workplace.

Whatever the reason, for the chef-instructors at a culinary school, the effects of this complaining may be more pronounced than they are for instructors in other types of schools. It seemed to undo a primary dynamic of the kitchen—the chef as omnipotent authority. Eve Felder, CIA class of 1988, who'd been my garde manger instructor, was now the assistant dean in charge of curriculum and instruction. She suggested the change in the dynamic may have begun in 1989, when the school first gave students teacher-evaluation sheets, officially called "Feedback Forms," to fill out at the end of each block. This was a revolutionary idea (and not a very pleasant one) to a chef who had been pretty much allowed to do what he wanted in his own kitchen. "My staff gets to evaluate me? Grade *me?*" Furthermore, everywhere in the industry, in every kind of kitchen, complaining wasn't done—you just didn't do it. This was a fundamental part of kitchen culture. Why? I don't know. Perhaps kitchen work is so damn hard that if you had any complaining gene in you at all you just got deselected out quickly. You let one complainer into a place this hard and hot and miserable, and pretty soon you'll be overrun by whiners. Or maybe it was simpler than that: Complaining in a kitchen just doesn't make any sense. It would be like walking through the Sahara and complaining about how hot it is. Obvious and irrelevant.

My favorite complaining story in a kitchen comes from Thomas Keller during his Rakel days: It had been a killer service and a long week, and one of his beat, sweaty line cooks couldn't wait to start breaking down his station to begin the work of cleaning the kitchen so he could go home. Then, at 10:55, five minutes before the kitchen closed, a server entered the kitchen announcing a late walk-in—"Order in!"—and slapped a ticket on the line cook's shelf. The line cook groaned. Keller fired the guy on the spot. The incredulous line cook said he was sorry. Keller told him to go home. The line cook couldn't believe it—said he was *sorry*. Keller told him to get out, told him if you don't like to cook, I don't want you in my kitchen. Keller meant it. And that was that.

You didn't complain in a kitchen—you quit.

Another Keller-related complaining story: Keller was evidently fairly demanding of all his cooks, and often what he asked didn't make sense to the one doing the work. He had one such prep cook picking basil. The prep cook had a pile of leaves in front of him and had thrown all the stems in the garbage. Keller, who was experimenting with infused oils—it was earlier in his career; he'd never use stems now, but at the time he was trying it—told the prep cook to get all those stems out of the garbage. This apparently was the last straw. The prep cook grabbed for the nearest knife and began chasing Keller around the kitchen. The guy had snapped. This is a more conventional form of complaining in the kitchen.

It all goes back to the fact that a professional kitchen is a place unto itself, a place where you can't lie. To allow people to complain opens up the doors to self-deception, laziness, and a lack of accountability. The work is hard; no one's forcing you to be here. If you don't like it, leave. If it's too hard, if you can't do it, we'll find someone who can—nothing personal—but service starts at 5:30 and there's a lot to do.

Certainly there has been behavior in revered kitchens on the part of the chef that would be considered criminal in the corporate world. It's hard to imagine the boss at your software company or ad agency jabbing your ass with a carving fork to get you to work faster, actually drawing blood—it wouldn't fly. But it happens in kitchens—a good thing houndstooth check hides spots. Thrown knives, sauté pans whipping past your ear—it happens.

But it's a different world today. You could get sued. The world of the restaurant has gotten complicated. In 1997 a hostess at the four-star restaurant Lespinasse in Manhattan, led by Gray Kunz, sued the maître d' for sexual harassment. Her actions, being a form of complaining by one of his staff, prompted Kunz to fire her. But hundreds of workers at the St. Regis Hotel, which housed the restaurant, protested the woman's dismissal, disrupting work and forcing guests to carry their own bags. The hotel rehired the hostess the following day. The issue grew so volatile that Chef Kunz left the kitchen for three weeks, till people cooled off. A half year later, he was gone (he said it had nothing to do with the event, that he wanted to open his own place—something that wouldn't happen for six years). Could that same Keller line cook file a wrongful-dismissal suit today? Maybe. Four-star kitchens have become haltingly respectable. In Keller's kitchens, everyone addresses everyone—from the lowest culinary school extern to Keller himself—as "Chef," a term of respect. There's no yelling and no throwing of utensils, and it's been years since anyone's chased Keller around the kitchen with a knife. Indeed, in the fall of 2004, the French Laundry fired a sous-chef for what was described by numerous sources as grossly unprofessional behavior involving physical and verbal aggression and intimidation.

The CIA, of course, happened to be training those people who would go out into the new professional kitchen and other segments of the industry. It believed the standard of professionalism was not relative to one's surroundings—standards applied to the corporate boardroom and skills kitchen in equal measure. But it was the power of the students to complain, combined with the changing nature of the workplace, the country's increasing ethnic diversity, and the growing sensitivity generally to discrimination and harassment, that was causing some Sturm und Drang among the teaching staff. What was acceptable behavior on the part of the chef-instructor and what was not seemed to be changing. Screaming was once considered an effective tool for getting something done in a kitchen—that didn't fly anymore, and no one had a problem with it, but did that mean you couldn't express anger? If you could, how much and in what form? If you wanted a kid to be accountable for his work, to be prepared for the day's lesson, say, come to class with a To Do list or having memorized key techniques and terms in cheese making, and he didn't, you could get mad at him, but nowadays, that kid could complain that your getting mad was intimidating. And, now, intimidation is not allowed.

Turgeon later described the effect of this on chef-instructors to me this way, a small example from a uniformly respected and admired teacher who, though considered tough, generates very few complaints: "When I was in Bounty, I didn't think twice about saying 'fuck,'" he told me. "But one day in here, I got really upset at a group that was underperforming. I turned and walked toward the sink and said 'fuck.' This was a Friday and I went home and worried about it *all* weekend. *Am I gonna get in trouble for that? Maybe the group thought I was yelling at them. Or maybe one of the kids is really sensitive and is gonna report me.*" Turgeon has had a student begin to cry in front of him. They're a different bunch these days. Many chefs say the student body has gotten younger, though during the past few years the average age of a student has dropped from twenty-four to only twenty-three. In Turgeon's class, the oldest student was twenty-three—except for one career-changer, a forty-one-year-old woman named Mary, who'd left mortgage banking to pursue her culinary ambitions. (That's a serious career change, but it seemed kind of a no-brainer to me. *Mortgage banking or working in kitchens . . . hmm, let's see.* Mary wasn't sure what she'd do with her culinary education but thought she was headed toward catering.) And another profound change: Most of these students didn't even want to be chefs. It used to be that sixteen out of the eighteen students would want to be chefs. "Now," Turgeon said, "it's half."

❧

All things considered, the timing of the student e-mail was apropos as far as my addressing this issue at the school and underscored its pervasiveness. The e-mail had been disseminated to the entire faculty by Jerry Fischetti, the associate professor who teaches Introduction to Interpersonal Communication. It had been written in response to a class assignment and was less dramatic itself than the response it elicited from the faculty.

"In my IIPC class," Fischetti wrote, "one assignment is to answer the following question: Comment on the statement, 'When emotions are involved, the emotions become the message.'" The student agreed with the statement and his response followed:

> On the opposite end of the spectrum, a person who is upset, angry, or hostile is going to send that message and that message only. In the culinary industry, it was a common practice for chefs to teach by methods

of fear and intimidation, not by compassion or patience. Some chefs teaching at the CIA, to this day, still practice those methods of teaching, and the effect on the student is discouraging. A student who is yelled at by an angry, upset chef only hears the negative aspects and not the lesson the chef is supposedly trying to teach. Hostile chefs create a lack of interest in the student, a desire to stop listening, to emotionally shut down and close their mind to learning new things—the exact opposite of what the chef-instructor is supposedly trying to achieve.

Turgeon immediately dispatched an off-the-cuff response, one that every chef who'd come to the warm world of the CIA from the dark and stormy world of restaurants appreciated, many of whom wrote similar responses:

Jerry, could you keep a record of this statement and send it back to this student after they have been in the industry for 5 to 10 years and let's see how their thoughts on this subject have changed. When the reality hits . . . your dishwasher just called out; your saucier just gave notice; the next months you foresee having just one day off; you currently are putting in about 80 hours a week; you just had to fire the front-of-the-house manager because they are stealing wine from the cellar; you need a new dishwashing machine because the old one is on its last legs; your business has been down the last couple of weeks because of high gas prices, and it's absolutely crucial that the local newspaper's review of you is a good one; and so on!

Now that's intimidation. And yes—chefs do yell sometimes!

✦

On the other hand, a number of students told me they didn't think the school was hard enough. Carrie Whealy, a twenty-two-year-old from Iowa, was among them. "I expected it to be really hard core," she told me. "I've been a little disappointed." She also said, interestingly, that she'd arrived at the school planning to be a chef, but now, almost two years later, recently back from her externship at Chez Panisse and with graduation six months off, she wasn't sure what she wanted to do. Perhaps go into writing, she confessed.

I was also spending time in Chef Pardus's class. I had dinner with him and several of his students—after service and before cleaning the kitchen and lecture—and I voiced what I'd heard from some students, that it wasn't as hard as they'd expected. They agreed unanimously. The chefs were great they said, but they didn't push you.

I was sorry to hear that. I didn't want to think that chefs here were going soft on students. Being hard and pushing me was the making of me, and I wasn't even a student. Not giving me the opportunity to take the easy way out was something that didn't just help me while I was at the school, it could be applied to everything I did. In a lot of ways, learning to cook saved my life. So to think that the school was filtering out what had been the most valuable part of it to me, personally, and doing so because it had allowed our culture of complaining to weave itself into the fabric of the school, was especially disheartening. Some chefs even wondered aloud if it wasn't the result of the school's pandering to consumers, trying to get and keep their business.

Nonsense, said Ryan. (Uncharacteristically, and with annoyance, he used a stronger word when I pressed the issue.) It's not a kinder, gentler kitchen, he said, and they aren't pandering to any consumer or competing for students' bucks. (They *are* competing for the very best students, Ryan said. The CIA accepts about 80 percent of its applicants, though the school notes many of the 20 percent are not accepted because the applicant doesn't complete the process, often because of the school's requirement for previous work in the industry.) But if by kinder and gentler, what was meant was more professional—that would be true, he said. If it meant that when someone was dressed down for not being prepared, it was their performance that was criticized, and that the student was not personally belittled, then that was true, he hoped.

"This institution as far as I know and throughout our history has never been about anything but continuing to raise the standards for our industry, for the profession, and for the individuals who are here," he said.

Yes, there were issues of how best to teach the work of the chef as the profession changed. More and more, the school looked toward how best to teach the individual rather than institute a blanket approach to instruction.

"There are two thousand three hundred students here and probably twenty-three hundred approaches to take," Ryan explained. "Does that require faculty members to be smarter? Yeah. Does it require them to work harder? You bet—and what's wrong with that? So I don't see any of these things being mutually exclusive, and I don't see them as being anything but a natural evolution."

Some of the faculty had noted the changing nature of their work and the continual struggle to be rigorous without being intimidating, an especially tricky tightrope given the extraordinary diversity of the student body—from sensitive high school graduates to knuckleheaded cooks to forty-one-year-old former mortgage bankers.

"I don't think people are confused, Michael," Ryan said, doing his best to temper my annoying persistence on the issue. "I think that people are struggling in accepting their personal responsibility, whether here or elsewhere. It's hard to accept responsibility. It's easier to walk by a piece of paper that's on the ground and pretend that you don't see it than to stop and to pick it up. It's easier to fool yourself into saying, 'Oh, somebody's going to come down on me or a parent might call me, therefore I can't push these students,' and that's not the case. Do we have to be more sophisticated about it? Yeah, absolutely we do, that's the way the world works. We're not cooking the way we were a decade ago, either."

That was a good point. It did come back to cooking in the end, and I liked how cooking metaphors were always quick at hand.

One of the chefs who had taken the new teaching environment most deeply to heart was my chef, Chef Pardus. He had a reputation for being a hard-ass. He had pushed me and challenged me, but he never intimidated me. I was bigger than him and this helped, since he could kick my ass on the line. Also, we were both in our thirties at the time—I wasn't an impressionable youth easily intimidated. He was unfailingly challenging, articulate, passionate, and really smart in his approach to food. But a lot of students now complained about how hard he was. They either liked him or hated him (the surest indication that something powerful is going on—you couldn't have a tepid response). True to form, he wanted to be the best teacher he could possibly be, and so he struggled mightily with softening his style without lowering expectations of student performance or diminishing his own passion. And he had an ongoing dialogue with the assistant dean, Chef Felder, a longtime veteran and spiritual torchbearer of Chez Panisse, who was another chef I had no end of respect for.

"I agree that tempering emotions is a necessity, you're correct in that and I will continue to struggle with it," Pardus wrote in an e-mail to Felder while I was there.

I'm having trouble separating the training of professional cooks in cooking fundamentals from holding them accountable for organization and forward thinking. If I nurture them every step of the way through the braising process, compensating for a lack of organization so that they don't become "intimidated" and shut out the fundamental cooking technique—am I succeeding?

On the other hand, if they are very well organized and have planned well because they are afraid of the negative repercussions of unpreparedness, but they undercook the braise and it's tough—have I failed?

I would rather have both a well-planned and successful dish. Unfortunately, many of our students come to class with the attitude that "showing up is everything."

I can work on my motivational skills, but fearing the wrath of the Chef is a time-tested tool for getting young cooks to follow directions.

"The perpetuation of the belief that 'fearing the wrath of the Chef is a time-tested tool for getting young cooks to follow directions,'" Felder wrote back,

disturbs me in the deepest part of my soul. Yes, fear is a motivator no doubt, but I come from the belief that one lights the fire of passion in a young person to be the best they can be through positive interactions and by setting very high standards for them to attain.

I equate this belief with how I cook as a chef. I cook from the understanding of what the item needs. What will make that vegetable taste the best that it can taste. I don't try to "master" the item. I look at the essential character traits of the vegetable and match my cooking technique and combination of flavors with those traits. In my core, for me, I know that that is the best way in dealing with people.

Certainly in raising children, we know that setting parameters and guidelines of what is acceptable and not acceptable is of paramount importance. How I work with Emma is very different from how I work with Genevieve [referring to her young daughters]. Like a new potato versus a strawberry, they each need something different while I still adhere to my commitment of raising children who have a strong sense of love, kindness, respect, and responsibility.

I so would like to change the belief that one needs fear to achieve the highest standard. What does fear do to an individual? What is "mastery" without love and passion? How do we nurture intrinsic motivation rather than extrinsic? Fear is so extrinsic to me. It comes from the outside. The only tool that fear gives is a perpetuation of fear itself.

Sharing knowledge, role modeling, the concept of the "more you give, the more that will come back to you," breaking bread and engaging in thoughtful conversation, committing to our belief in each other's greater good, holding each other accountable, giving each other a break, seeing clearly, creating a space for dialogue, for mistakes, are principles that are so near to me and so much how I want to live, the idea that "fear" works is terrifying to me. The energy of fear rattles my bones.

. . . I was up a lot of the night thinking of how long it takes to understand a person and how lucky I am that I have people like you who
aren't afraid of exposing yourself and digging deep into our similarities
and differences. I appreciate your time on this topic.

She signed it, "Respectfully, Eve," and the conversation continued
long after I left the school. Felder was right and Pardus was right; Felder
expressed a utopian ideal, and Pardus described the reality as he experienced it daily in the kitchen with a score of new, very different students every fifteenth class day.

Felder's idea, echoed by Ryan, about cooking to the item, to the potato and the strawberry, is apt and what makes teaching today so much
more complex and difficult than it used to be (and probably so much
more effective). Truth is, the cooking world is filled with knuckleheads.
It's filled with humanity of every stripe. For a knucklehead, a group I
include myself in, yelling works. Fear is a splendid motivator. Turgeon
learned this way, too. Why did he start to hustle so hard at his first job
after the CIA, at Vidalia under Jeffrey Buben, what made him excel? "I
wanted the chef to stop yelling at me so much," he said, grinning at the
memory.

But there are a lot of people out there who don't respond to chefs
who, as one phrased it, "discuss with volume." Mary the mortgage banker
surely doesn't need some hard-ass screaming in her ear to clean her god-
dam station. Nor the thoughtful Carrie, who was moving from the hope
of cooking to the intent to write about it. How does an instructor pitch
his or her teaching to students with such diverse goals in the same class?
The only way I know of is smaller, more specialized classes, but until
that happened, Pardus and Turgeon, both CIA grads, both cooks and
chefs who learned by getting their asses kicked and by working really,
really hard, would continue to grapple.

"Hard to believe," Pardus wrote to me toward the end of the summer
when I asked about the issue, "but I've become an anachronism. I'm
looking at it as a challenge. If I can soften my delivery without diluting

the intensity, I will become the teacher I want to be: one who is tough and rigorous but engaging. Alienating students is not in the long term best interest of my career."

I wrote back to Pardus, telling him he reminded me of Cool Hand Luke after he'd dug that dirt out of Boss's hole for the last time—"*I got mah mind right, Boss!*" Pardus said he was afraid I'd say something like that.

After I'd finished in garde manger, and saw Turgeon in the hall, I asked him if he remembered to hug his students today. He grunted, shook his head, and looked away.

I'm sure I was annoying to them, and they knew they were taking a risk before their colleagues, if not the CIA president and his administration, just by *talking* to me, and for that I was truly grateful, but I couldn't help it. I loved this school and all these chefs. They were really passionate about what they did, and what they did was to teach people how to work with food and everything that followed from that—which, as far as I was concerned, meant pretty much everything.

And as far as the students went, there were good ones and bad ones, diligent ones committed to extracting as much information from this place as possible and others who preferred to let the information wash over them. In my observation, the students who complained said more about themselves than about the school or this or that instructor—they defined themselves as people who put blame elsewhere rather than take responsibility for their actions. The harder they argued their point, the deeper they entrenched themselves. Those students who said that the school wasn't tough enough, that the instructors didn't push hard enough—they were the ones you wanted on your team.

CHAPTER 4

❧

Waiting for Bibimbap

"I want to welcome you. I'm Michael Pardus, your instructor in K-1 for Asian cuisines."

This was the pre–Day 1 meeting in which the chef set the ground rules for the next block or course of study and did his best to ensure that all were prepared and ready to roll the moment the block began.

With the curriculum revamp in 2001, not only had the name of the class been changed to more accurately reflect the cuisine (it used to be "Oriental" cuisine), it had been lengthened from one half block—seven days, followed by seven days of charcuterie, to a full block. The eighteen students now seated around a long table in the Continuing Education Center's dining room were currently finishing up their three-week block in American regional cooking, a course that also had been expanded from a half block (split with fish cookery) to a whole one. This made a huge difference. Pardus noted that in his class, for instance, instead of spending a scant one day each on Japan, Korea, Thailand, and Vietnam, they spent two. India and China got three days. This was enough for a brief overview of these styles, and importantly, the students got to prepare their menus at least twice rather than once. So, if your Thai papaya salad and green pork curry were lame, you had a chance to figure out why and try to fix it the next day. Previously the food with which most students were least familiar went by in a blur. Cuisines of Asia still remained a sprint, but there was now time for the class to develop a routine—they were still mastering basic restaurant service in addition to the food itself, rules of sanitation, station setup, and the order-fire-pickup that began at 6:00 sharp.

"I don't care who gets the food as long as it gets there. I don't care who cleans the floor as long as it's clean and half of you aren't in the courtyard smoking," he says, running through the rules of his kitchen after handing out tracking schedules, who's on which station on which days, what each station is responsible for, and a sheet spelling out exactly what he means by being prepared. "I know at five-thirty if the sous-chef has done a good job. . . . I really emphasize how you organize yourselves. Come to class fully armed with all the information you can bring to show you are prepared. You have daily assignments. I do not collect homework. This is so you cannot do a Google search of key terms and cut and paste."

Key terms included materials and methods—such as *paneer* and *katsuobushi* on days for the cuisines of India and Japan, respectively—about eight to ten a day.

"You do this, you don't understand your menu or a recipe, or anything, you ask me at three-fifteen, you'll get a gentle, patient person. Never hesitate to ask me. What's a severe bias cut—hell, what's a bias cut? What's it mean 'medium-low wok'—what's medium low for a wok? You come and ask me that at five-thirty, I'm going to tell you to go take a walk around the block, because you aren't prepared.

"I have a reputation for having a really hard edge. But I'm very passionate about what I do and when people don't join me in my passions," he says, and his lips curl into a tight grin, "I get a little cranky. . . . I'm really into it." Pardus has traveled in Japan, Thailand, has connections in Singapore—they speak English there, he tells the class, so it's not an intimidating place to extern, if they want that, he can help them line up work—and he has begun this year to organize a culinary tour of Vietnam. This is his fourth course during the ten years he's been at the school. "It's been my best so far," he tells them.

My final days back at the CIA would be the first four days of his course, cuisines of China and Korea. The menu included Hot and Sour Soup, Smoked Bean Curd and Celery Salad, Lacquered Pork Ribs, Crispy Tangerine Chicken, Moo Shu Vegetables, and Shanghai-Style Fish with Bok Choy and Fried Rice. Pardus's kitchen, like Turgeon's, was on the basement level of the main building and so had no windows and was long and narrow. Its dry-storage cage contained unfamiliar items, such as *nam prik pao* (a Thai chili paste), various fish sauces, noodles made from mung bean starch. There was a bank of ranges, but there was also a tall box used for steam-roasting and smoking pork ribs and pork shoulder butt and Peking duck; a tandoor oven; and three traditional restaurant woks with about 135,000 BTUs beneath them (a normal range produces about 20,000)—lift a wok off its base, the dozens of jets of flame below looked like rocket-engine output. Cooking in one of these numbers was an education—the kind of experience you can get only by doing it. The wok got so hot, you couldn't let your food sit still in it; you had to keep your food dancing above the surface continuously or you'd burn it. Above these woks were wall spigots for cleaning them with a big wood-handled brush, then tipping the water out into a trough that channeled it to a drain behind the stove.

It felt good to be back in class. You arrived and got straight to work—no lecture or preamble from the chef, no dithering while others got their shit together. In K-1 we gathered product and began making our dishes, developed by Pardus, Shirley Cheng, and their colleagues in Asian. At first, Pardus said he felt a little intimidated and unsure—how authoritative could a white boy from Connecticut be on Asian cuisines? Eventually, after a lot of study and travel, he thought he might have an advantage over Shirley Cheng, from Chengdu, China, or Prem Kumar, from Kerala, on the southern coast of India. They cover seven regions of the Eastern world, and while Cheng or Kumar would no doubt bring an authoritative depth to their native regions, they also had their own biases. Pardus hoped he'd bring both knowledge and balance to every region.

Early on the first day, a student approached Chef Pardus with a chunk of ginger she'd just peeled. "Do you want this grated or minced?" she asked.

He said, "Minced," then paused. "Ya know, why don't you get me a piece of ginger, a peeled carrot, and a scallion at your station, and I'll show everyone how I want them done." The first day, he answers a lot of questions and demos a lot of the basics they'll be using each day.

"Hey, folks, come on down here so I can show you something real quick," he called to the class when the ginger, carrot, and scallion were ready at the station. But he scanned the long steel table, lined with food and cutting boards, and said, "Where are your tasting spoons? How can you cook without tasting?"

"We're that good," a student in front of him said.

"I'm gonna call you on that one," Pardus returned. "That's the kind of statement that's gonna come back and bite you on the ass. I'm the only one allowed to be cocky here." He grinned, then moved on to peeling ginger: "Instead of using a knife or a peeler, use a spoon. It gives you a better yield and you can also dig into the crevices. When you mince it, don't cut it into random chunks"—he makes a frenetic chopping motion—"and talk about what you did over the weekend. You bruise it. I want a nice, clean, dry mince."

Next he demoed a scallion—long cuts on the bias, noting that there are all kinds of biases you can use on a scallion, but he wanted, he said, "nice, long, pretty, thin, feathery pieces. . . . I'm holding my knife like they taught me in Skills. Don't worry about raging speed. Do it right."

And he demoed a carrot. Rather than squaring it off, removing the rounded edges, he sliced it on a bias into thin sheets, then fanned the sheets like a deck of cards on the board and rocked his knife across the sheets to create a quick julienne, uniform in width but of differing lengths. "No waste, a lot faster," he said. "Are these good enough for a consommé? Probably not. Are they good enough for a stir-fry? Absolutely."

And on we went through to service, three and a half hours that zip by. This is another part of the life and spirit of the kitchen—the nature of time feels different here. Time goes by really fast in a kitchen, but not in the sense of your not being aware of it, an effect often described by artists and craftsmen when they become deeply engaged in their work. It's the opposite. You're intensely aware of time—service is at 6:00, after all, and you've got to know where you stand relative to that. But because time moves at a rate that's different from normal clock time, you simply have to learn to sense that those nuts you put in the oven or those beets roasting in foil ought to be done by now.

One result of this unique time dynamic is that it's easy to spend twelve hours in a kitchen and have it feel like a normal day at work. Are you tired? Yes, but not that tired—it's not like time spent sitting at a desk or taking call in your hospital's ICU for twelve hours or a shift in the mailroom. There's something about the combination of working with food—the nature of the craft of cooking, its physical and mental demands—and the irrevocable deadline of service that changes one's sense of time. The relentless daily service is critical to the dynamic. It keeps you engaged in the time you might otherwise tend to forget about altogether, as a painter or woodworker does. You can't be heedless if the deadline of daily service looms—when you will either be prepared (and have a good night and your soul is nourished) or you will not be prepared (and you get your ass kicked and your soul is bruised).

I thought about this squishy time business because I'd spent that morning, starting before seven, in the Caterina kitchen, the school's showcase restaurant serving the public, watching another class study balsamic vinegars, then prepare for service. By the time I got out of Pardus's class, after dinner, cleanup, lecture, and a quiz, it was after nine and getting dark. And I felt great, tired as if from a good workout, not beat. This was a beneficial aspect of the kitchen. But also it led some chefs to work too hard—those chefs who wouldn't leave the kitchen feeling good, because if you felt good it meant you could still do more work, and so they invariably worked past that point of feeling good, always trying to do more, because they were chefs and that's how they lived. A fourteen- to sixteen-hour day is fine, but if it's all you do, seven days a week, it's gonna run you down and crush you eventually. You had to know your limits; you had to find the right balance of work to nonwork time.

※

Theo Roe's Skill Development I ran simultaneously with Pardus's class, and I'd make periodic dashes from one to the other for numerous reasons. I was curious about how Skills had changed, because it had been so important to me, was the place where I learned what I needed to know in order to learn the rest. Roe, moreover, was a brand-new teacher, and this was his very first class—all new instructors begin by teaching Skills, as is appropriate, I suppose. Roe, I discovered, had been a sous-chef under Pardus when Pardus was running the kitchen of Mustards, in the Napa Valley, Cindy Pawlcyn's seminal bistro, then followed Pardus to Sonoma when Pardus took over the Swiss Hotel. And, finally, I wanted to know the students who were currently entering Skills at the CIA. This was perhaps the most surprising of all.

I don't think what I found was unusual, but it felt dramatic. Before Roe's class, I'd attended a meeting of incoming students, about ninety or so, and afterward met by chance an accountant, a sales and marketing professional, and an attorney—two women, one man—each in his or her forties or early fifties, entering culinary school, what some people still considered a trade school, Dr. Ryan's views notwithstanding. From there I headed to Roe's class. His students, having arrived early, lingered outside under and around a gazebo. I met a personal injury lawyer and a New York City landlord, a cop from Wichita, and a Boston social worker, each in the early to mid-forties. Dan, a Chinese American still in his twenties, had grown up in the restaurant owned by his dad in Brooklyn, then had been on Wall Street for five years but wanted to return, he said, to the work he felt he ought to be doing—restaurant work. A UCLA graduate who'd worked in L.A. entertainment and also the dot-com world before it burst was among them, along with Guy Anderson, thirty-six, who'd left his job as a director of communications for West Virginia University. And there was also a fifty-three-year-old orthopedic surgeon named Phil Farris, from southern Louisiana. He'd been working in hospitals since age fourteen, but when two close friends died of heart attacks, he took it as a warning to seize the day and decided to follow his passion for food. He was such a foodie, he said, he felt like a Jew wandering the desert until he arrived here, and realized, "I've found my people!"

He'd enrolled hoping to one day open a restaurant in Belize, where he owns some land, but then discovered, he said, "now I don't know, there's so many opportunities."

On their first day, after a thorough tour of the kitchen, the first order of business was to begin stocks, and it was helpful to have an orthopedic surgeon such as Phil in class. Chef Roe discussed various types of bones and how they affected the final stock—young bones have less flavor but more gelatin for body; older bones have more flavor but less gelatin; joints are loaded with gelatin; meat still on the bones is loaded with flavor. Roe lifted a large joint from a tub of beef bones, and Phil commented as if they were rounding on a patient and lecturing his interns.

"Anytime a bone meets a bone there's going to be a lot of articulated cartilage," he said, the class huddled around a pot on the stove. Roe held up the bone as Phil pointed. "This is the femur, and you'll see at the distal end—the far end of the femur—here you've got your articulated cartilage. And that's the meniscus," he said, apparently delighted to see the connective tissue, the fibrocartilage, he'd so often repaired in aging and sports-damaged knees. Good gelatin means good body in your stock—ask your purveyor for extra articulated cartilage.

There was, indeed, an extraordinary range of students here. Far more eclectic than when Chef Roe, class of 1994, had been here. Theodore

Roe, thirty-eight, from State College, smack in the middle of Pennsylvania, was a big, solid chef, six-two at least, blue eyes, brown hair, and an aw-shucks easiness in his conversation, whose early ambition to be a ski bum hastened his fall into cooking (he'd worked in kitchens throughout high school). He did his CIA externship at Mustards and there met Pardus.

I found Roe down in his cubicle—chef-instructors have desks on the top floor of the main building and typically share space with another instructor—with his *Pro Chef,* the CIA textbook, open to "Egg Cookery" and studying his computer terminal. I'm a fan of eggs, and we discussed the subject and agreed that much finesse was required for superlative eggs. Eggs lead Theo immediately into a personal testament to the importance of excellent egg technique.

One of his first jobs was as a breakfast cook at a Marriott in Denver. It's pretty hard to get much lower in the cooking hierarchy, but he'd cooked *thousands* of eggs there. Theo comes right out and says, "I'm not hip enough to live in New York"—a quality I can relate to—but because of the thousands of eggs, he moved into a regular line cook's position, thirty hours a week, at a very hip joint on the Upper West Side of Manhattan, above his station in every way.

"I worked at Café Luxembourg," he told me, "part time, while I was a student here at the college—the administration likes to refer to the Culinary as a college these days, and I guess it makes me feel important. A friend set me up with a tryout for their brunch service. Because of my breakfast cooking experience at the Marriott, I was able to jump right on the hot line. First, the Marriott taught me how to properly cook eggs, which believe it or not, is a skill all to itself. Another good thing about being a breakfast cook was it not only taught me how to read tickets and expedite, but it also forced me to be clean and organized. Chefs hate disorganized slobs."

If you are a cook, there is something to be learned everywhere you go, even if you are a Marriott breakfast cook.

It intrigued me, also, that this former breakfast cook was now in charge of training tomorrow's chefs. Roe had obviously come a long way. *How did the CIA—the leader in American culinary education—hire chefs?* What did they believe a chef must know in order to qualify as a teacher of tomorrow's chefs, how good did they have to be, and how did the school evaluate a prospective chef's knowledge and skill and taste?

As it turned out, I found, they hired chefs not unlike the way a restaurateur hires a new chef for his or her establishment. Prospective chefs fly in and try out, cooking for Tim Ryan and Henry Woods, associate dean for faculty development, and up to six others, answering questions about their food to test their knowledge. If they pass, they are asked to give a lecture and demo to a class, on, say, egg cookery, or making polenta.

But just as the student body had evolved, so had the incoming chef-instructor.

"Our ideas of what it takes to be a successful chef-instructor have changed," said Woods, the man in charge of the hiring process, a 1978 graduate of the school. "It's a more complex world. Being a real good cook, fifteen, twenty years ago—that was OK. But it isn't anymore." For instance, they used to hire a pastry chef for their baking and pastry curriculum. They now have categories of chefs for this program: artisan bakers, production bakers, and pastry chefs—everywhere, the chef world was specializing. Of the three hundred or so applications Woods sees each year, the candidates most likely to be hired are those who have been referred by current chef-instructors. The least successful candidates, he said, are CIA graduates who apply on their own, thinking that the school is the same place they graduated from.

When an applicant looks good on paper—eight to ten years in the industry, good cover letter, good résumé, in midcareer growth rather than burned-out-and-looking-for-a-nine-to-five-with-weekends-and-holidays-off job—Woods invites the chef for a tryout.

The first thing a prospective instructor must do is cook a four-course meal for eight people. "The price of admission," Woods says. "They have to demonstrate they have the fundamental skills." If they don't, *sayonara*.

Thus, on Mondays, when the Escoffier restaurant is closed, one or two prospects will try out in that kitchen, which has a built-in, big semi-circular viewing window. The chefs have four and a half hours to prepare and present their courses: a consommé, a salad, a fish course, and a meat course.

Consommé takes some craftsmanship and knowledge. Can they make a perfectly clear beef soup—date-on-a-dime-at-the-bottom-of-a-gallon clear—one that doesn't taste solely of the garnish they put in it but has a rich, full-bodied beef flavor? Salad: They've been able to go to the CIA's formidable storeroom in order to pick ingredients that satisfy them, and the CIA staff will evaluate how complex the salad is. Did the chef simply use mesclun greens, or did he or she choose a variety of ingredients, perhaps roast some vegetables, perhaps toast or candy some nuts? How was their vinaigrette—simple or complex—and was the acidity right? The chef is presented with a fish and a meat, and must devise a dish for each on the spot. Does the chef know what the fish is, does he or she fabricate it well, serve the right portion size? And is it seasoned and cooked properly? Does the chef make a fumet from the bones or decide on an easier, nonstock-based sauce? And then the meat: a similar set of evaluations and expectations from the judges.

Having sent out the last course, would-be instructors then leave the kitchen to sit before the panel—usually several are Certified Master Chefs—to be grilled about the food they've just cooked and served. Do they speak well about it, do they have clear explanations for how and why they handled the food as they did, why they paired this meat with that garnish? Sometimes, Woods said, the panel will like the food but sense no passion or energy from the chef, qualities a chef-instructor must have. Other times, the food will be borderline, but the chef wows them with a passion for food and cooking, or with exceptional articulation of a subject, and may be hired on the basis of this.

If they pass the chef practical, they are then invited to teach a class. If they succeed here, they will be given an offer. If they accept, they'll be trained in teaching skills for six weeks before they begin their first Day 1, the maiden voyage in Skill Development. Which is where Theo Roe is now, a bit slow to react, a bit plodding and unsure, but not lacking confidence in his knowledge and technique, simply finding his teaching legs.

For his chef practical, Roe did a Beef Consommé Royale ("Royale" signifies a plain custard garnish, a form of egg cookery, notice; one whole egg and three yolks per cup of cream, according to Escoffier #496, chilled, then diced); a salad of organic lettuces, pickled globe beets, spiced walnuts, Chatham goat cheese, and a Dijon vinaigrette. He was given striped bass for his fish and a couple of chickens for his meat. He poached the sea bass and served it with a citrus butter and an herb salad. He broke down the chickens, roasting the bones for a natural jus; he made a forcemeat with the dark meat and piped that into slits he made in the breasts, which he partially sautéed first, to render fat out of the skin, then finished in a low oven to ensure they would cook all the way through without drying out. He served the chicken sausage–stuffed breasts with herbed spaetzle.

"My cooking tryout was intimidating," he recalled. "But I guess they liked it."

The chef tryouts all have an assistant for help, if they need it, to peel shallots, chop mirepoix, locate equipment, and the like. Frank Jerbi is the Escoffier kitchen Fellow—a recent graduate who assists the chef, a six-month paid position. Frank thus works for the chef tryouts. He can gauge the quality of the chef by how much the chef leans on him. The more work they ask him to do, the worse they tend to be. One chef, for instance, had to ask Frank if he thought he had enough egg whites for the consommé. "I don't think that's gonna do it, man," Frank told him. The guy didn't pass, Frank's advice notwithstanding. Frank was Roe's assistant and said Roe was "cool," hardly asked for any help at all.

Pardus did his tryout at the winery kitchen of Markham Vineyards, in St. Helena, in the Napa Valley. He threw up in the parking lot beforehand, but he felt better once he got cooking. He, like Roe, did a Consommé Royale and pan-roasted chicken. He garnished his salad with roasted tomatoes and a goat cheese crouton. The most interesting part of his tryout, though, was receiving the odd small fish they gave him—smooth, shiny skin, looked like pompano only really small. He finally decided they must be pompano and was right. They were too small for eight portions, he said. The proctor agreed and got him some tiger shrimp, and he made a forcemeat with these. (Forcemeat is a display of craft the judges love to see.) Pardus seasoned his with citrus zest. He made a stock with the fish bones as a sauce base. He thought it was a good dish, tasted great. But, before the panel, when Tim Ryan asked how he dealt with the texture of the shrimp farce, Pardus immediately realized his error: He should have pushed it through a tamis, a drum sieve, so that it would be completely smooth on the palate. Thinking fast, he said he'd seasoned the shrimp with citrus zest before pureeing them and didn't want to tamis out the flavor. Ryan surely spotted this as the BS that it was—but he probably didn't care; what would have been important to Ryan was whether Pardus *knew* in the first place to tamis the farce for a smooth, clean texture, and he did.

I would imagine it's a nerve-racking experience, even if you're doing something you do all the time, like breaking down chickens and cooking fish. But cooking techniques are not what usually brought a candidate down, but rather bad decisions—thought mistakes. "You'd be stunned by how many people try something they've never done before," said Woods, naming the biggest cause of failure in the tryouts.

⌗

Frank Jerbi is twenty, young for the management position he holds, the sous-chef of this restaurant kitchen. He has brown eyes and straight brown hair, and his pallid complexion shows off deep circles beneath his eyes, the mark of overtime and weekend jobs. I admired the confidence with which he both instructed students and with which he cooked. He said the chef tryout was easy—he could pass it no problem, and from a purely cooking standpoint, I didn't doubt him. My first day in the kitchen of the Escoffier Room, the school's oldest restaurant, one devoted to classic French cuisine, he made the consommé. "I've been making consommé twice a week for a year," he said. "I love it."

I appreciate the craft of the consommé, so I asked him to describe the finer points of making it.

He shook his head and said, "It's the ratio, man."

Now I really liked the guy—ratios are truly what cooking's all about. It's not about the ingredients; it's about the proportions of those ingredients: 2 eggs per cup of liquid make a custard; 0.3 ounce of salt seasons a pound of ground meat; 3 parts fat, 2 parts flour, 1 part water make a pie dough; and 100 percent flour, 60 percent water, 3 percent fresh yeast, 2 percent salt equals bread. This is where cooking begins. Are the ratios variable? Sure—I like less egg in a custard, and maybe another cook wants less salt in ground meat—but the point is, you have your own convictions, which are matters of preference, and preference is relative to standard ratios. Only once these are committed to your soul can you truly begin to cook.

I asked Frank what the ratio was for his consommé, a stock made clear with egg whites, its flavor fortified with meat and aromatic vegetables. He rattled his off: 5 quarts stock, 3 pounds meat, 1 pound mirepoix, 10 tomatoes. "Plus whatever scraps from garnish I have" (the soup is garnished, in part, with leek, carrot, and celery julienne, the cutting of which yields a good amount of flavorful trim). This was straight out of *The New Professional Chef,* one of the school's texts. He salted to the chef's taste—Chef Le Roux, from Brittany—the chef liked things really salty, he said.

Frank, too, appreciates the finer points of consommé. He said he cut the mirepoix—2 parts onion, 1 part each of celery and carrot—in a julienne, rather than in a rough cut. When you mix egg whites, vegetables, and ground meat into stock, then bring it to a simmer, the egg whites coagulate around the meat and vegetables and rise to the top of the pot in the shape of a thick disk, called a raft or a clarification. The way it clarifies a stock is that the proteins of the egg white form a mesh, and as it rises, it collects all the particles that make the stock cloudy. Frank said he cut the mirepoix in thin sticks because he felt as they overlapped within the raft, forming their own mesh, they made the raft sturdier. I liked the notion that the vegetables, whose purpose is to add flavor, mirrored the network of proteins. I don't know if it really mattered, but it was an elegant idea and worth the extra effort to someone who liked to cook.

Also, he has a special tool for his consommé, a four-foot length of plastic tubing. By the time the raft has formed, the stock is mainly clear, and you can see this as it bubbles over and through the raft. You must keep cooking it so that the vegetables and meat give up their flavor to the liquid (the egg white also traps flavor molecules and gelatin). But you should cook it only so long, because eventually the vegetables will break down, and their particles might recloud the stock. Once the consommé has cooked for the appropriate time, it is then strained through a coffee filter to remove all the solids. Typically, one pressed a ladle through the raft to get the stock out. You had to be careful, because you inevitably break up the raft when you do this and threaten the clear stock. When Frank's consommé was done, he set it on the counter above a five-quart container and a strainer lined with a coffee filter. He stuck the plastic tubing down into the consommé and siphoned it out. This method disturbed the raft as little as possible and saved quite a bit of time as well, the elegant fluid issuing from the tube as if from a spigot.

In the Escoffier Room, this consommé was not simply served as is or even with ordinary garnish. The restaurant has added the name Bocuse to it, and the signature *B* above the ranges, in honor of the Great One (this class, in fact, currently had a Troisgros offspring working sauté; the restaurant preparing Italian food currently had a young Vongerichten in its ranks; and, as long as we're dropping names, the school made no secret of the fact that Bocuse sent his own son here). Thus, the consommé Chef Le Roux served was the one Paul Bocuse made famous at his Lyonnais restaurant—Consommé Elysee, formally, but Le Roux called it by the name of its creator. The broth is garnished with black truffle, foie gras, julienned meat (beef or chicken, depending on the broth), julienned vegetables, then sealed with puff pastry and baked at service till the dough rises into a golden brown dome. The diner breaks into the flaky crust to release the heady aroma of truffles in the piping hot broth. Damn good dish.

Frank intended to finish a year's fellowship here, then continue in the bachelor's program, for two more years of study. He'd been a line cook through high school, and it was hard for me now to picture him out of his whites, out of a kitchen. He was a genuine cook—you could see it in his eyes—he had that aged look already. When I asked about how the CIA was changing, he said immediately, "It's getting kind of touchy-feely," adding, "I need someone yelling at me to motivate me."

He and Chef Le Roux got along well. Le Roux had been a new skills instructor when I was in Pardus's Skills class, but whereas Pardus was now nearing forty-seven, Le Roux was fifty-nine. He was a veteran of some of the great classical kitchens of New York—Le Pavillon and La Côte Basque among them—a man of few words and infrequent smiles, dark eyes, gray hair, a sweet man, who I suspected was a really good cook. Married with two daughters, he noted with evident regret that his girls had been all but completely raised by their mom, because he was always working so hard as a cook. He had been at La Côte Basque when a major shift in French dining occurred in the United States in 1980: formal tableside service—big racks of roasted meat carved, served, and sauced tableside—became contemporary plates constructed by the kitchen brigade. Le Roux remembers it as a kind of trauma, suddenly everyone plating everything in the kitchen. "After the first day, I was exhausted," he said. "And *I* was *fast*." He went home thinking, *I don't know if I can do this—I've got to reevaluate the way I run my station.*

Frank now did certain tasks the chef entrusted only to the Fellow, such as make the consommé, make the chicken-mushroom farce for the sautéed chicken dish, and cut the foie gras.

Xavier Le Roux, who emigrated from France in 1966, had risen through the cooking ranks apprentice-style, as is customary in that country. He was an old-fashioned chef, well respected at the Culinary. I tasted some of the sauces for his fish entrées as he was instructing the poissonnier on Day 1, with service a few hours off, how to make them and how they should taste—sorrel sauce and a fresh "herb jus" using tarragon, chives, sage, basil, marjoram, and parsley. They were superb, colorful, light, and bright. I spent most of my time there just watching and talking to this French chef, mainly focusing on changes here. Yes, the students did seem to be getting younger, he said. He didn't think it was a kinder, gentler kitchen today; it was what it was. "I'm here to introduce you to restaurant cooking," he would tell his class during the hour lecture that preceded dinner, prep, service, and cleanup. "I'm not here to teach you how to sauté."

He did note that the number of European chef-instructors here had diminished markedly. At one time, Germanic accents predominated here, or seemed to, but the new ranks replacing the old were more likely to be young American chefs than European ones.

What did the French chef of the Culinary's classic French restaurant think of the new style of experimental cooking popping up here and there? What, for instance, did he think of Ferran Adrià, the ground-breaking Spanish chef and poster boy for the avant-garde movement? "Why do you need to freeze foie gras and turn it into powder?" was his response. Give him a nice, thick piece properly sautéed and he was happy.

But most food wasn't that way today, he noted. "It's still classically based," he said. "The name has changed; it's fashion. Instead of 'red wine sauce,' they name the wine and the region." That is, it's still about the basics.

Nor was Le Roux narrow-minded. He often let students put specials on the menu. One student recently made a beef consommé and infused it with tarragon so that it was clear but tinted green. The student gelled this consommé with agar, a seaweed-based carbohydrate that will keep a liquid gelled even when hot. When the consommé was poured onto a sheet pan and set, it could be cut into noodles. The consommé noodles became a main garnish for a lobster bisque special.

Frank, a traditionalist, obviously thought it felt "weird" to eat hot gelatin. Le Roux shrugged and said, "That's the cooking of tomorrow," apparently happy to remain in today. Le Roux was old-fashioned, too.

"He didn't speak to me for the first three months," Frank said fondly, quenelling the chicken-mushroom farce for the stuffed chicken breast into simmering water. "He was just makin' sure I knew he was the man." Frank tasted a quenelle, then brought one to the chef. As the chef raised the quenelle to his mouth, Frank said, "More cream, more salt."

Chef Le Roux tasted, then nodded, and as Frank turned to leave, Le Roux said, "Kick it up a notch!" and he looked at me and chuckled.

⇒•⇐

Cooking is both simple and infinitely complex, and so is a cook's relation to it. When I'd been at the CIA, learning skills, I'd had lunch at the Escoffier, and it had been my favorite restaurant of all. I loved the formal tableside service, a lost art in America. I loved the classic food for its high craft. But I had changed. This kitchen, which I once stood in awe of, now seemed overly busy and awkward. The food was not as good as I thought it should have been. The sautéed sweetbreads were sliced too thin, and so were impossible to cook right. The foie gras terrine was also sliced too thin, shorting the sense of luxury that made foie gras special in the first place, and it was oxidized around its perimeter, a quarter-inch border of unappealing gray. Escoffier was a teaching kitchen that restaffed every seven days, granted, but these little things, which I'd never have noticed when I was first here, now bothered me. The food showed me just how much I'd changed since I'd first arrived eight years ago as a journalist.

I still got a chill when I entered my old skills kitchen, K-8, where Mediterranean cuisine was now taught and served. This very kitchen—with its two banks of ranges on each side, three gigantic steam kettles, and central aisle—was the spot where my life pivoted, and it was filled with the ghosts of my former classmates: Adam Shepard, a cook in the artist-monk tradition, the best in our class, with a knife hand damaged in a carpentry accident. He now lived in Brooklyn with his wife and toddler son, and had just opened his own restaurant, a Japanese noodle house called Taku, near his apartment. The *Times* had given him one star, and he was delighted to have been reviewed. Adam is the kind of cook who would make a duck pâté at home, chopping the meat by hand (which he'd done shortly before I'd last seen him).

Ben Grossman had left accounting in his midtwenties to pursue cooking. He'd been our group leader. A bit before my return to the CIA, I'd been sitting with some friends at an outdoor table on the Upper East Side of Manhattan, around midnight, when I heard my name called, incredulously. Ben was walking his dog. He was a chef at the Cub Room, in SoHo, but would leave soon after, upon the birth of his first child.

Paul Trujillo had been cooking on a clipper ship.

Erica Norman was a cook in Philadelphia.

I'll never forget these people. Learning to cook changed my life. They are a part of me, forever imprinted on my brain as associations with the trauma of learning to cook.

Thus I walked through this particular kitchen one day with Dan Turgeon and experienced quite a bit more than one would normally experience. He'd asked me if I wanted to grab some lunch while I was in his class, and this was the kitchen he chose. But the ghost of Turgeon was there, too, and this ghost and the chef-instructor beside me were different people. I felt hyperaware, as if the kitchen tiles in K-8 were charged with this lost time—Lola and Travis and Paul and Erica and Ben and Adam were still there. Here I was, moving through my first CIA kitchen along with the chef from my last CIA kitchen. I carried a plastic tray, and a beautiful student named Carlie carved lamb for me from her station. Her smile was bright, and, like an angel who knew I was tripping on this experience, directed me to a fellow student, who'd made some excellent duck rillettes. This student smiled vividly, too, and I felt time moving slowly, but as Turgeon and I headed toward the door, I recalled the oxidized foie gras. Dan Turgeon, the man beside me, was inert to me now. I continued to admire him as a cook, a chef, and an instructor, but it was Turgeon the ghost—most vivid and most valuable to me when I hated him, when he could make my life a misery—who made me feel that I was losing something by returning to the CIA as a writer and not as an aspiring cook.

※

As if to underscore this point, the cooking gods sent a fiasco my way. I'd chosen to spend my final days back at the CIA in Pardus's Cuisines of Asia class. On Day 4, the first day of Korean cuisine, five groups moved through their day's food assignment: a spicy beef soup called *yukkae-jang,* various kimchi preparations (Pardus liked to ferment his own), stir-fried glass noodles (*jap chae,* based on sweet potato starch), and others, including a fried trout dish, ingenious from a sales standpoint. In Asia, serving and eating whole fish on the bone is common, but it's hard to sell in America—we don't like fish bones in our fish. So Pardus stole an idea from his friend Michael Huynh, chef and co-owner of New York's Bao 111. Huynh, a native of Vietnam, wanted to serve fried fish with the bone, as they do in his country, but knew it wouldn't sell. What he decided to do was to take the fillets off the fish and run a skewer through the fin, spine, and head, so the fish would be shaped like an *S,* as if swimming. He then breaded and fried the fish skeleton along with the fillets, and put the whole fish on the plate, the bones separate. Pardus did his dish with trout and it looked really cool, the fish swimming on a bed of julienned red peppers, julienned nori, sliced scallions, julienned egg crepes, and toasted sesame seeds, served with a sauce of soy, ginger, vinegar, and Korean pepper paste.

I was helping the group saddled with the vegan dish, which Pardus was asked to offer, a request he agrees with. Chefs and cooks, myself included, too easily dismiss vegans—they can't truly care about food, the reasoning goes, given how they limit themselves. For a chef running a business, this was bad policy, and Pardus knew it. When Pardus got the vegan crowd on a packed Saturday night at the Swiss Hotel in Sonoma, he'd tell them, "Can't help you tonight, but listen, you come back Tuesday—bring your friends—and I'll do a whole vegan menu for you!" The vegans loved the special treatment, and Pardus filled his restaurant on what would otherwise have been the slowest night of the week.

Pardus had played up in lecture the night before an extra dish that was on our station, something called *bibimbap*—a dish that's fun to see, fun to make, fun to eat (it's even fun to say): a warm salad with stir-fried julienned skirt steak, spiked with the Korean pepper paste (which has, Pardus said, "an effusive fruitiness before the heat kicks in"), and topped with a fried egg. A spicy Asian version of the French bistro staple frisée salad with lardons. In Korea, the dish is a catchall—*bibim* meaning "thrown together" and *bap* meaning "rice." Anything thrown together with rice can justifiably be called *bibimbap*. But it's an important part of Korean culinary culture, and some cities, such as Chonju, are noted specifically for their *bibimbap*.

The members of my group were organized; they had an extra set of hands—mine—and I pressed them to do the intriguing *bibimbap* because it was my last day at the CIA, maybe forever. This was going to be fun, I thought, little bites of skirt steak marinated with ginger, garlic, scallions, and pepper paste; crunchy matchsticks of daikon and red radish, carrots, and cucumber; a chiffonade of iceberg lettuce and shiso leaves (a mint relative). Michael Grenko, a guy in his early twenties who hoped to open a restaurant with his dad, got to work on cutting veg while I did the marinade and cleaned and cut the skirt steak.

From 2:00 to 6:00, everyone's pretty much just prepping for service, much like any restaurant kitchen. The difference between here and a restaurant was that here service would last only twenty minutes and feed between forty and sixty people. Also, at a restaurant, you wouldn't expect a lecture after service with the possibility of a quiz. But it was a good routine and not difficult; there was time to think about your food and to poke around and see the other group's food, to break away to watch Pardus demo the scallion pancake or to discuss how much salt was used to ferment the kimchi.

Shortly before six, Grenko asked what I wanted to do at service. I told him whatever he wanted to do, I'd do the other. "I really like to stir-fry," he said. I said, "OK, I'll fry the eggs." I didn't really care what I did—I just wanted to produce the dish. We'd prepped about ten orders, and I'd cracked fifteen eggs into ramekins to be ready and had four clean sauté pans hot in the oven. Pardus said, "We'll sell five and keep five for family meal."

Pardus voiced his annoyance at the way Grenko was set up, with his mise en place in awkward spots of our station. Grenko fixed the problems, and Pardus got a small steel pan with plenty of oil smoking hot and dropped in an egg. "That's a little too hot," he said. The egg white deep-fried puffy around the outside and then turned crisp along the edges before the egg was done. "Pay attention to how you regulate your heat," he said. He put down rice in a bowl, then the hot stir-fried salad, then slipped the egg out onto the top, and moved on to the next station to demo their Korean dishes.

At service, *bibimbap* orders came quickly. Michael had his stir-fry done before my pan was completely hot. I dropped the first egg in—there was just barely enough oil and just barely enough heat. The egg stuck a little, but I managed to finesse it off without breaking the yolk.

The idea, when cooking an egg on a plain steel surface, is to have enough of a film of oil that's hot enough to cook the egg white before it sinks through the film of oil and touches the steel, where it *will* stick if it hasn't coagulated in that fraction of a second. Also, the pan has to be perfectly clean or the egg will stick no matter how hot the pan.

By the time I'd gotten the first egg done, three more *bibimbaps* had been called. The next egg went into that same pan. It stuck a bit from the last egg and I broke the yolk trying to free it, so I put pan and broken egg aside. Three pans left, two on burners and hot. I dropped in the third egg, and, thank God, it slid around in the pan on a sheet of hot oil. I was already behind, and the people who'd ordered the *bibimbap* had their arms folded, watching me. I moved to the waiting bowl of salad, lifted the egg with my nifty slotted fish spatula, and—oh my God—the egg stuck to the spatula! Sonofafucking *bitch!* I shook it and broke the yolk, dropped it back in its pan, grabbed a new pan (down to two), and borrowed a clean spatula.

I more or less went down in flames from there. The remaining minutes are a blur of broken yolks and ruined pans, which Pardus himself had to rush to the pot sink to clean to try to get me through this mess and save me from complete and total humiliation, a small cluster of unfortunate students standing aside, watching, waiting for *bibimbap*. On the last egg, I found my rhythm, which was of no use at that point, of course. Service was over. I could stick it up my ass and hold it there, I suppose.

I'd had twenty minutes to fry ten eggs—I couldn't even do five. I'd been shellacked and sent to the showers before the first inning was over. I was out of the game. I wasn't good enough. I couldn't fry an egg to save my life.

Welcome back, writer.

❧

"I'm constantly being told by certain people around this school that fear is not a good motivator."

This was the beginning of our nightly lecture, and it wasn't starting out to be pleasant. The rest of the kitchen had done well that night, leaving me alone in my mortification. I was a different person now. But everyone, including myself, had been a little lax in cleaning the kitchen. And Pardus had to nip this in the bud.

"That fear and intimidation are not good tools to use in an educational environment. You make me doubt that." He paced back and forth along the bank of ranges. "I berated you two nights ago because the kitchen wasn't clean. And yesterday the kitchen was clean. Why? Because you were afraid I was going to berate you again. Today, I praise you, tell you what a great job you did before you went to dinner, and you get all giddy. And then I have to go around, I have to inspect the kitchen, I have to point out the same stuff I pointed out two nights ago.

"So when I'm caustic and harsh and yell, things work. When I'm pleasant and patting you on the back and saying what a good job you're doing, everything goes straight to hell. Why is that? You have to answer that yourself and ask yourself which you prefer. Because I'm really leaning toward being a hard-ass. But on the other hand, I'm trying to find a better way to do this myself. It's up to you. If you can find the discipline within yourselves to get things done without being yelled at, then fantastic, and if not, then I'm afraid that's the only tactic that I have at my disposal to use. It's entirely up to you."

An egg fiasco, followed by a Dad Lecture. What a miserable way to end my days at the CIA.

✦·✦

PART THREE

The American Chef

❧·❧

CHAPTER I

Edge Cuisine: Grant Achatz

That very night, head hung, beat, I retreated to my car across the vast, crumbling parking lot behind the towering walls of the CIA. By grace, a dose of divine sugar to help me swallow the pill of the *bibimbap* fiasco, I ran into Krishnendu Ray, a lecturing professor in the bachelor's program, a sociologist from Balasore, a small provincial town on India's east coast, and later New Delhi, and in a way, the Sage of the CIA. It was he, for instance, who wrote to his colleagues the most thoughtful response to the student e-mail critical of chef-instructors who yell. After citing an academic source on reasons for anger in a kitchen, he reflected on anger's sibling:

> Humor, especially bawdy humor, is the other side of the same coin, which compensates for the angry outburst, cements the imagined community of bad taste, and makes us men. Nothing unites people more than their self-conscious bad taste, which by being vulgar, creates a distance between us and them out there with their repressive pretensions. Humor is equalizing where anger is hierarchical—both necessary for an imagined community.

Hence, in spite of its best efforts, the CIA has been unable to legislate away either the chef's angry outburst or his bawdy jokes. Instead
the Institute classifies them as unprofessional behavior, which makes
them both rarer but also so much more tempting to use, and more
powerful as subversive anti-corporate speech.

Just a sociologist's observations.
Best, Krishnendu

When I saw him ahead of me in the parking lot, I jogged to catch
him. I'd been trying to get in touch with him but we'd kept missing. I'd
visited his class in 1996 (he was lecturing, as I recall, about a theory that
all religion was simply an attempt to control women's sexuality—this, at
a cooking school!) and wanted to talk with him about the CIA then and
now. Kris has an easy smile and a calming manner; he regretted not getting together and asked me to call him when I was home.

When I phoned later in the summer, he told me that he was about to
publish a book, *The Migrant's Table,* about how food choices reflect the
dilemmas of ethnicity (this arising out of his doctoral thesis for SUNY–
Binghamton), and that he would soon take a teaching post at New York
University as assistant professor in the Department of Nutrition, Food
Studies and Public Health. When he first arrived in the United States in
1989, a scholar studying political economy and international development, interested especially with immigrant issues that concerned food,
food was not a proper focus in academia. It was OK for anthropologists
to study the eating habits of indigenous peoples, but not for a sociologist
to study his own family's table. Since then, however, the food revolution had penetrated the Ivory Tower, and a sociologist's study of contemporary food culture was now valuable. He noted, by way of example,
that he'd been asked by Princeton's Institute for Advanced Study to
deliver a paper on Italian cuisine, the first ethnic cuisine, he'll argue, to
go haute in America. He was now at work on a book that touched on
my own work: His was tentatively titled *Men in White* and would ad-

dress, he said, the chef's rise to prominence in American culture, drawing a strong parallel between the chef and the surgeon, each of whom began as a kind of low-life wretch and became a figure of authority, power, and reverence. I was eager to speak with him about that and hoped also to garner a quick glimpse of his shrewd and candid observations of the CIA.

The CIA both amazed him and often made him chuckle. All these rules, he thought when he first arrived in 1996—unlike anywhere he'd been before. "What other place prohibits colored underwear?" he asked me. He suspects the rules have evolved out of the fear that chefs might fall from grace, return to their wretched state, and so they try to change their language and behavior to mirror the corporate world where professionalism is more standardized.

"Chefs' humor is very bawdy, very working class, masculine," Kris said by phone from his office, "and now that has to be given a patina of professionalization, which creates funny doublespeak. The purest, cleanest, most proper chef pronouncements are basically undercut by a private world of vulgarity. If a chef is speaking politely to you, nicely to you, and not making filthy jokes, he doesn't trust you—I'll bet that. Which creates a peculiar schizophrenic culture. Which Bourdain plays with. Bourdain I think is so attractive because he outs that."

The chef's vaulting into popular culture, as Bourdain has done, has created a situation not unlike that of the musician or painter in the American arts scene.

"Most painters, most actors, are poor and wretched," he said. "Some are really stinkingly filthy rich and visible, and I think that's where cooking is. The CIA's attempt to turn it into a certification system like medicine and law—I don't know how much of that is going to be successful because of certain skill requirements. What you have to learn in medical school appears to be substantially more complicated long term than what you have to learn in cooking school. Not because cooking is inferior, but because there haven't been substantial technological transformations in cooking. So I don't know whether that wager is going to work completely—the wager of certification, that this is how people are going to be and this is what professional means.

"Though we try desperately to do that through attire and rules and proper behavior, and basically eliminate working-class attitudes out of a working-class institution. Bad behavior, bad boys behaving badly, is out. It gets sublimated, gets invisible, but it's the culture of the class. You try to legislate it away, that's why we sound so shrill. Dress codes and everything else—so loud and repetitive and so endless. You sit with faculty at lunch, the most important discussion they have is which student is out of dress code. . . . They know the past, and they know their own past. That's why it's doubly poignant, it's the fear of falling. They know what their real selves are, they can easily slide into some nice racist jokes and sexist comments, we know the temptations—that's why it's a little like being a born-again.

"I think as we cook less at home," he went on more generally, "cooking becomes more magical, and if that goes hand in hand with affluence"—that is, the more affluent you are the less you have to cook—"then you buy it like art, like craft. And like craft, it's riding up the escalator of status. Precisely because we can't do these things. We don't even know how to begin to do these things. And so cooking begins to turn magical. And then for magic to happen you need magicians to claim that it is magic, which is what chefs are now doing."

The gender aspect he found interesting and telling—that now women are increasingly influential in professional kitchens. The CIA demographic described it accurately. Only a handful of women graduated from CIA programs through the 1960s. For a time women could not enroll at the CIA because the building didn't have separate facilities to accommodate women, and until the 1970s there wasn't enough demand by women to make the construction of such facilities worthwhile. "The CIA never stopped women from entering," Kris noted, "they just couldn't get *enough* women, which is revealing. As long as women are doing the cooking at home, they don't want to go to school to learn it. They stop cooking at home suddenly, and their percentages go from zero or one percent through the 1970s—by the end of the 1980s, the post-feminist generation has grown up: young girls have grown up who no longer have the idea that the girl is in the kitchen, so now they're ready to come back to the kitchen, in a professional sense—and the demographic goes up to twenty-five percent in the '80s and '90s, which is quite dramatic, in fact." (As of the end of 2005, women made up 37 percent of the total enrollment, with 27 percent in the culinary arts and 76 percent in the baking and pastry program.)

And this he concluded underscored the fact that cooking for show, cooking for performance, becomes meaningful only once we have stopped cooking and others have stopped cooking at home.

Again, it can't be called magic if we all do it. For cooking to remain magical, for chefs to maintain their status as celebrities, to be thought of as artists rather than laborers, it's critical that we continue to pay other people to do our cooking for us, which ensures that the process will remain mysterious. But more than that, he'd said, we have to have magicians who "claim that it's magic." It's the chef claiming it's magic. Does that make the chef a shaman or salesman? Perhaps a little bit of both.

Also interesting to note is that as more and more people become interested in cooking, more do begin to do it at home. So what does that do to the magic aspect? I asked. "Magic will turn into fashion and the quest for the next new thing," he said, "which is much more temporary."

Krishnendu provided my perfect intellectual launch out of and away from the CIA and into two kitchens of CIA graduates: a woman and a man of roughly the same generation (she graduated in 1988, he in 1994) but who couldn't be more different in terms of their style of food and style of restaurant.

❦

Grant Achatz was one of the most impressive cooks I met while writing *The Soul of a Chef*. He worked the fish station at the French Laundry. He was young, twenty-three then, in 1998, yet he'd been at the Laundry for a year and had spent a year at Charlie Trotter's. These were two of the greatest kitchens in America; Grant's positions were coveted and difficult to land. Indeed, he'd mailed a letter a day to Keller to get Keller to respond, and ultimately, after receiving about twenty letters, Keller did, if only to stop getting the letters. Enhancing his actual youth was his even-younger appearance, with fair, light red hair cut short; a narrow face; sincere, brown deeply set eyes; and abundant freckles—a look befitting his disposition, that of a sweet, soft-spoken, earnest Midwesterner.

I liked Grant immediately. He stood out at the French Laundry even among a brigade that was almost uniformly standout. There was something about the very appearance of French Laundry cooks that set them apart from other cooks in other kitchens. Part of it was cleanliness. They worked clean—their jackets weren't coming out of their aprons; they didn't have blood all over themselves. There was an elegance, a natural efficiency, to their movements. But also something more. Their faces were unusually vivid. Someone else mentioned this to me—I think it was Steve Reiner, the *60 Minutes Wednesday* producer—he said: "They even look different." He was right. Somehow the intensity of work there, the demands for focus and 100 percent commitment, somehow result in—I don't know how else to put this—a clarity of being that is actually visible. It sounds crazy, but it's true. You go to the French Laundry or Per Se, you look around, and if someone is not comfortable, doesn't quite belong, you can *see* it. They don't shine. Their discomfort, their inelegance, appears as if through a smudge on a lens.

That said, there was something even beyond this look about Grant. He was impressive in his movements, in his determination, in his articulation (uncommon in chefs as a rule, and especially uncommon in twenty-three-year-old cooks), and in his skills as a line cook. Being a line cook at the French Laundry is something. During any given service, Grant was responsible for prepping, cooking, and plating about nine separate dishes. And we're not talking steak-frites. His were complicated dishes with multiple components, along with expectations of perfect cooking technique and on-the-money internal temperatures.

The most interesting thing Grant taught me then was the importance of cutting your own shallots. The importance of this didn't have to do with the quality of the shallots, either, but rather with how you thought about them and how you used them. In some kitchens, it's fine to dump your peeled shallots into a food processor and pulse them till they're reduced to a kind of shallot medley, everything from juice to mince to big chunks—a compromise made by lazy cooks. In other kitchens, a single prep cook will mince the shallots for the entire line. Grant learned to appreciate chopping his own shallots, even though he scarcely had time for it.

"It affects your psyche," he told me. "If you take a half hour to chop shallots, you're going to make sure they don't get wasted." This was a remarkable thing for a twenty-three-year-old cook to have sensed and learned—and, moreover, articulated.

⊰⋅⊱

When I next sought Grant out, six years later, he was the executive chef of Trio, in Evanston, Illinois, just outside of Chicago. He'd been named a Best New Chef by *Food & Wine* in 2002; he'd won the Rising Star Chef award from the James Beard Foundation in 2003, given to one chef age thirty or younger; and in 2004 he'd earned four stars from the *Chicago Tribune,* which said he was "the most dynamic, boundary-stretching chef to hit town in a long, long time."

I arrived in Evanston on a night the restaurant was closed and so was able to have dinner with Grant and his wife, Angela, at their home. Grant grilled some sausages and corn still in its husk while Angela finished the potato salad. We ate in their backyard near the Weber, while their two boys, Kaden, age two and a half, played, and Keller, age six months, gurgled. When I asked Grant how he was doing, he shook his head as if still disbelieving it. "Really good," he said, "amazingly good."

He'd arrived at Trio July 1, 2001, and this summer, 2004, would be his last. He planned, he told me, to announce to his staff in a few days that he'd be leaving Trio on July 31 to open his own restaurant in Chicago called Alinea.

The reason I'd wanted to return to meet him again was not only to explore the trajectory of a young cook moving up in the chef world but also because of the *kind* of food he was serving. Trio cooked what was sometimes referred to as "out there" food. Weird food. What-is-it? food. *Is*-it-food? food. For example, I'd heard "pizza" came as a tiny square of white paper, stuck on the tip of a pin. Even Thomas Keller, Grant's mentor, had told me, "I'm a little worried about Grant."

Others, though, were claiming he was a visionary, working at the outer boundaries of the new edge cuisine led by Spanish chef Ferran Adrià at El Bulli and English chef Heston Blumenthal at the Fat Duck. The media, charmed by Grant's humble Midwestern attitude and impressed by his resolute seriousness and culinary daring, were already gushing. "What Achatz is doing in his 13-table restaurant is nothing less than redefining fine dining in this country," wrote David Shaw, the late Pulitzer-winning reporter for the *Los Angeles Times. Food & Wine* previewed his new restaurant, proclaiming it "may be America's best new restaurant"—and ran the story three months before the restaurant even opened.

I was skeptical about this kind of cooking in which the method overshadowed the food itself, in which classic dishes were so deconstructed they didn't look like anything you could even recognize. When you're not even sure what you're supposed to put in your mouth or how, isn't this going too far? But I was also curious: Was the food any good? Was there something to merging molecular chemistry and gastronomy? At age thirty, Achatz was perhaps the most notable chef in the country working this type of food. Certainly, he was able to reach the edges of culinary reason, at so young an age, only because his foundation was so solid. At his core he was grounded in classic technique that had been honed in two of the best and most forward-thinking restaurant kitchens in the country. Without the basics, a cook is lost. Having perfected the basics, a cook can go anywhere. Grant was trying to go where no one else had gone before. He was a young culinary James T. Kirk and Trio was his *Enterprise*.

❧

Grant had arranged for a room at a good rate for me at the Homestead, the hotel that houses Trio, located on a leafy street in Evanston, a few blocks south of Northwestern University. He suggested that I have dinner at Trio before I spent substantial time in the kitchen so that I'd come to the table with as few expectations as possible, and so I did.

I arrived in the subdued dining room, where about twenty-five people were seated. The room, lit by overhead dome lighting, was handsome, decorated in earthy browns and funky modernist art on the walls. Trio's four-course tasting was priced at $85; the eight-course chef's tasting menu, which included lobster, lamb, and beef dishes, at $120. Service was gracious and, knowing who I was and that I intended to spend the week in the kitchen, assumed correctly that I'd want the Tour de Force menu, the largest of the three tasting menus, twenty-eight courses ($175) that described the complete range of the Trio kitchen, a genuine culinary adventure.

Twenty-eight courses does not mean twenty-eight large plates of food, of course, or even small plates of food. One "dish" was simply a frozen circle of verjuice the size of a Communion wafer, a refreshing intermezzo toward the end of the meal. Some "dishes" came with no dishes at all, or even silverware. The first course was a small slice of Sri Lankan eggplant that had been poached in a spicy liquid and had a crisp sugar top, as if it had been brûléed, served on a fork—one bite, good flavors sweet and spicy with a nice crunch to go with the soft eggplant.

The next course: wild steelhead roe, tealike tosaka seaweed, and tiny cucumber balls, wrapped in a package of something reminiscent of rice paper—what was it? Tasty, mild, not weird. Interesting.

It was, rather, the third course that signaled I was not in a conventional fine-dining restaurant: salmon with pineapple and soy sauce—another one-biter. The whole deal was presented on what the staff called an "antenna," a skinny rod about fourteen inches long rising at an angle through a heavy circular base. Not only was there no plate, all silverware had been removed from my table. The cubes of salmon and pineapple had been skewered on this antenna, and a soy sauce foam, stiff as shaving cream, had been dabbed on the pineapple. The creation bobbed gently before me, beckoning, like a little pet or something. I'd seen this thing arrive at other tables, and it was invariably fun to watch people's reactions to it and what they did and how many angles they looked at it from—as if it were modern sculpture in a museum, but not something you put in your mouth—and to note how long it took them to go down on their food. Now it was time for others to watch me. And so I did—I went down on this thing. It tasted really good—salty, sweet, savory. But facing the bobbing little number, staring it down, and then actually getting it into your mouth—you didn't need silverware, you didn't even need arms—was odd and vaguely unsettling. I like using my hands, I decided.

And the meal caromed off from there, cruising, banking, breaking, one missed shot, and more than a few gorgeous swishes. The fourth course was among the latter. "Chilled English Peas *ramps, eucalyptus, yogurt, ham*," the menu read. In my notes I called it pea soup. (I take notes throughout a meal like this, which is especially pleasurable to experience alone—the only way, as far as I'm concerned—I'd have been frustrated if anything beyond the food demanded my attention.) It was a chilled pea soup, dotted with fresh green peas, in a bowl with a wide, flat base—delicious in itself, kind of a no-brainer if you've got great peas. In the center of this was a disk of something white and creamy, on top of which was something icy and opaque, and on top of this ice—a granité, it looked like—were transparent pink balls, like pale salmon roe. The soup was also garnished with four shavings of Smithfield ham and small bright green leaves.

A very pretty and elegant-looking dish, conventional apparently—soup with garnish. And delicious. The peas and pea puree were a delight, something minty in there too, but not mint, hard to place, and the peas went perfectly with the ham (why not—as appropriate as a ham bone in split pea soup). The creamy center was a tart yogurt. The granité on top—*hmm*. Ham. *Ham* granité? OK. And the roe on top? That minty, unplaceable flavor—what was it? On the menu it said "eucalyptus." Of course. Eucalyptus leaves—and eucalyptus . . . roe?

Who cares, this is a delicious dish, I thought.

The next dish had become something of a signature for Grant, the Black Truffle Explosion: It's simply a ravioli filled with truffle juice with a slice of black truffle on top, a single bite that explodes in your mouth, exactly what it says on the menu. Delight.

The meal went on, but all the elements of the mind behind it were already in evidence: the unusual serving devices *(Look, Ma, no hands!)*; conventional flavors in unconventional forms (ham granité, soy foam, and that rice paper wrapping the salmon roe and cucumber balls would turn out to be sake, gelled with agar); unconventional flavors in unconventional forms (eucalyptus roe); and perfect cooking technique (the peas).

But—very little cooking technique at all this early in the meal. That would come later, as dishes heavier on protein arrived—the beef and the duck and the lamb—much of it cooked sous-vide. (The Cryovac machine, which vacuum seals food in plastic, was evidently in more frequent use than the sauté pan.)

The lamb dish, for instance: Strips of lamb loin were cryovacked, then dropped in hot water until they were perfectly medium rare. They were then served with sunchoke puree, lamb sauce, ajwon (the seed of an oregano-like herb indigenous to the Middle East), and a little packet of stuff in a small rectangular cellophane pouch that the server called "bag of texture." The lamb was perfectly cooked and had extraordinary flavor; it was grown by Keith Martin, in Pennsylvania, a guy I'd met while working on *The French Laundry Cookbook*, who fed his flock nothing but the finest grasses and alfalfa, which he grew himself. Indeed, because there were no flavors of searing, the lamb sensations were so vivid I actually saw in my mind's eye Keith's alfalfa fields—the flavor was so amazingly grassy and floral.

But because it wasn't seared or grilled, but rather gently warmed, it would lack the complexity of flavor and texture that a good sear gives to red meats. Thus, the "bag of texture," five items—capers, garlic chips, oregano leaves, sunflower seeds, and lamb that had been cooked to melting tenderness sous-vide, then pulled apart—deep-fried. Savory, crisp, crunchy, nutty—all of it delicious.

Desserts, likewise, ran the gamut, from interesting and solid—a great chocolate plate, including a very-high-fat bittersweet chocolate, on a flaxseed-and-pistachio cookie (flaxseed?!), a yeast sorbet (?!), and pistachio sauce—to somewhere beyond interesting (homemade bubble gum concluded the meal).

And then there was the out-there food—that "pizza" I'd heard about. A half-inch square of white paper, lightly dusted with tomato powder, fennel pollen, garlic that had been dehydrated and pulverized, and salt, affixed to the paper by a brushing of the fat rendered out of baked mozzarella. It tasted very much like pepperoni pizza; it lacked, of course, the heat and aroma, the chewy cheesiness, the fat, the protein, and the starch (though the paper was rice-based). Before Grant was born, I enjoyed having Space Food Sticks, a product that played off the popularity of the space program in the late 1960s, but Grant's dishes were straight out of the Jetsons. The food wasn't unpleasant by any means, but was this eating? Not always. The kitchen would sometimes chuckle when a table new to the restaurant would order the pizza as an appetizer while they looked over the menu.

Then there was the "shrimp cocktail"—which needed even bigger quote marks than the pizza. Trio's shrimp cocktail came in a mouth spritzer set in crushed ice. That was it. *Spritz, spritz*—tastes just like shrimp cocktail!

The chips and dip ("Chicharrones con Salsa") were fun—braised pigskin, cleaned up and fried puffy, and served with avocado that had been cured with salt and other seasonings, then pushed through a drum sieve into skinny "worms," as well as the gelatinous seed-goop from ripe tomatoes, seasoned with garlic, chiles, cumin, and coriander. The dish composed mainly of seeds—kiwi, plantain, and passion fruit—along with curls from the meat of young coconut, all dressed with lime vinaigrette, was a little nonsensical (there's a reason we don't eat fruit seeds), but it made me *think* about seeds. A fine-dining restaurant such as this usually serves a foie gras course. On the Trio menu it read "Moulard Duck Foie Gras *blueberries, cinnamon, tapioca, sorrel.*" The ingredients alone were enough to nudge this dish into the "odd" column, but more so: They arrived at the table in a glass tube, about an inch in diameter and about seven inches long, and made a strata of color along its length. Only a little instruction was required ("Cream end in your mouth first," the server directed), and *schluppft!*—into the mouth. Like something you'd be doing to get drunk faster at a frat party. But it was tasty. The flavors (blueberry and *sorrel?*), amazingly, worked. The foie did not have a strong flavor, but instead gave the whole deal a very rich, luxurious feel. Grant had certainly figured out a surefire way to encourage the diner to eat multiple, separate ingredients in a set order—foie, blueberry puree, cinnamon tapioca, then again, foie, blueberry, tapioca, then conclude with sorrel puree and cinnamon jelly, a plug of it—to make this parfait really pop in to your mouth.

The dinner lasted about four hours. Never once did I feel antsy. It was a delight all the way through, truly dining as entertainment in a way I'd never experienced before. And I was full, but not bloated. I'd enjoyed plenty of wine throughout the meal, but I didn't feel drunk. This kind of thing is difficult for a chef to pull off. At a French Laundry over-the-top meal, after the second dessert course I'm praying the server will arrive with the *mignardises* tray and not another set of silverware; when the server *does* comes back with yet more silverware, I want to hoist up a white flag. This meal at Trio had been extraordinary. You wouldn't want to eat this way every day. The *Los Angeles Times* article recounted a woman who got up and left after the third course, grumbling that she just wanted a *steak.* But the ingredients, methods, flavors, textures—all of it came together to create a new kind of dining experience. At least for me.

What was going on back there in the kitchen?

❧

Trio's kitchen is as traditional as the food is non. Entering the large rectangular space from the dining room, the hot line—the kitchen's about forty feet long—and a bank of service counter is to the left, leaving a wide open path for the expediter (Grant) and numerous servers to come and go down the center of the kitchen. To the right is a coffee and beverage station followed by a raised built-in booth that serves as the chef's table, where a table of four can eat and watch service at the same time ("Kind of a pain," says Grant, "but people love it"). Desserts are finished and plated at the far end of the kitchen.

The Trio kitchen is celebrating its tenth anniversary—her opening chefs were Rick Tramanto and Gale Gand, who have gone on to considerable acclaim at their Chicago restaurant, Tru. Shawn McClain, who took over the kitchen when Rick and Gale left, now runs the Chicago restaurants Green Zebra and Spring, and was nominated in 2005 for a Best Chef Midwest award from the James Beard Foundation. Grant's following McClain makes this string of chefs an unusually successful one for a restaurant, owned by Henry Adaniya, who's proving to be something of an impresario for choosing stars in the making; the formal name of his restaurant is, appropriately, Trio Atelier, *atelier* being French for "studio" or "workshop." (His choice to replace Grant would be Dale Levitski, a veteran of Blackbird in Chicago, one of the city's best restaurants, but the change wouldn't last. Adaniya would close it in February 2006.)

The place looks conventional in action, as morning routine gets under way, a dozen or so cooks at their stations banging out their mise en place—pasta dough being mixed, melons reduced to perfect parisienne balls, enormous cèpes being peeled (I'd been served the mushroom dish and eating an entire fat cèpe was as satisfying as eating a steak), butchering and portioning meat, picking and washing lettuces, and in a back room, the pastry room, gum being made, sorbet bases being mixed.

David Carrier, age twenty-eight, a sous-chef and a former commis at the French Laundry, moved through a box of asparagus. "This is what happens when you can't get good asparagus," he laments. Many of the asparagus came in kind of ratty on top, and so he was picking each itty-bitty bud off the tip of those that were any good, part of a course featuring white and green asparagus with a chamomile vinaigrette (as well as littleneck and geoduck clams; a wine sorbet made from the wine they served with this dish, Argiolas Vermentino, from Sardinia; a poached quail egg and what looked like a raw hen's yolk but was in fact an apricot puree, its exterior gelled with sodium alginate and calcium chloride so that it sat like a yolk waiting to break; and what the server had called "a fines herbes sponge," about which, more later).

They do their lobster the way the French Laundry and Per Se do it now, by sous-vide. They include whole butter in the plastic pouch and drop it into 130-degree water.

John Peters, age twenty-nine, also a sous-chef and a veteran of Vong, Jean-Georges Vongerichten's Chicago outpost, was the butcher and currently cut Keith's lamb loins into strips (they called them "snakes") to be bagged and cryovacked for service.

Nathan Klingbail, age twenty-four, had heard about Grant's taking over Trio from his former boss, the chef at the Amway Grand, in Grand Rapids, Michigan, a kitchen where Grant had once worked. "It's been three years and I ain't bored yet," he said as he worked through his prep list. "My parents didn't understand why I would work these hours"—twelve- to sixteen-hour days for subsistence pay—"but after my dad saw *Into the Fire,*" a special series that profiled various kitchens and aired on the Food Network, "he said, 'I understand.'" In the world of professional cooking, which in the vast majority of kitchens is dominated by the crushing monotony of daily prep, this was an exciting kitchen to be a part of.

The bizarre language of his list attested to this:

- T1 snakes/chokes x2/sprouts/choke sauce/seed sauce/Aj sauce
- Bag: g-chips & oregano & capers & lamb & seed
- T2: shroomz/tongue/romaine/cress/arugula/puree/sauce/smoke

Roughly translated, his morning's work focused on the "Elysian Fields Farm Lamb *sunflower plant, bag of crispy texture*" and the "Ribeye of Prime Beef *spring lettuces, morel mushrooms, smoked tongue.*"

Brett Jeffry was twenty-three-year-old "unpaid slave labor," in his words, and he was delighted to be so. Brett was midway through his externship from the CIA, not long out of Turgeon's class, in fact ("He's the only guy who really talked about how busy it is, the importance of speed," he said of his favorite chef-instructor there). Brett was so organized and focused he applied to extern at Trio as soon as he arrived at the CIA, months before he even set foot in a CIA kitchen.

Another extern had been nicknamed "Milk Crate" after he was caught sitting on one (you don't sit, ever, when you're in the kitchen, you just don't). Milk Crate broke from his prep at 12:20 to vacuum the carpeted mats along the line.

Carpet along the hot line . . . hmm, haven't seen that since the French Laundry and Per Se. And the blue aprons that everyone wore, the pervasiveness of the pint-size deli cups to hold sauces and mise en place—the feel of the French Laundry was palpable and visible. The water for blanching green vegetables was salty as the Atlantic. The veal stock looked and smelled exactly as it did at the French Laundry, pale brown and heavy with the sweet smell of tomato.

"Straight out of the book," Brett said. He shook his head incredulously. "You taste it—*oh, man.*"

Mary Radigan, who'd remained friends with Chef Pardus after graduating from the CIA a year and a half earlier, was working pastry in back (though she made it clear to me she was a cook, not a pastry chef). "It's a different learning experience here," she said, recalling hours spent picking the individual cells of a grapefruit apart for a textural garnish for lobster—the popping in the mouth, the sweet-sour flavor a perfect seasoning for the shellfish. "A different way of looking at food." She planned to leave Trio to stage (or trail) at Blumenthal's Fat Duck and travel in Europe and, she hoped, return to Chicago when Grant opened his new restaurant.

Her boss in pastry here was Curtis Duffy, age twenty-nine. Curtis had that vivid appearance of precision, ease of movement, and confidence reminiscent of the French Laundry cooks. He was from Columbus, Ohio, and went to culinary school at Ohio State University. He'd spent his formative culinary years, two and a half of them, at Charlie Trotter's. He, John Peters, and David Carrier were the core of the Trio kitchen staff.

Trio's is a roomy kitchen, the atmosphere is relaxed without being lax, and the cooks seem to form a cohesive and friendly group. Had I not already eaten the food, I'd have said this was same-old, same-old. But it's not, which becomes clear only at service, after everyone's station has been wiped down and pressed white cloth has been taped down at the pass (with painter's tape, as at the French Laundry), in the center of the line, after Grant has set his station: serving spoons; a hotel pan with several rolled damp white towels with red pinstripes, to be used for wiping plates; ten "antennas," the sculptures built for the salmon-and-pineapple dish, and twenty "squids," silver prongs rising out of a small circular base used to hold one of Grant's best dishes, a tempura of shrimp, Meyer lemon confit, and gelled cranberry, all held together on a vanilla bean skewer; a Diet Coke; a mug filled with a variety of markers; the long strip of metal that holds the tickets. Below were glasses to hold the smoke for the smoked tongue and other dish-specific vessels. The crew at the back of the kitchen, under Curtis's direction, plates early courses (such as the pea soup) as well as desserts, and this station likewise is dressed in a starched white tablecloth fastened down with painter's tape.

The kitchen is especially busy in the beginning of the evening. About half of Trio's customers this week (usually about 40 or so a night, small for this time of year) will order the Tour de Force, which means a long dinner, so most who eat here come earlier rather than later. At the restaurant where I once worked, four of us would handle 150 reservations. Grant used 12 people to cook for 40 reservations. True, the restaurant sat 65 and they'd done as many as 100 in a night—but, still, the high ratio of cooks to diners was more along the lines of a Michelin three-star kitchen rather than a restaurant in the American Midwest.

"Chef," Elaina, the front-of-the-house expediter, a thin woman with short blondish hair, says to Grant, "the gentleman at table thirty-four said he hates eggplant, but he agreed to try it. He tried it and he said he hated it. Is there anything else we can send them?"

Grant nods and to the line says, "Fire two cheese and crackers." Molten cheddar inside a crackery dough—kind of like a crispy ravioli.

All stations are quickly busy, but the service is thrown off early when Stephen Parkerson, a CIA extern, loses a shrimp—floured and battered and fried, it falls off the vanilla bean as he's moving it to the little pronged sculpture, the squid, resulting in a rush to fire another. This throws him off, and when he's off, Nathan beside him has to pick up a little slack, and it goes like dominoes down the line, just a bit, just enough to make this first hour a little bumpy; especially when one of the line cooks, Jeffrey Pikus, notices he's low on bacon—very thin, flat, dehydrated strips served with the roasted cèpes—but doesn't do anything about it, kind of hopes he gets lucky. The line is fluid, everyone helps each other—and deli cups filled with frozen sorbet fly through the air from pastry to the hot line and back—these cooks can float among one another's stations, but this also allows for the domino effect when one person gets thrown off.

Elaina, carrying a plate, again approaches Grant, who's studying the tickets, and says, "This lady on thirty does not like asparagus." Grant shakes his head—*You'd think they'd read the menu*—and says, "Ask her if she'll eat cauliflower." A few moments later Elaina returns to say, "Chef, she will not eat cauliflower."

"Go get a list of what she won't eat," Grant says.

Elaina is back in quickly to say, "Table forty-four is clear."

"Two lamb," Grant calls to the line. Then, "All right, thirty-three?"

Elaina says, "Chef, table thirty-three is clear."

"Two beef!"

"Two beef!" David Carrier calls back.

Elaina: "We're up on table forty-five"—meaning someone has left the table; they won't serve food until everyone is seated.

The four diners at the chef's table are avidly watching service and nodding and pointing, evidently impressed and delighting in their front-row seats.

Elaina: "Chef, the vegetarian on table forty-one wants no meat, no fish, poultry, or mushrooms. That includes truffles."

Grant reads the table's ticket and calls, "Three shrimp and a fennel!" Then he writes on the ticket the necessary replacements for each of the vegetarian's eight courses.

Two servers bump each other on the way out, knocking a strip of bacon off the mushroom and jolting other garnish. The server returns the plate to David on the line to salvage it, but he says, "It's not going to happen" and sends the plate to the dishwasher after removing all salvageable items, importantly the bacon. With the lost 'shrooms here and four more Tours ordered, it's clear Pikus doesn't have enough bacon to make it through service. Another line cook breaks away to get some strips roasting between Silpats—but they won't be dehydrated as Grant has intended for the dish. He's pissed and says to Pikus, "It's no use lying to yourself." He says it quietly and matter-of-factly, but you can see Pikus is miserable and humiliated and pissed at himself, even as he never stops hustling through this service, his personal ass-kicking.

Elaina: "Chef, I haven't seen that duck go up on thirty-three."

Grant: "Don't worry about it."

He hands her two beefs. White rectangular plates with a medallion of beef cap—the unctuous cut of beef above the rib eye—a ball of sautéed spinach, sautéed morels, a circle of salt and pepper, and a medallion of beef tongue, on which David Carrier places a leaf of spring lettuce. Each is in a distinct area of the plate, spread out from the others. Grant puts down perhaps a half teaspoon of two main sauces, one a forest green watercress puree and one a meat stock based on the reduced poaching liquid for the tongue, and various garnish on each item. The last garnish to go down is smoke. Carrier holds a piece of applewood over a gas flame to light it, brings it to the plate, blows out the flame, and holds a glass over the smoke, then puts the smoke-filled glass over the tongue and lettuce. The smoke flavors the tongue but more important will fill the air at the table with the aroma of wood smoke when the diner lifts off the glass—something I found surprisingly effective when I'd had it. But these dishes are very elaborate, with as many as a dozen components, and take two or three people a minute or more to plate. Elaina takes the beef dishes and leaves for the dining room.

One server calls out to pastry, "I've got a no-berries on table thirteen please."

Grant hands two duck plates to a male server who turns so quickly that the garnish of radish and hearts of palm falls. Slim "coins" of alternating radish and hearts of palm are precariously balanced on a plank of jelly made from Australian rain forest plums, but these do not hold together well. Grant takes the plate back and rights the garnish. He hands the plate back to the server who turns and it falls again, but the server keeps going toward the dining room. Grant has turned back to the line but realizes that he saw the garnish fall again. He turns, says loudly, *"Hey!"* and holds out his hands in disbelief, as if to say, *Why do you make me work so hard—when you see something's not right, don't serve it, fix it.* Caught, the server returns and the problem is repaired.

When the rush is finished and the line has a moment to wipe down their station, David says, "A little hairy there for a second." Grant throughout was nothing but calm, even when he'd been frustrated. And the remainder of the evening goes smoothly.

Throughout the day, a stage named Luke, a tall blond L.A. cook, had patiently worked his way through about a hundred crates of asparagus but during service was free to observe, and Grant would eventually send him a few dishes to try.

I asked him why he was here. He said his girlfriend wanted to move back to Chicago, her home, so he'd be looking for work. "I've staged at Trotter, the French Laundry; I've eaten at Ducasse and a couple Michelin three-stars," Luke said. "People are saying this is the best restaurant in the country, so . . ."

I asked him what he thought about what he was seeing. "I've never seen anything like it. . . . During the day it's like a normal restaurant, but now this is different—I've never seen anything like it. This is crazy." The smoke on the plate, the apricot liquid that looks like an egg yolk, the eucalyptus roe, the fines herbes sponge. I'd helped make the sponge today. Piles of fines herbes (a traditional four-herb combo of tarragon, chervil, parsley, and chives) are juiced. This liquid is then put in the bowl of a standing mixer and set in ice to keep it cold. A little of the juice is heated enough to melt a sheet of gelatin. This gelatin is then added to the mixing bowl, and it's whipped till the liquid froths to triple its volume; the foam is then put in a hotel pan and chilled. The gelatin sets before the bubbles pop, and so after it's completely chilled, you have what is like a foam pillow of fines herbes juice. At service a cone of it is carved out using a teaspoon and added to the asparagus plate as a garnish.

The soy sauce for the salmon-pineapple antenna is stabilized by gelatin in the same way, though this is kept at room temperature and so maintains a more shaving cream–like pliability. A mixing bowl filled with the stuff is part of Grant's mise en place at the pass for "saucing" the antenna.

This is the out-there food of his reputation: the smoke; the sponge; the no-hands; the carrot–mandarin–smoked paprika "leather" (kind of like a fruit roll-up for adults, something that's likely appreciated by adults who have kids, as Grant does); the mozzarella blown into a bubble, injected with tomato water, and served on basil—a reinvented *caprese* salad; a pheasant dish served in a second dish filled with pumpkin seeds, apple, and hay, over which at presentation the server pours boiling water, so that while you eat the pheasant, your head is filled with smells of, as Grant described it, "a quintessential Midwestern fall." The list goes on. Honestly, you'd never expect it from this earnest, freckle-faced kid from a little town in Michigan. During service, when people ask to come back to meet the chef—which Grant is honored by—some of the guests think the server is kidding. "He's the chef? How old is he?" During the day, there he is, in his black pants, black clogs, and blue apron, patiently wrapping salmon roe, seaweed, and cucumber balls in sheets of gelled sake, the quietest person in the kitchen. Was he really "redefining fine dining" as some were claiming?

❧

After the final desserts are sent out, all begin cleaning the kitchen. It will shine before the cooks gather for a meeting (a review of tomorrow's reservations—do they have all the food they need?—and a reflection on the night behind them: "I feel like we underestimated tonight," Grant says, "and we got burned. Does anyone else feel like that?"), and then leave, after midnight. They'll be back again around ten A.M. tomorrow—short days given the relatively small number of covers.

Grant does not go home. Instead he heads to the office to sit in front of his computer for the next two hours. He'll think, he'll search the Internet. He'll answer e-mails at considerable length and of uncommon eloquence—for a chef, at any rate. He'll check out eGullet, one of the most popular and well-run sites for culinary discourse, to post comments or answer food questions under the member profile "chefg." It was on the Internet that he found the base to make chewing gum, a source that would deliver Australian rain forest plums, and, after he read an article in *The New York Times* about Australian finger limes, those too (the *Times* article had noted that you wouldn't find them anywhere in the United States; Grant took this as a challenge to serve them and headed to the Internet to get them—the shipping charge alone is $300). What artisan-craftsman could help him design and create unique, dish-specific sculptures to use in serving his unusual food—the antenna and the squid? He found and wrote to forty of them via the Internet.

"The Internet," Grant says, "is *the* most underutilized chefs' tool."

On the wall behind his printer is a large dry-erase board, a two-column list that more than anything describes the culinary brainstorm perpetually swirling in Grant's mind. Most of the items are still just ideas, but when an idea is realized and put on the menu, Grant likes to note the date by the idea.

- How can we make "snow"?
- How can we make bubbles that don't pop?
- Can we make a dome of bubbles that disappears when touched?
- Bubble or taffy, caramel or gelatin?
- Alginate explosion (9/25/03)
- Sashimi on breadstick or tube of crispy seaweed with filling of ? and powder
- "Dry shot" in starch cornet → into bag of textures (1/27/04)
- Savory "roll up" carrot w/orange, ginger (1/23/04)
- Savory pectin soy-sesame bars
- Forced air—aquarium pump
- Masamum curry chips/replace pizza?
- Raisins on vine coated in??
- Cereal?
- Transglutimate!!
- Caramel-coated vinegar bomb as P.C.
- Saddle "byaldi"
- Starch usage! invisible flavors (12/3/03)
- Pectin skin
- "Candy Kane" 3 flavors . . . n. olive/vanilla/cranberry? "Grinchesque"-like shape
- Deconstruction of dish w/simple form w/different shapes. Give diner a flavor map to follow.
- Malt 11/7/03
- Oyster in sesame meringue (1/21/03)
- Mist bottle application (virtual shrimp cocktail 1/23/04)

- Chocolate soda (12/31)
- Bubble gum (1/23/04)
- Tempura shrimp with M. lemon, cranberry (on a *vanilla* bean) (10/18/03)
- Salsify wrapped in ??? w/clams, mussels, dill, oysters, *sausage* (12/5/03)
- Crispy nest of   w/asp
    - → traditional flavors
    - → unusual flavors
- Menu in graph form
    - → color tells sweet/savory
    - → hue shows intensity
    - → axis is neutral
- Eating without hands! (2/13/04 "antenna")

"A menu should read like sheet music," he says, so that the diner could know at a glance the progression of a meal, see the intensities, the truffle explosion (a knockout single bite) versus the verjuice (a light, clean, small intermezzo) versus a big meat dish. Grant seems always to be on, his brain perpetually thinking of new ideas, new manipulations of food.

He'll leave the restaurant office by two A.M., he hopes, and can be home by two-fifteen. His wife, Angela, whom he met at the French Laundry (she worked front of the house), has been trying to mandate a home time of no later than two, and she's been only partly successful. Now with two children under three, he needs to be home for longer than eight hours, at least four of which are typically spent sleeping. He gets up when the kids get up—"because if I didn't get up and start being with them, I'd feel guilt," he says. Asked about this schedule, Grant smiles and says, "I love it."

Running a restaurant of this caliber and with this emphasis on experimentation and innovation is hard work. But for the past half year he's been trying to propel this four-star restaurant while also putting together and opening another one. This new work requires knowing not just how to work a hot line and run a food cost, but how to put together a P&L sheet, do cost projections and site searches. "It's been hard," he says.

Especially as this new restaurant has to be perfect—this is the one, this is it, this is where he stays. And so he wants the structure of the entryway and dining room to mirror the food experience; he wants people to be put a little off their guard by the design; he wants the kitchen to be the kind of place that evolves as his cooking evolves. "It won't have a standard brigade setup," he predicts, "and maybe it won't have a line of ranges and a flattop. It will have a lot of portable induction burners, instead." His eyes grow bright, and he smiles at the absurdity of a normal kitchen layout, such as Trio's, accommodating his food during service. "Right now," he says, "we have fish station calling to pastry station for a sorbet that's going on a vegetable dish!"

He's got the financial guy and partner, Nick Kokonas, who will lead the money-raising efforts and be a primary investor himself.

Kokonas, a thirty-eight-year-old Chicago native, is completely new to the restaurant business, a fact he sees not as a detriment but rather as one of many reasons this venture is exciting. "I build businesses," he says. "They're all the same as far as I'm concerned."

Kokonas is a trim, dapper, handsome man with short dark hair and a Mediterranean complexion typical of his Greek roots. He attended Colgate, backed out of going to law school at the last minute because it didn't feel right, and instead took a job as a trader on the Mercantile Exchange for five dollars an hour. (He notes that the high pressure and the need to make fast decisions in that job are not different from the requirements of a good line cook in a crunch.) Kokonas did well, advanced, and eventually started his own business trading derivatives. The business grew to ten employees and soon opened branches in New York and San Francisco.

He also invested in some dot-coms, one of which was sold to Pearson Publishing for a profit that, with his derivatives business and other investments, was more than enough money to retire on. The derivatives business had grown to seventy-five employees, many of whom he didn't even know, and this was one reason the work no longer excited him— he liked the personal nature of work. He decided instead he wanted to play a lot of golf and take his kids to school. A smart, energetic guy, though, and he kept his eye out for the Next Thing.

In the winter of 2004, a friend called him to say he had lunch reservations at Trio but something had come up—would Nick and his wife, Dagmara, like them? They thought *Why not?* and went, expecting a customary high-end meal. Kokonas can no longer recall what the first course was, but he remembers his emotional response to it: "This is different, something different is going on here." He asked the server what was the deal, and the server replied, "We got this new kid from the French Laundry and he's blowing our minds."

Since retiring, Kokonas had begun to take an interest in wines, and from wines developed an interest in good restaurants. He and his wife had been unprepared for their lunch—didn't know what to make of it or how to evaluate it—so they made a reservation for dinner. Again, they were, he said, "blown away." He and Dagmara decided to reserve a table on the first Wednesday of every month. "I became convinced that Grant was doing some of the most interesting stuff in the world," Kokonas says now. But, he added, he sensed a disconnect between the place and the food.

When he first laid eyes on Grant, he couldn't believe this food was coming from, he said, "this kid who looked like he was fifteen years old." As the Kokonases were regular customers, Grant would always chat with them when they came to Trio. Kokonas would say, "If you ever want to talk about a partnership, let me know." Grant thought about it.

Kokonas, on another visit, said, "You know what? We should build a restaurant together."

Grant asked, "What kind?"

Kokonas replied, "Whatever kind you want. It's your vision."

Shortly thereafter, Grant e-mailed Kokonas two pages outlining that vision. When Kokonas read it late at night, he got so excited that he woke Dagmara up to tell her, "We're going to build a restaurant with Grant."

Grant wanted first to hash out a business plan to see if they were on the same page; he didn't want to find himself with a money guy who would try to muscle him in directions he didn't want to go. Kokonas said to Grant, "I don't care about a business plan right now. I want to know if we can be friends. Because if we can't, this is going to be a miserable experience and I don't want to do it."

And that was how Alinea began. Grant—who had only cooked while others handled business affairs, had little experience with things like profit-and-loss statements and lease agreements—typed up a rough two-page business summary. Kokonas read it and that night, and well into the next morning, wrote from Grant's proposal a thirty-page business plan, which remains basically unchanged today. The goal was simple, Kokonas said: "We want to build the best restaurant in the world."

⋙⋘

Every aspect of creating a restaurant, Grant says, has so far gone smoothly, except for the one thing he thought would be easiest of all—finding a place and negotiating the lease. He's located a good building, but working out a deal remains a struggle he doesn't know if he can win.

But he doesn't dwell on this—he's got service tomorrow, and the infinite world of gastronomy to explore for new ideas and new products. He's got a wife and two kids he adores, a four-star restaurant, a schedule he loves, work that is his life; he's at the top of his game and in the upper echelons of American chefs. And he's just turned thirty years old.

⋙⋘

One of the things I liked about Grant was remarked on by Nathan Klingbail, a fellow Michigan guy, one of the few members of the brigade who sautéed protein during service (sauté pans were infrequently used in this kitchen). As I helped him pick through and clean a box of wormy morels midday, I asked him about Rocco DiSpirito—one of my favorite topics as it always resulted in emotional responses from cooks.

Nathan recalled an episode of the NBC reality show *The Restaurant,* in which Anthony Bourdain and Eric Ripert ate at Rocco's on Twenty-second Street during the filming. Bourdain and Ripert were getting kind of squishy by the end of the meal, but early on Bourdain got some cold food, and Nathan chose this point to remark on: "When Bourdain said he had cold food, and Rocco went back and said, 'Stop serving cold food!'" Nathan shook his head. "If someone served cold food here, Chef, he'd"—Nathan swings his elbow down—"and work your station better than you've ever seen *anyone* work it."

This truly earned, among chefs and cooks, the ultimate devotion—made you, in a way, untouchable. And it explained more than anything why Grant, for all his Midwestern humility and PBS elocution, commanded a deep respect from the kitchen staff: Not only did he run this restaurant, not only did he do the hiring and firing, not only was he a nationally respected chef and culinary innovator, Grant Achatz could, at any instant, take over your station and work it better and faster than you could do it yourself on your *best* day.

⁂

Grant Achatz was all but born into restaurants. His entire family worked in them or ran them. There were—he had to squint, really thinking about it—eight different food and beverage operations within the family at various points, beginning with his grandmother, who, after working in restaurants for many years, opened a place of her own, Achatz Café, in 1976, at the age of fifty-five. When Grant's mom went into the restaurant on Saturdays to bake pies, Grant went, too. He couldn't reach over the edge of the dish sink so he stood on a milk crate to wash dishes. He was five and a half. In 1980 his parents opened a restaurant, Achatz Depot, and Grant started working there. By age twelve he was a prep cook. By age fourteen he was working the line a couple of days a week after school and on weekends, and when he got his driver's license, every day after school and on weekends.

Grant always loved to work. He didn't like to go out much, but when he did he was glad he had money—he equated money, and the feeling of having it, with work, he said. His parents instilled in their only child a good Midwestern, Germanic work ethic, or perhaps it was simply part of his genetic fabric. He did well at school when he liked a subject (art, architecture) and not well when he didn't (English, math). He liked cooking more than school. Cooking was immediate.

But by the end of high school, Grant understood the limits of what he was doing and the limited nature of the food. He was flipping burgers and eggs at a Midwestern family-style restaurant. When he served gravy, it was, he said, "whitewash—flour and water." The food had descended from his grandma, who'd grown up during the Depression and World War II. Her motives were based on economy, and culinary innovation was based not on infinite possibilities of gastronomy but rather on restrictions and deprivation. She'd grown up in an era, for instance, when fat was too expensive to use to make a roux for a gravy.

A food revolution was under way in America, and Grant needed to learn about food and cooking in the best and fastest way possible. Beginning at the CIA in 1993 not long after he finished high school, he graduated in 1994, not yet twenty-one years old. Because he wasn't of drinking age while in school, he wasn't even tempted to go out, nor was he inclined to, anyway. He preferred to stay in his dorm room and read cookbooks. He was very naive, he says, when he went to culinary school. He didn't know what Michelin signified. He'd tried once to do an emulsified butter sauce and it hadn't worked ("I didn't really learn to do that until the French Laundry," he says now). But he did well at the CIA, liked almost all his classes, especially wines and the Escoffier Room. He didn't like breakfast cookery because he and the chef didn't get along (he thinks it was because he could flip eggs better and faster than she could).

Immediately after school he returned to his extern site, the Amway Grand, mainly because they promised to send him to Europe if he did, but he wasn't comfortable there. So he applied to and ultimately got a job at Charlie Trotter's in Chicago. He'd been carrying around the April 1995 issue of *Wine Spectator,* which named Trotter's the country's best restaurant, and so he applied there. Why would you start anywhere other than the top? Kind of a no-brainer for Grant. He worked there a year, but he never felt comfortable in the kitchen—just didn't feel right, didn't like it, wasn't happy. There was an antagonistic relationship among the brigade because they all had to fight their own way just to get through service. "You get there at nine," he says, recalling that kitchen, "just so you can get everything done and then at three o'clock Charlie changes the menu. It's chaos." Grant just assumed this was the nature of kitchens at that level. He promised himself he'd last out a year, and he did. But when he was finished, he was so discouraged by the experience that he was debating with himself whether or not to keep cooking at all. If this was cooking at its best, was this what he wanted to do?

To clear his head and to "regain my balance," he says, he and a girlfriend bought plane tickets to Europe—"the Holy Land," he describes it—and traveled. He ate at several two- and three-star restaurants, and was uniformly disappointed by them—too fussy, condescending, and overpriced. He and his girlfriend joined a bike tour in Italy and one day were cruising the hills outside Florence. The six of them decided to stop at a small restaurant for lunch. "I don't remember the name, I don't know the town, and I'll probably never go there again," he says now, "but it was one of the top five meals of my life." It was a completely organic experience, he explained: romantic, a beautiful day, a rustic restaurant in the Italian hills with an actual grandma back in the kitchen and long communal wooden tables so worn by diners that they shined. You could see the old woman putting the brick on the chicken, dropping the pillowlike gnocchi into the water. It was his first-ever experience of authentic regional European food, and it blew away the Michelin stars by a mile. "It was exactly what it was supposed to be," he says, meaning the perfect fulfillment of what it set out to be. That meal was a revelation.

Part of the impact was the surprise of it, the chance encounter, of falling into one of the greatest meals of one's life by accident, not expecting it, and suddenly, *Wow,* a new understanding of what food—cooking it and serving it and eating it—was all about. That is exactly the kind of impact he's striving to achieve with his cooking and space-age food, and it was shown to him, ironically, by rustic fare and centuries-old techniques in the hillsides of Italy.

After his return, Grant began to apply to the best restaurants in the country. He still hung on to that *Wine Spectator* issue, now more than a year old. The other top restaurants mentioned in it were the Inn at Little Washington, outside D.C.; Valentino, in L.A.; and Masa's, in San Francisco; as well as the Lark, a respected restaurant near his home in Detroit. So he applied to them. In another part of the magazine was a blurb about a two-year-old restaurant called the French Laundry. The food sounded kind of cool. It was by now the summer of 1996. Thomas Keller that spring had won the James Beard Foundation award for Best Chef California, and the French Laundry, with its unusual name and romantic location, had begun to develop its own mystique among cooks throughout the country. For the French Laundry, Grant did something he didn't do for the four others: He created a stack of letters addressed to Keller at the French Laundry in sealed, stamped envelopes. He still can't explain why, given how little he knew about the restaurant, which wasn't nearly as renowned then as it would be in a year, when *The New York Times* called it "the most exciting" restaurant in America.

"One of the most bizarre things in my life," he says now, when asked to explain.

By August, Keller had had enough letters and contacted him, saying, more or less, as Grant puts it, "All right, all right. What the hell's your problem?"

Grant went out to trail for two days. "I had no idea what I was getting into," he says.

The first time he set eyes on Chef Keller, the man was sweeping the kitchen floor. Grant had never seen a chef sweeping his kitchen floor—it was always an underling who swept the floor—and this guy was supposed to be the best in California. Grant worked for two days and when it was over, Keller asked, "Do you want a job?"

He did, and this move, more than any other, has directed his life and his mind.

In the fall of 1996, Grant drove out to Yountville, in the heart of the Napa Valley. His dad accompanied his only child to help with the drive and see what this place was all about. Grant had been trying to describe what he'd seen there, what Keller's food was all about, but he had a hard time articulating it. When the long drive was over and they'd unpacked the car, Grant called Keller to explain the situation: My dad's here, I want him to understand the food and where I'll be working, he's leaving tomorrow, is there any chance at all we could get a reservation? (Chefs are almost uniformly hard on the lowest ranks of the cooks; you've got to keep them in their place, treat them like serfs—on your *good* days, if you're feeling *generous*—otherwise they're lower than dirt and don't let them forget it. This is protocol—all great kitchens are like this, and Keller's was no different.) He told Grant he didn't know what the situation was but he'd find out and call back in an hour. He hardly knew Grant, the twenty-two-year-old who was beginning in the kitchen as a *commis*, a prep cook, the lowest rank. But Grant had asked anyway and was surprised—as surprised as Keller to receive daily letters from Michigan, surely—to hear Keller say that they should come in at 7:30.

Grant had gotten lucky—Keller was feeling generous. Keller said that kind of offer was a matter of chance, what was going on that day and his mood.

"It was the most amazing meal of my life," Grant says now—was then and remains so, the turning-point meal in his career as a cook and a chef. He got the Oysters and Pearls, what has since become one of Keller's famous dishes: a warm tapioca sabayon served in a small elegant dish, on top of which floats a layer of oyster juice and a fat belon oyster. On top of the oyster is a quenelle of sevruga caviar, garnished with chives. It's an absolutely fabulous dish. Grant remembers thinking he had never seen so much caviar on a single dish. Garnish! He had the rouget with parsley puree, a *palette d'aix* (a mixture of poached garlic and hard-cooked egg yolks, shaped into a disk, breaded with panko, and fried), garlic chips, and parsley leaves, another French Laundry classic, one of Keller's favorite dishes to cook over and over again, beautiful to look at and lovely to eat. Grant would one day be cooking it over and over again, too. But that night, he marveled that every tiny pinbone of this little Mediterranean fish had been removed—the effort and care it showed. This food, wine, and the relaxed service, combined with the romance of Napa, the French Laundry garden, and the stone building—he'd never experienced anything like it. A perfect meal.

And then Keller came out to say hello. This was rare in those days—Keller didn't like to come into the dining room, preferred to keep the two worlds completely distinct. When the *mignardises* were delivered, Grant and his dad said thank you and asked for the bill. "You're all set," the server said with a smile. "You're not getting a bill."

Now Grant was completely floored. No bill? This, truly, was another world.

What moved Keller to be so generous to a virtual stranger that night in the fall of 1996? Grant wondered aloud if it didn't have something to do with Keller's seeing a father and son together. Keller's parents had divorced when he was young, and he'd never been close with his father (a situation soon to be reversed), and Grant thought maybe Keller saw a relationship between a father and a son that he wished he'd had as a young cook.

Grant is still amazed and grateful for that meal and Keller's generosity. It was the beginning of the critical professional relationship in his career, one that is now a great friendship. When Grant won the Beard award for Rising Star Chef of the Year, Keller was ecstatic. "I think he was more excited when I won the Beard Award than I was," Grant recalls. "He was jumping up and down. I swear to God, I'd never seen the guy show emotion like that."

You could say that Keller has no kids of his own, but in fact he does. A lot.

≫·≪

Thus began Grant's four years at the French Laundry, during which he rose from commis to sous-chef and was forged into the cook and chef he is today. Truly those were his Kung Fu years—he, Grasshopper; Keller, his Master Po. He learned pretty much everything there—from how to handle foie gras to the importance of mincing your own shallots and sweeping the floor.

"I grew up in the French Laundry kitchen," Grant says. "Thomas taught me how to cook in the philosophical sense. In the literal sense as well, but more about how to treat food, how to express yourself through food, get excited about it. Being submerged in that environment for so long made me realize a lot of things about what it is to cook. There's a lot of cooks in the world. There's a lot of cooks who just cook, and there are cooks who think about what they're cooking, care about what they're cooking, understand what's happening with their cooking, have a vision for the final step of the cooking. I think that's what he projects really well, that this isn't a mechanical execution, or that that's a small percentage of it. It starts up here"—he touches his temple, pausing for the words. "From emotion, whether it's passion about a particular ingredient, the process that you're going to use to manipulate that ingredient, or the end result once you have it in your hands. I had never seen that before."

While the cuisine Grant does now at Trio doesn't look anything like Keller's food, Keller's food is clearly reflected in the technique. How Grant learned to tie the torchon of foie gras, for example. "We use that technique to mold various things as well. How we make veal stock, how we sauté fish. It's all encompassing. If, in the act of doing something, I check myself and say, Where did I learn this? Nine times out of ten it's gonna come from the French Laundry and him."

But there was also the more intangible, and powerful, lesson of how to be a cook. "Like the push," he says. "Very few people push themselves to their limit. Me and Eric and Gregory"—Eric Ziebold and Gregory

Short, who would also become sous-chefs along with Grant—"we were in awe of the way Thomas pushed himself."

"You never questioned it," he continued, recalling the crushing work-load, because Keller was doing it himself. "You just fucking did it." (The only time I've ever heard Grant swear.) "You've got a hundred and two reservations and nineteen VIPs, and he looked at you and said, 'Do you have time to do this dish?' You didn't even *think* about not saying yes. *He* knew you didn't have time."

But, Grant says, "If he gives you the nod of approval, that's *it*—you're *golden.* Life is good."

Life was especially good when Chef was happy. Ultimately, Grant learned to read his tells. When he heard the double click of Keller's clogs—the heels go *click-click*—or when he saw Keller pick up a chive tip and stick it in his mouth like a toothpick, he'd look across the pass at his friend and fellow cook Mark Hopper, who'd heard and seen it too, and they'd exchange an easy grin, because they knew it was going to be a good night.

He remembers with ultra-clarity the night Ruth Reichl ate there, the meal that compelled her to pronounce, as only *The New York Times* can do, that the French Laundry was the most exciting (read: "best") restau-rant in the United States, launching this near-mystical place into the stratosphere. September 1997, a Thursday night, a group of eminent food writers in town for a symposium, not just at a single table but scat-tered throughout the restaurant. The energy in the kitchen was high and good. Thomas was writing the menu for the most important table, the four-top containing the restaurant critics of *The New York Times*— and the *Washington Post*. (The *Post's* Phyllis Richman told me she had organized the meal and, with a lingering trace of annoyance at her prom-inent colleague, said, "She scooped me!") Thomas looked over to Grant on garde manger and said, "Grant, make me a pasta dish." So Grant decided on a ravioli, stuffed with sautéed chanterelles, a piece of seared foie resting on top, and a sauce—looking back, he thinks it was almost too simple, but at the time he thought it was "really cool." But even more than the creation was the fact that Chef had asked him, basically a young line cook, to give him a new dish to serve to the exalted table.

Sixteen-hour days, five days a week, working at that level, it's hard, but it was also thrilling to move up through the restaurant as the restaurant itself rocketed into orbit. After two years, various tensions within the French Laundry family told him he'd better leave while the going was good, and so he left to work for a Napa winery, La Jota. Keller is fiercely loyal to his employees, and he expects the same loyalty back. Grant had left too early and for the wrong reasons, and Keller was furious.

This was late 1998, when we were completing *The French Laundry Cookbook*. Among the final duties I had by then was to write Keller's acknowledgments. All three sous-chefs—Grant, Gregory Short, and Eric Ziebold—had worked hard with Susie Heller (who was writing all the recipes) and Deborah Jones (who shot the photographs), taking time out of their day or using their days off to make dishes for Heller and Jones. Keller thanked Gregory and Eric, but refused to include Grant— he was too angry.

After a year, Grant returned to the French Laundry. And Thomas, admitting that he was wrong not to have acknowledged Grant, included his name in the fourth printing. Grant stayed on another two years as a French Laundry sous-chef, and when he felt that it was time, finally, to leave, he spoke with Keller, who this time gave him his blessing.

It is time for you to leave, Grasshopper.

❧

When Henry Adaniya (who began as a cook more than twenty-five years ago, moved into service, and then became a restaurateur and the owner of Trio) read Grant's résumé and application, he didn't throw it away, but he did put it aside. Adaniya was losing his chef, Shawn McClain, and had posted a want ad on the Internet. Grant had responded to it. Adaniya saw Grant's age and thought, *Yeah, a lot of young line cooks at hot restaurants are looking to make a name for themselves. No thanks.*

A bit later, though, Adaniya was talking to a purveyor and Grant's name came up. The purveyor urged Adaniya to check out Grant. So he did—he sent him some exploratory e-mails with a range of questions, everything from menu details to how he'd run a business to what kind of junk food he ate. He was less interested in Grant's specific answers, Adaniya says, than in understanding "what is the essence of his character." And it was through e-mail that Grant first distinguished himself to his future boss. "He writes beautifully," Henry told me. "His vision is clear. He was honest. He knew where he wanted to be, and how he wanted to do it. He also had a manner that expressed wisdom."

So he told Grant, OK, we'll bring you out. Grant sent a very clear list of what he needed, and plane tickets were arranged. A few days before his tryout, in March 2001, Grant called Adaniya and said he didn't know if he'd be able to make it. Adaniya didn't know what to think.

Nor did Grant. After two days of working his usual shifts at the Laundry, but with a high fever and severe chills, Keller sent him home. The next day he was still unable to shake the chills and fever, so Angela took him to the emergency room, where doctors were urgently concerned about his rocketing white-blood-cell count and worried about possible bacterial meningitis, an illness that causes potentially fatal swelling around the brain. Grant did what any self-respecting cook would do. He called his boss and asked if he needed him to come in to work that night. He'd never called in sick—you just didn't do that.

"Where are you?" Keller asked.

"The emergency room," Grant said.

"You're crazy, Grant—don't come in."

Grant spent several days in the hospital and recovered, though the doctors never isolated the cause of the illness.

Instead of going back to work, though, Grant took off three more days to fly to Chicago and try out at Trio. Now he *really* felt guilty.

Arriving gaunt, gray, and weak, having lost nearly 20 of his 160 pounds, Grant began to cook. He continued to impress Adaniya before Adaniya had even tasted a thing, first by his demeanor and organization, then by the critical fact that he served the food when Adaniya had asked for it. Unlikely and unbelievable as it may sound, in many try-outs, Adaniya said, chefs sent out the first course at 3:00 and at 7:00, he was still waiting for the rest of the meal. Grant was good to the minute—first course at 3:00, second course at 3:12, and on through seven courses, all French Laundry stuff, Grant recalls, except for a little morsel of foie gras. (While I'd been hanging out in the Trio kitchen, Grant gave me a small disk, about an inch in diameter, a half inch thick, and said, "This is why I got the job." Foie gras, encased in a paper-thin chocolate-sugar tuile—it was strange and very delicious, the complex chocolate acting as a seasoning for the rich foie, the delicate sweet crunch a textural contrast to the foie's smooth richness, plus the little engineering mystery: How did he get that coating around the foie?)

Adaniya's response throughout the meal: "This is something I haven't seen before. This is out of the box."

He intended to offer Grant the job, but when Grant explained his vision of the restaurant (what it has become today), Adaniya said it was too radical for what he described as "an extremely conservative town." Grant wasn't interested in catering to the conservative diner, and the two parted ways.

But, as Adaniya continued his chef search, chef after chef served him meal after meal of the same old fine-dining dishes. Each time a new plate came, he thought, *This is just the same as everything else. I want something unique.* So he resumed his conversation with Grant.

"It was really, really risky," Adaniya recalls. "How do you serve this new space-age food? My staff was afraid of it. They didn't know how to present it to the guest."

❧·❧

"If I hadn't done the stage at El Bulli," Grant says, "I'd still be cooking French Laundry."

In the summer of 2000, Keller intended to take his three sous-chefs to Spain during the French Laundry's summer break. He suggested that

Grant go early to El Bulli and spend some time in the kitchen led by Ferran Adrià. Grant accepted. He flew by himself not knowing how he'd make his way to El Bulli, on Spain's Costa Brava. By chance—and this is one of the lucky things about being a chef, part of the chef karma—in Barcelona's airport, he bumped into a group of prominent chefs, including Suzanne Goin of Lucques in L.A., Paul Kahan of Blackbird in Chicago, and Wylie Dufresne, who would soon open WD-50 in Manhattan, which would serve out-there food as well.

Grant said, "Where are you guys going?"

"El Bulli," they told him.

And so he piled into a bus provided by the Spanish cultural group funding the American chefs' trip and joined them for dinner that night. While it surpassed the expectations he'd gotten from reading about the place, his colleagues, with the exception of Dufresne, were not as receptive to the "space age" cuisine.

He began his stage the next day and was disoriented from the start.

"It was all so unfamiliar to me," he said. "I felt like I had been exposed to some great restaurants in this country, and I thought I had a good understanding of the highest-end kitchen. As soon as I walked into that kitchen my feet were off the ground. I couldn't see a sauté pan, I couldn't see a stockpot simmering, the smells, the sights, right down to the language—I had no idea where I was. Aesthetically, it didn't look like any kitchen I had been exposed to. The ingredients were all very different and the techniques that were being applied were all very different. It was almost like I was on a different planet all of a sudden. There's nobody butchering meat, there's no veal stock going, there's no this, there's no that—what the hell is going on here?!"

It was here and at Adrià's "lab"—"They want people thinking they're back there with test tubes and Bunsen burners but that's not what's going on; looked like an apartment when I was there; a couple couches, a TV, a cooking suite, big library"—that Grant got his first serious taste of experimental cooking, agar and alginate and unusual sugar work (including the sugar "tuile" technique), reducing solids to liquids and reshaping them as solids again but in a different form and playing with heating and freezing. It was like a light switched on in his head, he said.

At the end of his five-day stage, Grant, Thomas, Eric, Gregory, and their respective spouses met for dinner, and now Ferran did what any chef would do for one of America's most famous and revered chefs— sent him and his staff everything the kitchen had to offer and then joined them at the table for another four hours, though he speaks almost no English and the Americans spoke kitchen Spanish at best.

Grant's reaction to this meal was more complicated than what he first experienced a week earlier. While he felt more comfortable talking about the food with his fellow cooks than he had with the chefs he'd met, something restrained him. Keller was there, who'd more or less raised Grant as a cook. This was not the kind of food any of them had encountered before. Grant loved it but, he said, "I felt like I couldn't express my exuberance."

I asked him why.

"I felt a certain sadness that I enjoyed it, because it felt disrespectful," he said. Such was his devotion to his mentor.

But when he returned to the French Laundry, the El Bulli experience grew in his mind and, having always been inclined to push even French Laundry dishes to the edge, he now pushed even harder. El Bulli "showed me that there's another way to do this," he says, "another option."

He remembers the night it became clear that he had to leave the French Laundry, remembers the very moment. He was training a new cook on garde manger and ended up working that station. A group including Hiro Sone, chef-owner of the restaurant Terra, up the road in St. Helena, arrived for dinner, and, always generous to their colleagues, the French Laundry chefs planned to send out several VIP courses. Grant can't recall exactly what the two dishes were that he described to Keller for Keller's approval, but they were El Bulli–inspired, and one included foam. What they were wasn't the point; it was the way Keller looked at him when he described the dishes—he could see it in Keller's eyes.

"He didn't have the heart to say, 'This doesn't fit here,'" Grant remembers. "At that moment, I thought, *This is it.*"

It didn't happen immediately, of course, but it happened inevitably. This time Keller couldn't have been kinder about his leaving. Grant remembers his final two weeks at the French Laundry, early in the summer of 2001, as the best and sweetest of his whole career there.

❊

Grant took over the Trio kitchen in July 2001 serving food that seems by his standards today to be not simply traditional but archaic, no matter how French Laundry–derivative they may have been—items such as saddle of lamb for two with *pommes Maxime*. The restaurant was full until September 11, when business at Trio, as at restaurants throughout the country, vanished. By late in the fall, they were doing eight covers a night. It's hard to prep for eight covers. On the other hand, the lack of business, which remained grave all the way up until Valentine's Day, gave Grant time to think and experiment, hastening the innovations that would lead to his twenty-eight-course Tour de Force menu, shrimp cocktail–in–mouth spritzers, glass tubes, "pizza," "squids," and "antennas."

❊

It's one thing to watch someone prep and cook dishes, another thing entirely to work with the food yourself. You can take all the notes you want, paying close attention with all your senses, carefully noting aromas, listening for clues of moisture levels and heat, but cooking is a physical manipulation of actual materials. Touch and feel account for at least half the information you absorb when making a dish. When you just watch, you're only getting *half* of what you need to know.

Grant was good enough to include me in as many of the innovative techniques as possible. I began with the sake "wrapper." Agar, a carbohydrate derived from red algae, which is not new to the pastry kitchen but is to the hot kitchen, is a gelling device. The advantage of agar is that unlike traditional gelatin, it will maintain a gelled state even when piping hot. Here agar is dissolved in sake. The sake is then poured on a sheet of acetate. The sake quickly cools and sets up as an opaque sheet maybe a sixteenth of an inch thick that can be peeled off the acetate. Individual wrappers are cut from this, filled with the seaweed, roe, and cucumber balls that have been lightly pickled, and the wrapper is folded into a package.

Seems easy enough, but what you'd never know without doing it is how very, very delicate the sake sheet is. It will rip at the slightest tension or quiver of the finger.

The next preparation I worked on also used agar. Grant created a cranberry sauce to go with the shrimp. This, too, was gelled but in a pan and at a depth of about a half inch, thick enough to cut into chunks. A chunk of cranberry gelatin was skewered onto a vanilla bean. Next a strip of rind from a Meyer lemon that had been confitted, or salted (which transforms it into a beguiling seasoning device). And finally a delicate Maine shrimp is skewered onto the bean. These are then refrigerated until service. At service, a small amount of tempura batter is mixed (it will lose its lightness unless made just before breading); the shrimp-lemon-cranberry kebab is floured, dipped in tempura batter, and swum in hot oil: You don't just drop the whole thing in—Grant didn't want the whole bean deep-fried—you had to hold the end of the bean for the sixty seconds it took to cook. This was a pain if you had other things to do—such as respond to the dozens of orders being called out—or had to cook eight of these at once.

The effect was extraordinary, though. A light, crispy shrimp tempura, which when you bit into it virtually exploded with the hot cranberry sauce, which felt like liquid because of the heat but was still solid (an agar gel won't melt until about 185 degrees Fahrenheit). Part of the pleasure was the surprise of finding a "liquid" inside something deep-fried, so the use of agar here was very effective.

But—it was a mother to keep on the fat vanilla bean. Just skewering them, the gelled cubes wanted to split on you. And the shrimp, also, they were so delicate they wanted to fall off the bean, too. This was workable during prep time but quite a bit less so during service when you had to flour and batter the things, putting more stress and adding weight to the delicate constructions.

That station also puts together one of the labor-intensive duck garnishes—the radish–hearts of palm structure: alternating coins of each with some mint oil and microgreens rest on a plank of another gelatin. These coins didn't want to stick together in their arranged red-white pattern. Watching Grant repairing one of these, I was struck by how many items he served that were just on the edge of breaking. You had to have a really delicate touch in this kitchen.

Next I worked with Curtis, who was making the eucalyptus "roe." This was fascinating and fun. First he brewed the eucalyptus tea, a lovely darkish pink color. When it was cool, he added alginate to it. Whereas agar derives from red algae, alginates derive from brown algae. Alginates also are used to gel liquids; they will only gel, though, in the presence of calcium. What Curtis then did was fill a mini–squeeze bottle with the alginated tea and squeezed out drops of them into a solution of calcium chloride. The drops hit the calcium chloride and their exterior immediately gelled, forming delicate little balls of tea. The larger apricot ball, the size of a chicken yolk, is made using this same process.

Grant explained Trio's use of alginate and calcium chloride, which he discovered at a food-technology expo in Chicago, to the readers of eGullet, the culinary Web site.

> Self-encapsulation of liquids was something we had talked about at Trio since the beginning of our time here. The concept of it exemplifies the thought processes we have in the kitchen. You will frequently hear me say to a cook asking what to add to a puree to adjust the consistency is . . . itself. If you are making celery soup, what should the ingredients be to make that soup taste like the essence of celery? Well, celery . . . of course, not water, not cream . . . celery. The point I am trying to make is if you take a product and wrap it in itself it has nothing to dilute the flavor that you are trying to express. . . .
>
> At this point we had encapsulated liquid in pasta (black truffle ex-

plosion). At the sight of this new technique we figured we could eliminate the pasta and wrap black truffle juice in itself. We placed an order for the product. One week later the *NY Times Magazine* piece on Ferran Adria came out. There it was . . . caviar of apple and the infamous pea ravioli. One step ahead of us for sure . . . but we were on the right track no doubt.

When the product arrived we knew we couldn't do "caviar" or even super ball sized encapsulations due to Adria's precedent. So we posed ourselves with a challenge. How do we create an encapsulation the size of a hardball? A self encapsulated soup or sauce depending on the size desired.

Trio also used various forms of foams. I find foams dubious, and they are especially tricky because they've become synonymous with the worst of the new innovations or edge cuisine done badly. At Trio, one foam, the fines herbes sponge, was served as a stand-alone garnish, the soy foam as a stiff sauce, and a hot brothy foam covered his lobster tail like a cloud of sea spume. (I didn't care for that whole dish, "Maine Lobster *flavors of Thai ice tea, aromatic bread,*" the menu called it, though Luke, the L.A. cook, had eaten that dish and was gaga over it.)

I remained skeptical of foam. I didn't like the texture. There was something inherently phony about foam. It tried to be bigger than it actually was—a heaping spoonful of foam really amounted to a piddly few drops of actual stuff. It was mostly air. Also, I didn't like the look of foam. Foam is what you skim off your stock and discard; foam is what you stay away from when you're swimming in a lake. I don't want to eat foam.

Grant defended it. "Why is there so much veal stock?" he asked me.

I'm a veal stock fanatic so I tried to keep myself neutral, rattling off the obvious benefits of an excellent veal stock—body, flavor, moisture, richness.

"Exactly," Grant said. "Foam does the same thing, adds and enhances flavor, body. It's a sauce. But it also does the opposite of a sauce. It adds lightness."

I nodded but he saw I wasn't convinced.

It was early in service when we had this exchange. He was at the pass and he pointed to the pineapple-salmon combo bobbing on the antenna. "How else could I sauce that?"

Here he had a point I couldn't argue. You wanted a sauce on this thing. It wanted the moisture, flavor, and seasoning that a sauce delivered. But one of Grant's goals here was to serve a dish that didn't require using your hands, so the thing was bouncing around on the end of an antenna. A stiff foam was a good solution; the Thai ice tea spume hiding the lobster was another story, but this I completely bought.

"People are scared of things that are different," Grant went on. "They push food back. In the last five years we've created five new techniques"—and by "we" Grant meant the professional chef, the innovative restaurant kitchens working this edge cuisine—"and they're being challenged on a *moral* level! . . . It's like the devil!"

So what are these new techniques? I count eight:

1. Agar, the ability to serve gelled food hot, resulting in such dishes as "fettuccine" made from consommé.
2. Alginate and calcium chloride, the ability to create different-shaped gels and to encapsulate liquid in itself, such as the self-enclosed ravioli or the eucalyptus roe.
3. Pervasive use of sous-vide cooking, the ability to cook protein very gently and slowly.
4. Various types of foams, from solid to liquid.
5. The sugar tuile technique: Three different types of sugars—glucose and isomalt (a sugar replacement derived from beet sugar) and fondant—are melted and brought to the hard-crack stage, about 365 degrees Fahrenheit, poured out, cooled, and ground into a powder, sprinkled out on a special nonstick paper (called "Magic Paper") in the desired shape, baked, and cooled. The result is a

sugar tuile that will melt at a relatively low temperature and encase an object, such as a disk of foie gras, in a very fine, crisp layer.

6. Aggressive use of aromas—serving shrimp on a hot vanilla bean, for instance, beef with applewood smoke, pheasant with the smell of hay and apples.

7. Unconventional serving devices, such as the "antenna" and the parfait tube.

8. Unconventional temperatures—hot gelatin, for example, or frozen foie gras.

There are other techniques as well that might be included but aren't unconventional until applied to this kind of food—techniques of dehydration, for example (Grant dehydrates mushrooms, bacon, and other items). Also, edge cuisine might simply be defined by the extent to which food is manipulated—turning shrimp cocktail into a liquid or, in a dish Adrià made famous, grilled vegetables juiced, gelled, sliced, and served like Technicolor piano keys as "grilled vegetables."

"As a whole," Grant says, "when you group all these things together, it begins to define the movement. These are going to be the indicators of said cuisine. I think it's important to keep moving gastronomy forward at this level. . . . More than anything, they help us express the objective: innovation.

"I don't want to do what's been done for a long time," he goes on. "I want to create. To try to invent, whether it be a dish or a technique. That's exciting to me. Rather than perfecting something that's old, I'd rather perfect something that's new.

"Three years from now, we might not be doing anything with alginate, but the thought process that led us to that will still be intact. If it's not alginate, it'll be something else. The thought processes are what's really important."

"What's the downside to all this?" I ask.

"It's really hard," Grant says.

❧

I drove out of Evanston soon after, excited for Grant, and with my mind a little more open to the ideas and techniques defining this edge cuisine. I was comforted by what one of Grant's sous-chefs, David Carrier, had said: "No matter how avant-garde you are, culinarily speaking, you always wind up back in the basics." Indeed, I'm sure that Grant succeeded at Trio because his basics were as close to perfect as basics can be. He could do whatever kind of food he wanted and would succeed because of this, from bistro to edge cuisine.

Grant would close down at the end of July and enter a peculiar world of nine-to-five, with plenty of time to spend with the family. Strange for a lifelong line cook. He could get everything done that he needed to do each day and still have tons of time on his hands and get enough sleep. It gave him time to think.

Eager to follow the progress of Alinea, I stayed in touch by e-mail. He wrote me in November 2004:

> I left Trio nearly three months ago. I have made my humble reputation on creativity. In my opinion Thomas made his on technique and dedication, and Charlie . . . "the pursuit of excellence." Over the last three months I have contemplated my place in this discipline, where do I stand? Where is my future? I have come to the conclusion it is the creative process that separates me from many culinarians.
>
> That creative process has led me to the building of Alinea. Within that container I will craft an experience like no other. From the design to space to the cuisine, it will express my emotions. The true origin of uniqueness, the start of creativity . . . emotion.

More than a month later, in the week between Christmas and New Year's Day, he wrote a long e-mail detailing the restaurant's progress, the design of the space, the kitchen, the serviceware, the wine list, the menu—it was all coming together in an exciting way. The demolition of the interior of the building—on North Halsted Street in Lincoln Park, across coincidentally from Steppenwolf, the famous experimental theater company—had been completed, and the basic concrete-and-steel foundation had been put in place, and chalk outlines of the kitchen had been drawn. It gave him the chills, sometimes. City permits were all granted. He'd hired his kitchen staff, six of whom were at Trio. His two sous, Curtis Duffy and John Peters; his business partner, Nick Kokonas; and a general manager were working full-time, with two days a week being devoted to food development. He was soon to meet a private wine collector, a friend of two investors, who would be making a portion of his collection available to the restaurant. This was extraordinary given that creating a wine list can be among the biggest costs in opening a restaurant, something that most new restaurants must do gradually. Here they were basically borrowing a wine cellar, allowing them to open with a wine list of more than six hundred wines, four times the size they'd budgeted for.

Luck seemed to be waiting for Grant around every corner. "All of this stuff scares me a bit though," he concluded.

On one hand I feel I am doing the right thing by trying to open this thing at the highest level. I seem to have resources available to me that most don't when they open their first place. I have heard some grumbles in the industry that I am just a spoiled kid who has investors with deep pockets . . . some people talking shit I guess you would say . . . but that is not really the case. This restaurant will be nice . . . really nice actually, but it has been done creatively and responsibly all the way through . . . even the biz angle which is allowing it to achieve more than the raise should provide.

On the other hand there is something magical about the FL story . . . cooking on a four-burner stove with shitty sauté pans . . . Angela tells stories about sitting on milk crates while taking resos in the early days . . . the whole time watching it grow into the dream. . . .

I am not starting with the end-all dream . . . but probably at a higher level than most 30-year-olds could. It almost seems like a natural progression for me though, and a natural pressure. The Keller protégé, first chef job he gets the Mobil 5th star, F&W top ten, 4 stars, and the JB award . . . the momentum pushes me in this direction . . . my cuisine demands it . . . if I opened a 250K bistro people would say what the Fu?? Somehow I feel people expect me to come out swinging hard. If I don't, I fail. If I do, and fail . . . I fail . . . so I guess that only leaves one option.

Best,
Grant

CHAPTER 2

The Romantic Ideal: Melissa Kelly

The sound of the kitchen's screen door slamming shut says *Home*. The air is a balmy seventy degrees at seven A.M. in Rockland, Maine, the first week of August. You can see the big garden in full summer bounty from the windows here. Michael Florence mixes bread doughs at the back of the Primo kitchen, built into an old Victorian house on the craggy Maine coast. He works on a heavy wood bench with flour and water in this rustic kitchen with a massive central brick oven, still hot from last night's service. Michael will mix the starter, natural yeast, with water and flour, a little commercial yeast, let it rest awhile, then finish mixing with a little more water, extra-virgin olive oil, and salt. He'll pour it into a five-gallon plastic container to ferment, let the natural yeasts feed on the sugars and release their tangy lactic acid that gives sourdough its name. Because of the warm weather, which makes the bacteria a little more feisty than usual, the starter's been too sharp, and this concerns him.

"You don't want an overpowering acidic taste," he says, "just a depth of flavor." Michael is a craftsman. Quiet, fair, medium height and build, a cap over his short, light brown hair, he studied classical piano at a conservatory in Wisconsin. He'd like to do a recital here in Maine, but it's hard to find three hours a day for practice. Every day in the kitchen, though, he'll make the country loaf, four big ones. He uses a levain (a different kind of starter) for the whole-wheat boule. They've got another dough for the baguette, and he'll also make the pizza dough and feed the starter. Occasionally he'll do a rye, maybe a rye with hard cider in the fall, but not often. "A lot of people enjoy bread, but not everybody can make it," he says. Sometimes he'll leave a loaf of bread warm out of the stone oven. He cringes when the cooks rip a piece off, tearing apart the crumb. Making bread is a craft; he wants people to appreciate it.

He needs to get all his doughs mixed and fermented before Kristin Nicodemus arrives to begin pastry back here. Kristin, twenty-nine, has a degree in applied history and public policy from Carnegie-Mellon. She worked in education for a while but it wasn't right. "My true passion was in restaurants," she says. She met her fiancé, Aaron Leikman, thirty-three, in a Seattle restaurant. He'll be in at about eleven, will be working the line tonight. Aaron has a degree in ecology and zoology from Oklahoma University, as well as an associate's degree from the CIA. Joe Nastro—tall and thin with dark hair cut very short, who used to work with animals out West, has a B.S. in animal science from the University of Vermont, and may return to that one day—is on the wood oven tonight. The wood-burning oven, he says, "is like working with another human be-ing. It's temperamental. You never know what it's gonna do next." After the bread has baked, Joe will load the oven with wood and really crank it for service. A pizza will cook in sixty seconds in there. A roasted whole dorade, stuffed with lemon slices and fennel, takes about five minutes on a sizzle platter and comes out with the skin nicely charred.

While this kitchen staff has more nonculinary degrees than most oth-ers I've met, there are some purely culinary folks, such as Lindsey Kut-sai, twenty-three, who arrives in the morning to begin prepping her station, garde manger. A graduate of the Institute of Culinary Educa-tion, formerly Peter Kump's in Manhattan, she's been here a year, her first real cook's job. Art Rogers will be the last one in, the other line cook tonight—from Rochester, New York, a graduate of a hotel and restaurant school in New Hampshire and an unflappable line cook. Right now he's out on a breakwater casting into the Penobscot Bay, and he'll land eight or ten small mackerel, which will be grilled and used on a salad tonight, or with cucumbers or purple Romano beans, depending on what's plentiful in the garden. Rob Holt, the sous-chef, is off tonight, and Alissa Alden, twenty-one, who began washing dishes here six years ago, finishes up pastry in the evening.

This is Melissa's staff, her kitchen. Melissa Kelly arrives at 9:00 A.M. in her white T-shirt and navy blue overalls with the white pinstripes—the commis pattern in French kitchens—rolled high above her clogs to reveal thin, saggy white socks. Melissa is five-foot-four, dark hair pulled tightly back in a ponytail, and if you walk into her kitchen at most times of the day before service, you're likely to see her in this position: straight over a cutting board, neck cocked to hold a phone, talking to a purveyor, the press, family, or someone begging a reservation at the height of the season. Melissa is thirty-nine years old, was first in her class at the CIA in 1988, won the Best Chef Northeast award from the Beard Foundation in 1999, and became a media darling after she put the Old Chatham Sheepherding Company Inn, the Relais & Châteaux B&B and restaurant in upstate New York, on the map. She and Price Kushner—they're married in all but the technical sense (never had the time or a strong inclination to make it legal)—have owned this restaurant in the Victorian house since 1999. And while Price is nominally the pastry chef—his culinary background is breads and pastry—and he does oversee and often cook that side of the menu, he spends the majority of his time running the nonkitchen parts of the business and in the evening leads the front of the house. Melissa is the force of the kitchen, 9:00 A.M. to 1:00 A.M., seven days a week in the summer. Most of the remaining hours of the day, she's dead asleep amid piles of cookbooks and notepads, which cover the bed and surrounding floor in their home nearby.

When I asked when her next day off would be, she said without thinking, "Labor Day." Her last day off had been Independence Day and before that Memorial Day. "We close for all the barbecue holidays," she says. Summers are busy in Maine. If you're not busy here in the summer, you've got a problem. Capacity summers are the only way to get through winter.

"You could shoot a gun down Main Street and you wouldn't hit anyone for three towns," says Price of the winter population.

But even those months, January through March, Melissa likes to stay open five days a week, despite the fact that they consistently lose money—she does it to keep her staff employed. Otherwise, she's afraid, they'd have no choice but to leave her. Also, I suspect, she's happiest in a kitchen.

"I'm not a groundbreaking chef," Melissa says. "I like to cook. . . . I *cook*. That's what I do. That's what I've done my whole life. Food is it. I'm not a photographer, I'm not an artist, I'm not a boatbuilder, I'm not anything else. I'm a cook, that's who I am."

And so she's most likely to be in her kitchen just about any nonsleeping hour—not dressed for a photo shoot, in the office on the phone with her brand consultant, or scouting new restaurant locations—dicing the onion and peppers for the peperonata, a base for a grilled swordfish–mussels–saffron gnocchetti, or mixing yolks and flour in the KitchenAid for the hand-rolled spaghetti, served with Nicoise olives, capers, and ricotta salata, as well as eggplant, basil, and tomatoes from the garden out back.

"I don't know why I do it," she says in her slightly nasal, slightly Long Island voice and without looking up from her board. "I enjoy it, I enjoy the routine, the sense of accomplishment. Even last night going through the cooler and getting everything organized makes me feel really good.

"I love the circle," she adds, "the cycle of cooking. It is a life cycle, it has its own life." The finest moments of the day are when she's got four or five pots and pans going, she's stirring a risotto, butchering the lamb, dicing the onion for the sauce, throwing the onion ends into the stock, every act and every scrap propelling her and the food toward the finished dishes, moments when one movement works toward several different ends, and all those different ends fulfilling a singular goal. "I love when there's that full circle, to me that's the best feeling."

⇒⋅⇐

The food at Primo couldn't be more unlike the food Grant pursues. Melissa's is home-cooking food that emphasizes the best possible vegetables, meats, dairy, and fish, simply prepared. It's served in a house on a hill. To enter it, guests walk across a front porch, through a foyer, and into a vestibule whose main feature is a staircase leading up. There are three small dining rooms on the ground floor. Upstairs is a small bar (your best chance to eat at Primo in the summer if you don't have a reservation), a small dining room that has a more bistrolike feel to it, and an open room that serves as a private dining room for up to fourteen people. Servers descend via a back stairway that leads to the kitchen. The hallways and doorways, the molding, the tongue-and-groove floors, the staircases all kind of whisper *Home*. The servers and cooks, they all work in a house, not a building, and this has its own impact. Service is casual, and the relationship between the servers and the cooks is not just cordial, it's family-like, as much as front and back of the house can be, anyway. (Front and back is always a difficult bond.)

"I've never worked in a place where there was such a relationship between front and back," says Tina, one of tonight's runners. "But I don't think Melissa would have it any other way." The last place Tina worked, she says, "the kitchen wouldn't talk to you except to swear at you."

I noted in my pad that Tina hadn't said, "Melissa and Price." It's true, I think—it's Melissa's personality that dominates this place. The food, American regional products (much of it from the region of their backyard), used to compose Italianate dishes that would have pleased Melissa's grandfather Primo. Especially the saltimbocca, which Primo ate on a regular basis—his favorite dish, in fact—and the one dish Melissa never takes off the menu, for that reason. Pork loin pounded thin, sautéed, served on a tall bed of garlic mashed potatoes with a sage-Madeira-shiitake sauce and a garnish of shaved Parma ham on top. The way Primo liked to eat it. Primo, whose picture hangs in one of the dining rooms, died in 1987 at the age of sixty-nine, when Melissa was on her externship in St. Thomas. He'd had a triple bypass and was put on a special diet that forbade coffee, wine, and dishes like saltimbocca. Primo, a butcher by trade, was miserable without these fundamental pleasures and abandoned the diet. "So he basically did himself in," Melissa says now. For Primo, eating and drinking *was* life. And our eating and drinking has become his granddaughter's livelihood. Surely he'd be a proud man to know she'd earned awards and national attention for her skills with his saltimbocca.

The familial atmosphere of the place comes from her as well. She's like a busy young mom, approaching forty, and this is her family. When Lucy Funkhouser, who tends the garden and the hogs, gets pregnant, Melissa exclaims, "The first Primo baby!"

Most important of all, perhaps, her food spirit pervades the place, her convictions about life as they're reflected by the products she uses and the way she handles them—that's really what Primo is about. Not foams and alginates, but a garden. The garden is the magnetic north of this kitchen. A two-acre patch of land she and Price cleared of rocks and dug and fed. It was and remains an expensive investment, not the least of which is Lucy's full-time salary, and part-time gardeners in summer, a time-consuming facet of the business, and not just in the effort to care for the garden daily and pick its bounty, but in terms of daily cooking. It's harder to cook out of a living garden. Melissa must cook whatever that bounty happens to be when it's at its peak even if she wasn't planning for it, not wasting a leaf. It's one thing to fax in your produce order at the end of the night; it's another thing altogether to wait and see what Lucy brings her in the morning.

The mixed-greens salad, named "Lucy's," included the following greens when I was there: mizuna, amaranth, basil, bronze fennel, bianca riccia, mustard, tatsoi, sunflower, Red sails, arugula, Tango, and flowering coriander (in the fall there will be more red leaf, young chard, and baby kale). Dressed with a red wine vinaigrette, it's a unique and interesting salad, so much so that people who order it thinking they're getting a standard mixed greens don't always know what to make of it, or how to appreciate the range of flavors in a seemingly simple salad.

That salad, Lucy's Salad—and Lucy, age twenty-five, for that matter—and Art's mackerel that he hooks from the breakwater before work, and Michael's bread, and Lindsey's hard work and struggle to learn the skills she needs to be a good young cook, and the fishermen who call Melissa up to say they caught an amazing cod they want her to buy, or the sheep lady who brings Melissa two gallons of sheep's whey that she can turn into an exquisite ricotta, served on a warm, crisp slice of Michael's baguette with extra-virgin olive oil and coarse salt and some greens—that's what this restaurant is really about.

❧

Melissa and Price had crafted a restaurant of exceptional romance in what is one of the country's most romantic areas, coastal Maine. It was a kind of fantasy restaurant life, the life people dream of if they dream of owning their own restaurant—a young talented couple opening a restaurant on the coast of Maine, doing it their way, making the food they love, growing a lot of it themselves, from lettuces to fine heirloom-breed hogs. It was an ideal, and Melissa and Price had realized this dream, and I wanted to see that dream in action—or, perhaps, what the reality is behind such a dream.

Also, this was a woman's kitchen. Women had a different experience in the professional kitchen. A group of eight women chefs had formed an organization in 1993, Women Chefs & Restaurateurs, dedicated to the education and advancement of women in the industry. One of its board members, Ann Cooper, has written a history on the subject, *A Woman's Place Is in the Kitchen: The Evolution of Women Chefs*. Melissa had reached the top ranks of cooking in America, and I was curious about her experience as a woman in the testosterone-dominated world of restaurant cooking.

However, there was something harder to get a handle on, a quality in Melissa Kelly herself, something difficult to put into words that made her, before I'd ever met or spoken with her, especially alluring to me in ways that most other chefs were not.

⋘⋙

When you travel in culinary circles, hang out with chefs, read as much as you can, you pick up distinctions and begin to notice the details that gather to form a larger, truer impression of a place or a person. The most interesting of these details came from Sam Hayward, chef-owner of Fore Street, a restaurant in Portland, Maine. Hayward was in my hometown, Cleveland, invited by a local chef to participate with several other chefs from around the country in a dinner to benefit the James Beard Foundation. Hanging out the day of the event in the host kitchen, a place called Fire, run by chef-owner Doug Katz and his wife, Karen, I was talking with Hayward (who would soon win Best Chef Northeast from the Beard Foundation), and Melissa Kelly's name came up. I don't remember how—I likely asked him if he knew her, because by then I was already curious. Of course he knew her. With a chuckle, he commented on all the journalists who told him they'd "discovered" Melissa Kelly, and he mimicked Johnny Apple, the *New York Times* reporter, saying it: *"You know, I discovered Melissa Kelly."* Hayward seemed to think it odd and funny that reporters should have such a proprietary feel about her.

I remembered Apple's story. It was the first I'd heard of Melissa, though her restaurant had been named one of the Best New Restaurants in 1996 by *Esquire*. I'd just published my first chef book, intended to continue writing about chefs and kitchens, and happened to be finishing my brief tour as a line cook at the time the article appeared in the *Times'* "Dining" section, a whopping 3,800 words, as long as a Sunday magazine piece. "Hudson Valley" in the headline would have been enough to catch my eye, having recently lived there a year, but the phrase in the subheadline is what I noticed: "a young chef's sorcery." Once a hard newsman, Apple has become the paper's roving gourmand, filing travel, food, and drink pieces from across the country and the globe. He does call her "a sorceress" (and "a smiling slip of a woman," one of two references in the story to how thin she is).

Recognition from *The New York Times* like that about a chef you hadn't heard of sticks in your mind. So when subsequent stories about her appeared, notably about her leaving Old Chatham and renovating a house and restaurant in Maine, I always read with interest. Book work unrelated to food and cooking took me to Camden, Maine, a couple of towns north of Rockland.

On my last night there, a Saturday night, I drove down without a reservation. I had to wait a while for a seat at the bar, and so had time to spot Price (the walls are hung abundantly with framed magazine and newspaper articles of the couple) and introduce myself, then ask if I could meet Melissa, if and when she had a moment during service. Price said he didn't know, that they were really busy, and he'd love to seat me if he could, but as I could see, they were packed. So I hung out and watched and waited. It was a very comfortable place to be, even when this crowded, like being at a really big fancy dinner party at a friend of a friend's house. Eventually, Melissa came upstairs to say hello. She looked like a cook, in her pinstriped overalls, with an elusive, feline quality that made her seem shy and self-effacing, but also clever and sly. She said she had time to show me the kitchen and—this was the middle of service on a Saturday night in the middle of July—gave me a tour of the garden and introduced me to the piggies, Gloucestershire Old Spots. She then said she had to get back to work.

A lone table in the bar had opened up, and I was seated and ordered. The food was superb—an *amuse* of oysters prepared three different ways, halibut on a succotash—all of it memorable more for the pleasure of eating it rather than for any sort of unique preparation, unusual pairings, or unfamiliar ingredients. Memorable also because of the old house, its good karma, and Price and Melissa's welcoming nature.

But it was not the strength of that visit that compelled me two years later to contact Melissa and ask if I could spend a week or so in her kitchen. It was the whole scene—the house and the garden, the husband-and-wife team, each working practically every night, a chef who raised her own pigs, a chef who had no interest in being on TV, no intention of writing her cookbook, who preferred working the line to schmoozing the dining room, who wore commis overalls rather than a crisp jacket with her name embroidered on it.

Ultimately—and only after I'd returned from Maine would I realize this—that ineffable quality of Melissa Kelly that I found so hard to define, what made journalists proprietary, what made her so alluring was this: seduction. Somehow she seduced you. Not in any conventional sense, but rather with her whole being, with her movement either at the stove or in the garden—both deliberate and graceful, combining strength and lightness—with her confidence in what she was doing. She didn't need to speak. She was grounded. She knew exactly who she was and what she was doing, moment by moment, month by month, year by year.

"I like to cook," she says. She's usually cooking when she says it. "I'm a cook. That's what I am."

※

Tuesday, August 3, 2004, is a typical summer day at Primo. Melissa arrives at 9:00 and begins her lists. Even before she knows what she has she writes on a legal pad:

Soup:
Stock:
Butcher:
Prep:

And it's the "Prep" that typically fills up quickly (pea soup, herbs, mash, gnocchetti, peperonata, chix jus), and the priorities marked with an asterisk. She's moved through every inch of the walk-in cooler, to check to see what they have and what they'll need, and has brought out the striped bass to begin butchering them. Lucy will wander through the kitchen in jeans and a tank top, sweat already beading at her temples, and drop off her "harvest list," all the items she'll be taking from the garden. Today's list includes zukesla (a type of zucchini), zucchini blossoms, calendula, nasturtiums, tomatoes, eggplants, gooseberries, micros, one artichoke, cucumbers, fresh garlic, and tetragonia. Also available to pick, but not required today, are red leaf, pea shoots, young chard, young leeks, Genovese basil, an herb called cutting celery, and parsley. Of all the produce they use, about 60 percent of it they grow and harvest themselves during the summer months.

Melissa can usually bang out several items on her list before it's time for the daily menu meeting with her sous-chef, Rob Holt.

Rob is an affable thirty-five-year-old who carries a few extra pounds, is balding appropriate to his age, keeps his remaining light brown hair clipped short, and sports a trim beard and mustache. Originally from Dallas, Rob started out playing in a band years ago, then moved into cooking. It's always nagged him that he doesn't have a proper culinary education. He learned as he went along, as many cooks still do, but he doesn't know what he's missed or what he's lacking. And now he feels he's too old for school, thoughts that fellow cooks who have been to school (everyone else on this hot line has a culinary degree) thoughtfully concede. He's been here less than a year, having come from San Francisco, most recently the kitchen of Boulevard, Nancy Oakes's restaurant, where he did exclusively stocks, sauces, and soups. He liked that focus and after two years there decided to make a change. He moved with his girlfriend, Monica, across the country to work at Primo. Monica is a hostess here.

Kitchens are like families—but adoptive families, with distinct personalities. Sometimes you feel comfortable in them and sometimes you don't. Rob has never quite felt comfortable here, it seems, much as he likes his colleagues and the restaurant itself. And Maine in the winter he found to be deadly dull. He's given his notice and intends to head back to San Francisco to start work the first week of September.

This is fine with Melissa. She likes Rob—he's been good and dependable—but also recognizes it's not the right fit. Furthermore, she's really missed the line. She's eager to get back in there cooking. She loves to cook. It drives her crazy that Rob toward the end of service begins to flag, and when big orders come in late, she feels like an expectant father: "Push!" she says through the service shelf at her puffing sous. This is physical work and you have to be in good shape—it gets hard. I've heard many chefs after they hit forty say, *I just can't do this anymore.* But she's lean and mean and loves it—*loves* it.

Service is a long way off. A lot has to happen over the next six hours in order to be ready, and writing the menu is first on the list.

Melissa and Rob sit in the dining room where it's cool, each with a pen and a copy of yesterday's menu. The room is quiet. The old wooden chairs creak. The framed photograph of Primo looks down on his granddaughter, as does a gallery of other black-and-white family portraits.

"Are we getting chanterelles in today?" Rob asks.

"Yeah," says Melissa. She looks over her list and the menu. "Skate—gotta finish butchering that. That's going on." She slumps over the menu, just staring. Minutes of silence pass. These are her least active, least intense moments of the day, as if when she's sitting, her whole body takes advantage of the break. "We're going to use the rest of the confit on a pie," she says. "We sold twenty-five pies last night. That was *hard.* Our record is twenty-nine, so he was right up there." Joe was on pizza last night, which also serves some appetizers and the *amuse*—he'll tell you how hard it can get. An order for five pies is called followed by three pies—it becomes a space issue as much as a time issue. He's got to spin and stretch each dough ball, then garnish the twelve-inch disk (with duck confit and fig for the "chef's whim"; or artichokes, olives, ricotta, and basil; or mushrooms and roasted garlic and thyme and radicchio), and then fire it. But it's hard to find the space and hit the cooking time just right on all of them because they take only a minute. Plus he's got the wood-roasted oysters topped with Jonah crab, and Rob or Aaron beside him firing numerous roasted whole dorade. That station is either a killer or a breeze, rarely in between.

"We got tuna tonight for the ap," Melissa says, then scans the menu, and Rob does the same, for a quiet minute. *How should I do the bluefin?* she thinks. Melissa says, "I just talked to Jess. He's got some nice swordfish, and littlenecks from Prince Edward Island, and they're the size of mahogany clams. We'll use those for the dorade, and he's bringing some lobsters for Lindsey." (*Chilled Garden Pea Soup with a salad of lobster, mint, and preserved lemon.*)

Melissa will buy only large swordfish, telling all her purveyors this, sending the message that she'll not bring in any that haven't had a chance to breed.

"Swordfish from here is amazing," Rob says, hungrily. "It's like butter, the best I've ever had."

"Whey and milk are coming," Melissa continues. "We'll make sheep's-milk ricotta tomorrow. She's bringing two animals."

"We're gonna do lamb two ways?" Rob asks.

Another long pause scanning the menu, the dining room is quiet.

"I'm gonna verbal out the quail," Melissa says, meaning it will be a special described by the server, "and I'll put the tuna on. I'm not sure about the blossoms."

More pondering. Melissa's still in the aps section of the menu and suggests doing arancini. Rob grins, he loves arancini—"Street food in Sicily," he says—risotto croquettes: flour, egg, bread crumbs, and fried, often with different additions to the fillings. Melissa will wrap sticky cold risotto around mozzarella and anchovies, deep-fry them, and serve them on tomatoes from the garden.

"That's gonna replace the blossoms, we need to accumulate some. We usually do those every other day, and we've done them the past two days."

The squash blossoms—flowers filled with ricotta, fried, and served on a bed of grilled squash, red onion, cherry tomatoes, and a pesto vinaigrette—are an irony: they don't sell well when they're written on the menu, but when they're verbal they sell like crazy.

Rob, whose attention on the menu is now on the pasta section, says, "No more pappardelle, need more eggplant and sauce, and I can pick some nice basil for that."

"Agnolotti for the scallops tonight," she says.

"We have enough gnocchi," says Rob. "We need to wrap salmon." (*Salmon fillets wrapped in grape leaves, grilled, and served on green beans, roasted peppers, and couscous with cumin-spiced eggplant sauce.*)

"Fingerlings?" she asks.

Rob says, "Yeah, I'll do a little bit more." Those for the strip steak, and then for the striper entrée, he needs more coulis, saying, "Red pepper for the bass."

"I don't know about the fennel," Melissa says. "She's picking more today, we have to check it out. Also ratatouille. . . . We'll wait to put sword on tomorrow to get rid of the dorade and halibut." She runs down the menu. "Ten plus two verbals, that's good."

"You still want to go with marjoram for the lamb?" Rob asks.

"Yeah, it was in the braising liquid," she says. Then, remembering, she says, "We used to do a lamb at American Place"—Larry Forgione's seminal New York restaurant—"the saddle. We put a crust on it with cheese and brioche bread crumbs. It's a little bit of a pain. It's a great dish and that'll really make it sell. But one crepe, make it more blini."

"Squarish," Rob says.

"Yeah, that'll make it a really nice dish." (*A double chop with a goat cheese crust, grilled, served with braised lamb shoulder in a spinach crepe, called "Crespelle" on the menu, and baby vegetables from the garden.*) "Oh, I got black-eyed peas in today," she says.

"Are you getting chicken in tomorrow?"

"Yeah."

"Maybe do black-eyed peas with that."

"Yeah."

"Quail?" he asks.

"Yeah, have to order. . . . We've got beans, she's picking leeks today. Squash, lots of squash, eggplant. It's hard when you've got a lot of the same stuff coming out of the garden. You want each dish to have its own personality." She fiddles with her pencil, staring at the menu, sighs. "We could do something with citrus and radishes." Long pause. "Skate, I think of citrus and beets, but also capers." Pause. "Need to go with the citrusy direction." After a few quiet moments she reverses herself, says, "Keep it Italian with panelle, with fried chickpeas, preserved lemon in the salad. Piccata—capers."

"Maybe segment some lemons, parsley," Rob says, referring to the herb salad that will go with the skate.

"I was thinking tarragon."

"Lovage."

"Chervil's good, fines herbes." She thinks. "Tarragon, lovage, arugula, maybe chervil, preserved lemon in the salad with the skate."

"For the steak do you want a vinaigrette with that?" Rob asks.

"Yeah. We can go with the red wine with that."

Melissa looks back up and sees her note to put tuna on the menu. The citrus and radish will go with that. She writes in the margin of the menu, "Tuna—salad radishes citrus cooked on planc in wood oven."

The meeting often concludes not when they're finished, but when they sense they simply need to get into the kitchen and start working.

Rob stands first and as he's heading in, asks, "Do you have the panisse recipe?"—the chickpea flour that's cooked like mush, then poured onto a baking sheet and cooled till it's set, then cut into shapes and reheated at service, a bed for the skate.

"It's just like the polenta," she says. "Four cups chickpea flour, nine cups water, salt and pepper, cook it for a long time, till it starts to pull away from the sides." Rob nods and departs. She makes some finishing touches to the menu to give to Monica to type up.

❧

This daily menu planning also very much defines the style of restaurant and the style of cooking done here. Or perhaps it's better to say that this planning is an organic element of the whole, interconnected—the garden all but demands this kind of rotation of new dishes onto the menu. It's hard coming up with new ideas at noon for that night's menu every single day, seven days a week—and not just dinner for the family, but entrées that live up to the expectations that the press and her reputation have created. Though a complete overhaul doesn't happen daily, Melissa and her cooks change as much as they can comfortably manage. The menu printed for tonight will have twenty-five items on it—five pizzas, nine appetizers, four pastas, and seven entrées—not including the *amuse* (cold melon soup, perfect for August, served in a shot glass, garnished with sweet anise buds and Prosecco), and a couple of verbals. Two days later, the menu will have twenty-three items, ten of which are new since the Tuesday menu, and the *amuse* will have changed to a fish kebab. That's about average, five new dishes every day.

It would be far *easier* for a chef to have thirteen aps and thirteen entrées that don't vary day to day but are, rather, changed once every few months—and I emphasize "easier" because even *that* is taxing.

I remember hanging out in the French Laundry kitchen, which also had rolling menu items, at the end of the night, the brigade sitting around on stools in a very quiet, very clean kitchen trying to plan their dishes for the next day. Grant remembers how hard it was to come up with new ideas at 1:00 A.M., having arrived fifteen hours earlier, prepped till 5:30, cooked for service for six hours, and spent an hour and a half cleaning the kitchen, intending to be right back there the next morning. At the French Laundry, each station was responsible more or less for developing their respective dishes, with Keller's approval or suggestions. There, a dozen cooks served 90 people every night; at Primo, 5 cooks served 140, and all the new dishes came straight from the brain of Melissa.

Especially considering the garden. At the French Laundry, they have beds where they grow microgreens and a lot of herbs, but the truth is that to serve the kind of food that has earned worldwide acclaim, Keller (in fact, most chefs in America) has to rely on all parts of the globe—and a company called FedEx, which has probably done more to change what we eat in American fine-dining restaurants than any other single company—whether he's shipping in fresh hearts of palm from Hawaii, morels from the Pacific Northwest, or truffles from Europe. Keller had told me long ago that the chef's dictate to cook seasonally and regionally had become a virtual fallacy in the American restaurant kitchen, and he was mainly right.

The Primo garden, however, which produced more than 60 percent of the produce Melissa needed to serve a thousand people a week, contradicted this. Yes, it was true, Melissa conceded, that in Maine you had to fudge the seasonal cooking a little. People are already wanting peas in April and by June are clamoring for tomatoes. You don't get peas in the garden in Maine in April, and the summer comes so late, the finest tomatoes don't truly grow ripe until July at the earliest. And so a chef must cater to our expectations of the seasons—shipping peas in the spring, tomatoes in June, and root vegetables in the winter.

Melissa can't avoid this. But her garden is not simply a symbolic gesture, either.

"The garden helps create who we are," she says. "I hate just ordering. I love having it just come to me here. It forces my creativity in a different way. I don't just dream up dishes and then order everything for it. Today you can get anything anytime of year. If you want heirloom tomatoes in February, you can have them. If you want Meyer lemons in the middle of the summer you can have them—you can have anything anytime.

"And that's why I try and not buy very much, and just stick to the garden. I think it makes the food taste better, number one, and it makes me think about where we really are. Summer starts for me with garlic, and we move into zucchini and then we start a little with tomatoes and now we're in beans, and pretty soon we're going to be in bean, cucumber, and tomato *madness*.

"The food is more appropriate to the weather," she continued. I noted that she said "weather," rather than "season," a particularly salient point in Maine. "In spring I'll have sorrel. And nettles. It's great stuff that's natural, what you should be eating then. I can order sorrel but it doesn't make sense to me to have sorrel in the fall.

"Sometimes we don't get tomatoes till September, but people want tomatoes in June and July. You want spring things in spring, but spring doesn't really happen here until June. So it's a little bizarre here, but this is the Maine season. That's what we serve.

"It doesn't always work out the way you dream it to work out," she continues. "There are so many variables. One year we'll have tons of zucchini, the next year we'll have no zucchini. Plus the weather doesn't always cooperate. It's not an exact formula. I like that about it. I like that it forces me—radishes, I've got four pans of radishes. Instead of ordering stuff in, it makes me think about, *All right I've got this and this, what can I make?* and make each dish different and have its own personality and taste good and do the product justice and sell.

"At night when I go home, I'll take my clipboards with me. I'll take two things to bed with me. Sometimes I'll take five if I'm going to stay up. And I'll page through the books or even just look at the index, just for something to inspire me. Sometimes I'll look online at other menus, but I try not to do that, because I really don't want to do that. But I do, I look at Chez Panisse—that menu really inspires me. There are just a few that can help me. Lucques in L.A., her menus inspire me. And Number 9 Park—her menus inspire me." Suzanne Goin, that is, and, in Boston, Barbara Lynch. "It's kind of weird that I chose three female chefs—there was no thought behind that, I guess it's the way that they cook. Just to get some inspiration.

"Our initial investment was tremendous, because the greenhouses and building sheds and all the tools we had to buy—my God, we spent so much money. We spent a hundred thousand dollars a year on the garden the first few years. You think about all the seeds, all the water, a lot of water, the first few years we had no rain. This year's been great."

Just to haul all those granite boulders out of the ground to find some dirt to start with was expensive. One day they hope to dig a well that will feed the garden and the restaurant—when they have the time and the money.

❧

Early one morning, before the sun was too high, I found Lucy Funkhouser, the gardener, before she was too far into her day. Lucy was born in New York City, though her easy manner and slow lope through the lush rows make her seem thoroughly rural. She has thick, short dark-blond hair and wide-set brown eyes. She put two slop buckets in the back of an electric cart and pulled away from the hill of composting refuse from the kitchen toward the small pen where the pigs are kept.

The pigs are Tamworths, a breed from England that is naturally lean, she explains. Last year's Old Spots were incredibly fat. Right now, the brown pigs are skinny, the size of small dogs; they won't be hogs until the fall. The kitchen saves scraps for the pigs—vegetable trimmings, strained mirepoix, and the like—they also have a separate bucket for compost. Lucy dumps the slop buckets into the pen and the little brown piggies dive in, grunting with delight. "The breed's best suited to small farms," Lucy says, "but they aren't commercially viable."

With the hogs fed, Lucy gives me a tour of the various sections of the garden—it takes about forty-five minutes to cover just two acres.

Across from the pigpen, she's grown tall hedgerows of rye and lamb's-quarters ("really delicious and really nutritious") to promote beneficial insects, and these are in front of a long line of pole beans five feet high. The asparagus are perennial if you treat them right, and she's letting them grow out till they're bushy and fronded, now four or five feet high, so that the roots get fed. This is the fourth year of growing them and they're getting good, she says. Also in this bed are strawberries she's grown from seed, white alpine berries (these look like unripe strawberries and are bursting with juice and flavor), and red runner strawberries. She tends five thirty-feet-long rows of garlic, a type called German extra hearty, a hard-core variety (superior to the garlic with no real core, the kind typically available at the grocery store), and will harvest five hundred to six hundred pounds of it this year.

The garden also grows enough herbs, cut flowers, microgreens and salad greens (which Lucy plants weekly), and shallots to obviate the need to purchase them from a purveyor.

Toward the far end of the garden, beyond one of two greenhouses, she grows cauliflower, romescu, and a purple cauliflower called Graffiti. Some of the cauliflower are covered by a white-cloth row cover to protect them from flea beetles, which all the cabbage family are vulnerable to right now.

She grows radicchio, escarole, and lots of kale and arugula ("Melissa can never have enough arugula"), winter squash, buckwheat. Pea blossoms, various lettuces—Galactic (very dark red for drama); bianca; a frisée that grows as leaf lettuce; Tango, a frilly leaf; Sunfire; Black-Seeded Simpson, an old-fashioned reliable lettuce that's been grown since the 1800s—Sharon Taye melons, moon and star watermelon, which has a pattern of stars with one, sometimes two, moons on it. "It seems like so many of these heirloom vegetables were on the brink of extinction," Lucy notes, "and now they're the rage."

Beets, cukes, Swiss chard do well, but the celeriac, planted in March, were largely killed by cutworms. Cardoons—an Italian vegetable, a thistle like the artichoke, with a celery texture and an artichoke flavor—she grows because they're unusual and fun.

She's planned rows of clover between the rows of lettuces and vegetables, in the pathways, explaining that it harvests free nitrogen in the air and transfers it to the soil via bacteria that live on its roots.

She grows red Russian kale, Bright Lights, and white chard, Lacinato kale—a sage-green coolly rippled leaf—a variety of specialty basils, parsnips, leeks, winter leeks called Blue de Solaise, as well as Upton.

She grows forty-five kinds of heirloom tomatoes, a few plants of each chosen carefully to get the maximum variety of color and flavor (many are started early in the greenhouse, a tactic Lucy had been skeptical about but says works great). Tomatillos ("a crazy plant, so humongous and disorderly") and the related sweet-sour husk cherries that will garnish the foie dish tonight, their tomatillo-like wrappers peeled back to make it a finger food. Eggplant and peppers are not doing well; she erred in cupping the roots to protect them from bugs, expecting the roots would break through the cup but they were instead choked. Carrots, summer turnips, pink and white Japanese turnips, which she tries to start every ten days. Zucchetta, "the serpent of Sicily," a squash that will grow four feet long if you let it, one of forty varieties in this garden. Lucy says squash are fun. Tons of blossoms. She once got so excited, she said to Melissa, "I'm gonna grow you a hundred kinds of cool squashes."

She's planted six kinds of pole beans, big white butter beans, English peas, favas, which are peaking now (Melissa also serves the fava flowers, which taste just like the beans). The fennel is excellent this year, as is the New Zealand spinach, called tetragonia, a hot-weather substitute for regular.

In a small decorative garden, just across the drive from the kitchen's screen door, abundant herbs and edible flowers grow—the cook's garden, nicknamed "the mall" because of the variety it contains. The flowers are so vivid in the morning sun that Lucy says, "Those nasturtiums are looking very excited to be alive." She grows poppies for poppy seed; as well as salvia, an ornamental branch of the sage family; sunflowers whose yellow petals can go in salads. The two perennial beds directly behind the house were here when Melissa and Price bought the property. Lucy uses them for teas—lemon and wild bergamot, chamomile, anise hyssop. She's even growing a hearty kiwi plant that gives fruit as small and edible as grapes. Beyond this garden are some apple trees whose fruit is so gnarly that they can only put them in the foyer for aroma and press them for cider.

Lucy says she loves the process of "being able to grow food and see

Melissa make it into art. And I get to see it every night. It's different on a remote farm. Most farmers don't see that, most farmers don't even know how to cook what they grow."

"Melissa translates [what's grown] into the customer's language," Lucy continues. "And they have a trust in her. They'll eat her kale even if they wouldn't eat kale at home. It's a subversive way of getting people to eat healthy things, to get them to eat these simple things that people have been eating for centuries. . . . Eating from the land. Eating can be a little empty without that [connection].

"That's the main thing, and it's really fun to grow this awesome variety of vegetables and to use my creativity to augment Melissa's."

The style at Primo was cooking that suited a small rustic garden in Maine and anytime throughout the year; it was home cooking in the style Melissa had known growing up in an Italian family. Pork with mashed potatoes and a mushroom sauce, the saltimbocca; grilled duck on sautéed kale, potato gnocchi, mushrooms, and favas; that amazing cod that came in, roasted and served with potatoes, salt cod fritters, and a kind of succotash of corn, baby beans, and green coriander; sea scallops with fried green tomatoes and hoppin' john; wood-oven-fired pies with a thin, crisp crust.

❧❦

"I took it really seriously," Melissa says, recalling her first head chef position. Once all the cooks have arrived, Melissa typically works at a small sink station, between the line and the dishwasher's station, butchering meat, chopping vegetables, the simple mechanical work providing plenty of time for her to talk.

Her arms are disproportionately long for her body. "I've morphed with the job," she says. "My right arm is longer than the left because I always work the left side of the line"—requiring her to extend her reach to her right to grab pans hanging above the line; at her height she really has to stretch and, in the middle of service, do it fast. At the ends of her taut, slender arms are stubby, raw fingers. She speaks as she cuts and cooks a ratatouille; mixes, rests, shapes, and cuts the gnocchi; boils the butter beans; and gets the risotto started.

"I—was—*crayzee*," she went on, describing her first days as chef de cuisine at the Beekman 1766 Tavern, at the Beekman Arms, in Rhinebeck, New York. "People who have worked with me in the past who come and see me say, 'I cannot believe you are so calm.'

"There was no talking in the kitchen at all. I was crazy because I had to concentrate, I had to make sure everything was right and it was *so,* there was *so* much to think about. I was twenty-four, twenty-five—I was young to have that position."

Fifteen years ago, Melissa had short punky hair that she did herself and wore clothes to match. Funky punk or not, a five-foot-four-inch young woman only a few years out of the CIA, Melissa was not an immediately imposing leader at the Beekman. "I was a different person. I was more of a girl then, and most of my cooks were my age or older, and most of them were men.

"I often wish I could have done this," she says, "just known what it was like to do exactly what I did as a male. I think about that all the time."

After graduating from the CIA, Melissa tried to get a job with Larry Forgione at An American Place, the New York City restaurant striving to elevate and respect American culinary traditions, but he had no position for her. She found work in the hills of West Virginia at the Greenbrier, a formal resort known for its food. There, under Certified Master Chef Hartmut Handke, she learned volume and speed in the sprawling hotel kitchen and refined her line cooking in its small high-end restaurant, the Tavern Room.

By chance, Forgione happened through the Greenbrier. Melissa reintroduced herself, and he remembered her and asked her to call him when he was back in New York. She did and he offered her a job. Not long after she began, late in 1988, she missed her train in from Long Island. Waiting for the next one would make her late, and she couldn't be late. She didn't want to leave her car in the city all day, so she persuaded her brother to drive her in. It was snowing hard. By the time they hit the Southern State Parkway, the roads were white. A Mercedes traveling fast in the opposite direction lost control, slid across the median, and slammed into their car head-on. Melissa flew into the windshield. Her brother was unhurt. An ambulance took her away to Mid-Island Hospital, where doctors put fifty-one stitches into her head and made plans for additional plastic surgery.

Today, when she lifts her wide dark eyebrows, you can see where the scar begins, but it's not something you notice right away. You're more likely to notice her extraordinary nose above a row of large white teeth, a bright, frequent smile, and dark blue eyes.

And it didn't affect her work, apparently, either. She moved quickly up to sous-chef, then, in the summer of 1991, Forgione took over the moribund kitchen of the Beekman Arms, the oldest operating inn in the country, in a picturesque Hudson Valley town, and asked Melissa to be its chef de cuisine. Thus, the girl from Long Island had her very first chance to run a kitchen.

With Forgione's reputation and the postcard setting of the colonial-era inn, the restaurant at the Beekman Arms was destined to be busy from the get-go. This would have been difficult enough work for the twenty-four-year-old chef, but she was walking into an operational kitchen with a staff already used to its own standards. The man who had been the chef, a guy roughly ten years her senior, was now demoted to her sous-chef. Moreover, it had been the kind of kitchen, not unfamiliar to just about anyone in the business in the early 1990s or before, in which smoking cigarettes and drinking beer throughout service was not unusual.

Not in Melissa's kitchen.

"When I got there, I was like, you can have a beer at the end of the night, you can smoke a cigarette on your way out the door, you can take a cigarette break, but you don't smoke during service, you don't smoke during the day," she says. "There was friction there. I just didn't work like that. I didn't want my cooks to work like that. They needed to focus on the food. These guys, it was like they were at a party at work."

She immediately changed not only the food—to the innovative American cuisine she'd learned in Forgione's Manhattan restaurant—but the standards for serving it.

"They had a steam table with *stuff* sitting in it," she says, still astonished by the memory. "I said, this is going to be an ice bath now, we're putting ice in there and fresh stuff in there, and we're gonna cook it to order, we're not gonna cook it in the morning and leave it there all day."

Several of the cooks quit fairly quickly, but a couple wanted to stay, and Melissa said she'd give anyone a chance who wanted it, but they'd have to be willing to change their habits. A cook named Leo showed up looking for work, and he proved to be the sort Melissa was desperate for. "Do you have any friends," she begged him. She and Leo Castellanos, now chef at the Blue Plate in Chatham, New York, are still close. They cleaned the kitchen and painted it, and got down to the business of cooking. But even so, it was a struggle every day to be a twenty-four-year-old chef trying to give orders to a bunch of older line-cook dudes.

One day, early on, the kitchen was receiving a lot of deliveries. It was a crazy day—pouring down rain. All deliveries have to be inspected, accepted, signed for, and then stored—a time-consuming process in the middle of an already busy day. If you're ever in a kitchen and see a guy not wearing whites, holding a sheet of paper, and looking for somebody he doesn't know, it's a delivery guy wanting to get the order checked in and the invoice signed so he can get out of there.

One such delivery guy called out to the kitchen, "Where's the chef?"

One of the older crew nodded to Melissa. The delivery man said, "That's the chef?!"

Melissa turned around, looked up at the guy. He repeated, "You're the chef?"

"Yeah," she said.

The guy grinned big and wide and said, "Ya like bein' a chef, little girl?"

Melissa was speechless. If this had been a cartoon, steam would now start whistling out of her ears. "What? *What?*" And her crew began to laugh. Waves of heat began to rise off her.

"You like being a truck driver?!" she yelled. *"Go wait outside!"*

She made him stand outside in the rain while she personally checked in the order. It was a big order, and she took her time.

Recalling the event today still seems to make her chest heave. "I had to stand my ground," she said, "because it was in front of these cooks who razzed me every day. I couldn't let them break me."

Even to this day she feels it. "People look at you and they see something and they have no idea who you are or the road you've traveled."

Even here, at her own restaurant, as recently as a year ago, older male cooks will become overbearing to the point that she wants to say, "I didn't just start cooking, I've been cooking for twenty years, and you don't know what I've gone through in those twenty years to stand here today. *Don't tell me* you think it's good to do it this way, because you know what? This is my restaurant. I like to hear other people's opinions and I listen, but sometimes I'm just like, No, we're gonna do it this way. And not just to stand my ground. It's just because that's how I want to do it and this is what I built. This is my house and my restaurant and I'm gonna do it the way I want to do it.

"That's been a really hard thing," she says. "All the experience you go through and when you look a certain way, people just judge you on what they think you are, what they think you know.

"I've worked next to some great chefs. Working with Larry, I had an opportunity to work with some great chefs"—chefs such as Mark Miller, Paul Prudhomme, Alice Waters, Wolfgang Puck. "They were Larry's friends—they worked in the kitchen. They're just people; I'm just a person—that's what it boils down to. We're all just people but we all have different collective experiences. Just looking at someone and judging them, it's hard to deal with that. I still get it."

Just a few months ago she participated in a women chefs' benefit at the Biltmore Hotel in Miami. She was paired with a male French chef, and when she said she wanted all her peas shucked, he said they should just use frozen. She said, *No, fresh.* He said of his frozen peas, "They're good, I use them every night."

"It's not your dish," she said.

"I'm not shucking all these peas," he said.

"Yes, you are, we're using fresh peas."

The French guy thought this was absurd and helped for a while, then disappeared, which she was glad for. "I don't like anybody to do my own prep," she says. "I want to make my own dish, I want to make my own sauce. I'm doing one dish for three hundred people. I didn't need his help, then he was mad because everyone was saying it was a great dish [halibut with a pea puree, lobster, and spring vegetables]."

"It's a challenge being a woman in the kitchen—it's a huge challenge."

Chief among those challenges is, she says, "Being taken seriously on your way up. Women have to work a little harder to be taken seriously."

The different treatment, she notes, though, is double-edged. Sometimes women get the benefit of the doubt, something else Melissa doesn't like. "I don't want any free rides or for anybody to say that's how I got this," she says. "I got this through work."

To young women entering the business she says, "If this is what you want to do, maintain your level of professionalism. Stick to your guns—it's easy not to. There are so many shenanigans in this business, and drugs and alcohol, there are a lot of opportunities to make mistakes. I've seen girls do that. You've got to be professional. And keep your part of the bargain. . . . Maintain your professionalism and you can demand that back."

❧

Melissa ran the Beekman Arms kitchen for three years, transforming it into a first-class restaurant serving American regional cuisine. Owner Forgione, himself a 1981 CIA graduate, was by then in the first ranks of celebrity chefs in the United States. It was perhaps inevitable, then, that, following the success of the Beekman Arms, he'd try to do the same thing in Miami. This has been a common pattern: When a chef becomes well known, opportunities to open offshoots of the flagship restaurant multiply. Again, he sent Melissa to open the kitchen. The results were not so lucky. While no restaurant's demise is simple, a combination of Forgione's spreading himself too thin and insufficient support from his business partners, together with a scathing review in the *Miami Herald* ("An American Place Waterside Restaurant," the paper wrote in March 1994, "is an unfinished, uneven creation suffering from conflict and confusion, producing disappointment"), hit the restaurant so hard that Melissa was on the phone trying to line up jobs for her cooks before the paychecks began to bounce.

About the only good thing to come out of South Florida for Melissa was Price Kushner, a Florida native whose parents ran a linen business that brought Price to Melissa's restaurant and provided an excuse to show up even when he had no business there. They became friends; they dated a couple of times. "Then suddenly we were moving to San Francisco together," Melissa says, apparently still surprised by it.

On the West Coast, Price worked the graveyard shift at Berkeley's Acme Bakery, the country's leader in popularizing artisanal breads, and learned there a feel for dough, both literally and spiritually—"knowing how dough felt and how it should feel," he says—skills that would come into their own when he created the bakery in an aged carriage house at Old Chatham.

Melissa here began what was her most itinerant phase as a cook, working for periods no longer than months at several restaurants. She and Price originally moved to San Francisco so that she could take over as head chef of Restaurant Lulu, Reed Hearon's hip, high-volume restaurant. It wasn't a good fit, and she and Price would eventually move out to Denver, where he'd gone to school. An outdoorsman, a builder by nature, Price would renovate an old house while Melissa worked at Mel's with Melvin Masters. It was while they were in Denver that Melissa got a call from a husband-and-wife team who were planning to open an inn in Chatham, New York. While at the Beekman Arms in Rhinebeck, south of Chatham, Melissa had worked with a cheese maker, Ken Kleinpeter. It was he who gave Melissa's name to Tom and Nancy Clark. They invited Melissa out to cook for them. They liked her food. She told them, "I'm not moving out here just to cook breakfast." They ultimately decided to open a forty-five-seat room that could serve dinner as well. Her plan for Price, as Price notes, was that he would initiate a bread-and-pastry program there while she created a restaurant. Both would come to perfect fruition within a year.

Melissa had left Miami in the spring of 1994. In the fall of 1995, having held five different jobs during that year and a half, she returned to the Hudson Valley, opening the restaurant at the Old Chatham Sheepherding Company Inn that October.

It was during her year in the desert, though, that she'd had her most important cooking experience to date. Significantly—indeed, perhaps in order to have it—she would have to turn in her chef's hat, so to speak, and become a cook. She'd been the head chef now—the leader—of four restaurants. With this move, she would return to being a low-wage line slave. For the first three months, she worked without pay, moonlighting to pay the rent.

The restaurant was Chez Panisse, "the only restaurant in California I wanted to work," she says. And thus the only restaurant that could entice her to take a step backward, as it were, and to work for free. Chez Panisse is, of course, the famed Berkeley restaurant that has arguably given birth to more world-class and prominent chefs than any restaurant in America and probably the world—Jeremiah Tower, Mark Miller, Mark Peel, Deborah Madison, Joyce Goldstein, Jonathan Waxman, Steve Sullivan (founder of Acme Bakery), Paul Bertolli, Judy Rodgers, and now Melissa Kelly.

Melissa didn't feel completely comfortable there, either. Born in a place and time of intense political ferment (early 1970s Berkeley), Chez Panisse remained political in the back of the house as well—any restaurant as justifiably famous as this is bound to have a severe social pecking order, which this place did. If you didn't fit into your place here, you wouldn't be happy. (I met a cook at the CIA named Leather who'd externed there and grumbled that he'd done nothing but carefully wash and hand-dry the lettuce, about which the restaurant was fanatical, every day for six months—that was his one, his solitary, job. He spoke to almost no one.) Furthermore, Chez Panisse remained funky in a way that was stereotypical of its region. Cooks there were not expected to work full weeks and were encouraged to have other jobs or serious hobbies outside the restaurant. "They have these rules there," Melissa says. It was not in the business, that is, of training line cooks. One cooked and served food for reasons more lofty than a paycheck. One's work as a cook did not comprise who one was but rather facilitated and augmented other work. This is likely a unique situation in American restaurants, surely a reflection of the mind who created it, Alice Waters, along with the late Lindsey Shere, pastry chef and co-owner, or at least is typical of a handmade restaurant, one that's unique as a thumbprint.

But what are you to do if a line cook is who you are at your core? Melissa wasn't about to go work at a candle shop or get involved in local politics. She snuck a job at a bakery called Morning Glory, the solitary cook from midnight to 5:00 A.M., while working her way up at Chez Panisse, from 2:00 P.M. till close.

"Chez Panisse is an incredible restaurant and incredible place," she says now. "Amazing people that work there. Very political. The politics of the place is that you have to work there a long time."

She began at the Café, upstairs, like all new cooks after the 1980 extension opened. The big move downstairs to the restaurant was supposed to take a long time. Melissa, however, was a killer line cook and had the chef-leader experience to make the move with unusual speed. In order to cook downstairs at Chez Panisse, a chef ultimately must cook a meal for Waters and a few others, answer questions about the meal, and be approved—a successful, though harrowing, experience for Melissa. Cooking for Alice Waters in this way, in which you do everything, from buy and prepare your food for a three-course meal—rabbit ravioli, in Melissa's case, swordfish, a fruit galette with cheese ("I hate to bake, hate it," she says, another mark of the true-blue line cook)—as well as choose the wine and set the table, would be incredibly daunting even in the best of circumstances.

Waters liked the meal, and so Melissa moved downstairs, suffering the jealous who-the-hell-does-she-think-she-is rebuke from her colleagues, inevitable upon such a speedy advancement within the intensely familial atmosphere of a kitchen.

She spent a total of six months at Chez Panisse, and it gave her the critical component of knowledge she needed to move forward, primed the path toward acclaim at the elegant but rustic Old Chatham. Homey food worked fine in restaurants; people liked to order and eat do-at-home food; you didn't have to make fussed-over, high-concept haute cuisine. You could make your favorite meals, the food you loved the most, with the best possible ingredients, treating them well and serving them with grace in a comfortable room. You could make *money* with this kind of food. Here was one of the most famous, most influential American restaurants ever, doing exactly this.

That may seem like old news today, but you've got to remember that when Melissa was learning to cook in the late 1980s, and when she graduated from the Culinary Institute, the most revered places among aspiring cooks remained the severely French white-tablecloth temples such as La Côte Basque and Lutèce—the four-stars, they were the trophy jobs. Innovation at the time happened in nouvelle cuisine, food even fancier than classical haute cuisine, at places like the Quilted Giraffe, or the refined and innovative cooking at Le Cirque by the young phenom Daniel Boulud. If you aspired to be the best chef you could be, you had to be doing this kind of serious food. The idea that you could make and sell the food you ate as a kid in your Italian Long Island household in the late 1970s was a revelation to Melissa.

"It took me home," she says of her experience at Chez Panisse. "It took me to the place where I felt comfortable cooking, the food I grew up with, that I feel most comfortable with." Up until Chez Panisse, she continued, "I'd always felt there was a division between restaurant food and home food. Chez Panisse liberated me to do [home food] myself. Before that it would be a little more fancy or showy. The rustic thing wasn't happenin' for me at all. I didn't feel like it was acceptable at a restaurant, but after that experience I realized it's OK, people liked it."

The result, by the time Johnny Apple stopped by Old Chatham, would be things like sheep's-milk cheese wrapped in grape leaves and grilled, rack of lamb on a bed of pecorino-spiked polenta, and crown rack of pork stuffed with Italian sausage. And more attention followed the *Times'*, from *Food & Wine,* the *Boston Globe, Gourmet, Bon Appétit, Condé Nast Traveler, Travel + Leisure, Town & Country,* and others.

—▪◄—

Melissa works with the sheep's milk and whey early in the day when the kitchen stove is not in use except for simmering a large pot of pork stock, and it's just her and Doug, the young prep cook, in this part of the kitchen. The whey she has is the watery rich-rich liquid separated out of the sheep's milk during the cheese-making process at nearby Apple Hill Farm. When the proteins that compose whey are heated they clump together, they curdle, into what is called ricotta. She begins this process now in a large heavy aluminum pot. The recipe she uses is from the cheese maker at Old Chatham Sheepherding Company. To cook there was a luxury. Funds (originally deriving from owner Tom Clark's leveraged-buyout firm) were virtually unlimited. In a way, cooking this sheep's-milk ricotta returns her to those productive but difficult years. Tom and his wife, Nancy, oversaw—and continue to run—one of the largest sheep dairies in the United States, with more than a thousand sheep. In addition to the lambs they raised for the kitchen, they also raised hogs. Melissa had all the sheep's-milk cheese and sheep's whey she could ever dream of. The farm-raised lamb and hogs yielded meat of extraordinary flavor. You couldn't buy better quality anywhere on earth, and it grew right there outside her kitchen window. It was here that she determined how she wanted to cook—in a small kitchen with a big garden, working the line every night with a couple of other cooks, making the food she cared most about.

"We had pigs," she says. "We had the lambs there. We had sheep's milk every day—it was an incredible place to cook. . . . We worked really hard there for four years. Same as we do here."

Ultimately, however, a cook's dream though it might seem, she grew disenchanted by the owners and the boggling sums of money that were spent. "They didn't get what was really happening there," she says. "After a while I couldn't work for them. 'Do you see what you have here? Do you understand what's going on here—that we're working and you're just in the way right now?' They had no concept.

"A lot of people don't know," she continues. "*Most* people don't know, even as a cook you don't know half the stuff that needs to happen in a day or a week or a year [for a restaurant to run smoothly], and to understand that, it gives you a different perspective."

Melissa removes her instant-read thermometer, slips it through the metal clip perpendicular to the sheath so she can hold it comfortably above the heating liquid. When she sees it hit 120 degrees Fahrenheit, she adds salt for flavor. She continues to stir, and when the whey reaches 140 degrees, she adds the milk, about two gallons. As the temperature begins to rise again, small clots of curdled whey float to the surface. Melissa measures the temperature again, and at 194 degrees she adds about a cup of white vinegar, which curdles the milk proteins. She continues stirring as gently as she would an incipient consommé raft. Some of the curds stick to the bottom and caramelize just slightly, but she determines they don't taste scorched. When it is as curdled as it will get, she dumps the contents of the pot into a cloth-lined strainer. I taste some of the curd, true ricotta. It has a delicate, neutral flavor. A cup of vinegar into four gallons of whey and milk seems like a lot, but the taste is not acidic.

"What are you going to do with it?" I ask.

She pauses thoughtfully, then says, "I'm not sure yet, I was thinking of an appetizer to feature it. We'll see how it turns out." She scoops the drained moist curd into a deep one-third pan. "I wish the bread were made," she says, smiling seductively at the thought of it, "so we could put some of this on warm baguette and drizzle it with olive oil."

Later in the day, after the bread has baked, she sets beside my cutting board a small piece of toasted baguette with the warm ricotta on it. The fresh cheese is snowy white and streaked with the yellow of extra-virgin olive oil. It's got a light, milky, sheepy flavor, faintly sweet, and a firm, curdy texture—a delight. I can see why she misses having abundant whey—what a luxury that must have been.

There are few luxuries here. Only lots of work—satisfying work. And a good thing, too, because for all of Melissa's successes—for her struggle to rise to sous-chef at An American Place in Manhattan, then taking over the Beekman 1766 Tavern and the trials in Miami and California and Denver, for the Chez Panisse struggles and for the splash of arrival at Old Chatham, and for the ensuing and endless press she continues to receive, and now, Primo, five years old and booked solid all summer long every day except barbecue holidays—for working, as Price puts it without too much exaggeration, "probably a hundred twenty-five hours a week for fifteen years"—for all this, she and Price will scarcely make a dime.

Melissa's mom, JoAnn, knows—she's Primo's accountant. She does the books.

"They'll be lucky if they break even this year," she tells me, without a smile. Price acknowledges this. "Everything we have is in this restaurant," he says, "and everything we make goes back into it." They'd make money if they were this busy year-round but they're in *Maine*—February and March, needless to say, are not thronged with tourists, or even residents for that matter. Nevertheless, they're making ends meet, and this year they'll have worked through most of the debt they took on in 1999 when they bought and rehabbed the place. "And I know that's when things are going to start breaking down," Price says with an ironic grin. "I just *know* it. Like we've got to put a new roof on, and that's expensive, especially in an old house like this."

⋗⋅⋖

The day's routine almost never varies. Morning prep is followed by the menu meeting with Rob, followed by about four more hours of prep—all afternoon and up until service the kitchen is a hive of activity, and work space becomes territorial, especially when service arrives and begins the sidework, wiping down silver and glasses and stacking plates, folding napkins. At 4:15, Melissa writes the day's specials, the verbals, on the dry-erase board.

At 4:30, the servers, usually about ten of them during the summer, gather in a wallpapered Victorian dining room hung with old black-and-white photographs of Melissa's family. They busily scribble the contents of the board into their pads. Melissa waits quietly, apparently relaxing, taking advantage of this time off her feet. No hurry. If you work in the kitchen, the pre-service meeting, a ritual in virtually all good restaurants, is a time of strange calm.

When Melissa senses the servers are nearly finished, she begins: "The first turn looks hellish on paper, the second turn looks spread out. We have a hundred and nine." The night before, they did 131 covers—served 131 customers—which is almost exactly two turns in this 65-seat restaurant. They're likely to do the same tonight, with walk-ins and people eating at the bar.

She then begins at the top of the two-by-three-foot board. "Duck-sausage pie"—each day there's a "chef's whim" pizza, this one using duck confit and figs, same as yesterday.

"How much is that?" a server asks.

"Fifteen," Melissa says. "The antipasti is a fried-squid salad. Quail is wrapped in serrano and wood-roasted, served on a salad with red onion, a quail egg, and mustard vinaigrette. . . . The beet salad has our roasted beets with an orange-pistachio vinaigrette. . . . The duck confit is served on the bone with an arugula salad, a champagne vinaigrette. The duck is cooked with allspice, cloves, bay, thyme, garlic, and white pepper. . . . The salmon is wrapped in fresh grape leaves, not the brined ones we've been buying. They've been blanched and it's grilled, so they get a little charred and crisp. That's served with fresh beans. . . . The bass tonight is served with a ratatouille of summer squash and eggplant— that's from our garden. . . . The duck is served with potato gnocchi. . . . We have seven orders of the leg of lamb with couscous, mint, peas, and Thai basil."

There is no real order of events here—it's a general group meeting. Price, sitting to the side, says, "Everyone did a great job with the verbals yesterday." Price, age thirty-three, is an energetic presence. His five-foot-six frame is compact and athletic. He's got dark hair that hangs in curls, and he's got a bright and ready smile. He's an easygoing guy, happiest when he's out on the lake in a flat-bottomed skiff with his huge New-foundland, Otis, on his way to a little island at low tide to pick sea beans for one of tonight's seafood dishes. "People really change—it's August," he says to the servers. Everyone knows that August crowds tend to spend less, are more demanding, and are generally less savvy than off-season patrons. "So do your best to maintain your composure."

A server says, "The green zebras were a little hard yesterday, and I noticed some people were leaving them."

"Do you think that was because they were green?" Melissa says. "Sometimes people think the green zebras just aren't ripe."

"No," the server says. "They were a little hard."

Melissa nods OK.

Melissa scans the board, set on a table beside her, propped against the wall. "There are two changes on aps tonight. The oysters tonight are Pemaquid; they're roasted with a tomato-fennel glaçage, which is kind of like a hollandaise, but not really—it's whipped egg yolks, with a reduction of Pernod, shallot, dry vermouth, and tomato. We're folding some whipped cream into that, and that's spooned over the oyster. We'll have a little fennel sauce on there as well. The glaçage will get a little brown on top when it comes out of the oven. It'll get toasted bread crumbs with toasted fennel seeds ground into them."

"What's the best way to describe that to the customers," a server asks, "kinda like a hollandaise?"

"No," she says, "it's more like a gratiné with fennel and tomato."

"And it's called glaçage?"

"Glaçage—it's a classic preparation. And we also have a house-made sheep's-milk ricotta. The sheep's milk came from Perry Ells's farm and we got whey from Apple Hill Farm. They're making a sheep's-milk cheese as well. We used the whey and milk to make the ricotta here this morning. So it's house-made, served warm on a lightly toasted baguette, with a little arugula, Black Mission figs, and extra-virgin olive oil. Very simple."

The servers are eager to know how Melissa worked the magic on the whey. Melissa describes the process and also notes the difference between this ricotta and ricotta salata, which is salted, pressed, and baked. The nature of the curds that define ricotta is that they don't fall apart under heat—they don't melt. Instead, they simply dry out. Melissa likes to use ricotta salata, in strips using a vegetable peeler, grated, or in chunks on pizzas and pastas. The servers listen intently, many taking notes, presumably for their own use.

The easy discussion goes on in this manner until all the servers have asked everything they need to know, or addressed any issues, for the night ahead. Then Melissa at last stands slowly and returns to the kitchen, finishing prep, then cleaning up for service.

Unless she hears someone whistling. Once, while seated in this dining room toward the end of the pre-service meeting, she heard whistling and was out of her seat like lightning. *"Who's whistling?!"* she shouted, the only time I heard her raise her voice. *"Jesse?!"* She bolted for the dish station where the new dishwasher was merrily hosing down plates. Melissa is superstitious: Whistling in a kitchen means death to the chef, she said. Jesse agreed to refrain.

❧

Service at Primo, action on the hot line, is classic American restaurant cooking—two line cooks, a guy on wood-oven station, a garde manger doing salads and aps, someone on desserts, and Melissa expediting on the other side of the line, wiping plates as they're set on the hot shelf above the two line cooks, handing them to the servers and calling out orders and fires. It doesn't really look like much unless you know what to look for—and then it's like watching a cross between a sporting event and a soap opera. It's an incredibly intense world that you can't possibly know completely until you're in it yourself. It's like being in the OR except here, the only person who might die is you.

Lindsey was on garde manger, her normal post, night before last. Lindsey is a young cook, twenty-three, who's recently graduated from culinary school. This is her first real cook's job. She's beautiful in her fairness—pale lips, fair skin, loose curly blond hair pulled back, blond lashes and eyebrows. If you saw her outside a kitchen in street clothes, you'd never suspect she was a line cook. Even her voice and movements have a sweet delicacy about them.

"I don't even consider myself a cook yet—I'm still learning," she told me, speaking like a true cook. She continued to roll pistachio–goat cheese balls that go with the orange-and-beet salad. "Melissa works so hard. She's such a great mentor."

It was the beet salad that got her two days ago—but not in the predictable way. She was getting hammered, but Melissa had kept an eye on her and she was holding her own. The orders for beet salad kept raining down on her. In that situation, you keep thinking to yourself, *It's gotta slow down or even out,* and then the orders for that one dish come even faster. About three and a half hours into service, she was making what seemed like her fortieth beet salad—baby beets from the garden are roasted and sliced, served with red lettuce from the garden, segmented orange, and the pistachio–goat cheese "truffles," Melissa calls them on the menu, finished with a pistachio vinaigrette. She reached for vinaigrette to dress the greens. As she lifted the glass pitcher out of her mise tray, it slipped from her fingers, spilled all over her mise, and broke the salt ramekin.

When service is busy like this, and it was peaking, it's all you can do to stay on top of things when everything is going well. When you are a young cook and you lose your dressing and foul your mise for the one dish that seemingly everyone in the entire dining room is ordering, it's as if someone drives a stick between your spokes as you're cruising down-hill on a bicycle. You go flying. You sit up and shake your head clear and find yourself so deep in the weeds you can't even see where you are.

Lindsey collapsed. She couldn't work. Melissa had to run back and help her. There was just enough vinaigrette left in the container to make the salads ordered, but what if more came in? She'd never be able to do it—she wouldn't have time to remake the vinaigrette. But she'd have to—but she couldn't—but she'd have to—what would she do? All she can hear in her head is Melissa's voice, *"Ordering, beet salad. Beet salad. Four beet salad. Beet salad."* The thought paralyzes her; she can't get past it. Melissa says, "Don't *worry*—if you run out we'll make more." But Lindsey never surmounted the mental block and staggered through to the end of service, on the verge of tears.

The thing is, no more beet salads were ordered. She had exactly enough vinaigrette. There was never anything to worry about.

"You can't let that stuff run you over," Melissa said afterward.

The next day I asked Lindsey about it. She was still beating herself up. "I should let it go; I shouldn't be so sensitive," she said, peeling more oranges for that beet salad.

Those kinds of events stay with you forever. They're trauma scars; they never go away. One year after I'd been to Trio, I was in the kitchen where Jeffrey Pikus worked. I'd been at Trio the night he ran out of dehydrated bacon. The guests at the chef's table would never have known a thing was not as it should be. One of the commis quickly got some bacon roasted off, and all Grant said was a quiet, "It's no use lying to yourself." That was it. One year later I bumped into Pikus, who was busy getting ready for service, and I was curious about this trauma phenomenon. I said, "Jeffrey, you remember running out of bacon?"

Pikus paused for a fraction of a moment—for the nausea to come and go—then nodded once at me and said, *"Yeah."*

As if he could ever forget! You never forget! I guarantee you, had it been ten years from now and I'd run into Pikus and asked, "You remember running out of bacon that night at Trio?" he'd shake his head and sigh, the memory as vivid now as it was at the time. It's a powerful business, line cooking. It does things to your head.

But with Lindsey, it had happened before. Last time, it was with the chicory salad. "I've never seen anyone drop so much dressing," Melissa confides. "I tell her not to pick it up."

Lindsey tosses the salad with her hands—so she's got oil on her hands, she gets oil on the glass container—it's slippery!

Last time she dropped the dressing she did need more vinaigrette. Alissa was on desserts and had time to help, so she made more dressing while Lindsey worked to keep up with the orders, constructing the salad, which included a soft-boiled egg cooked to order—and it's either a good egg night or a bad egg night, when the shells stick and the eggs keep breaking on you as more and more customers in the dining room keep ordering the chicory salad!

Now Joe, on wood oven, sees what's going on as he's making his pies and putting up his aps. He sees that Alissa is making the vinaigrette wrong, and he had to get pissed at her—because it was a night when Melissa wasn't there (a rarity, but it happens)—and Rob, supposedly the sous, wasn't doing a thing about it, was just working through service as expediter. Joe was furious.

Joe is tall and lean, with a sensitive demeanor. He came in on his day off to address the issue with Melissa. He remained furious that there was no leadership when Melissa was gone. So Melissa now had to go talk with Rob, and Rob's response was *I'd have helped if I'd known.* This in turn made Melissa furious. "It's your job to know," she told him. "You have to be aware." In this way it is a family soap opera—a chain of emotional events—from Alissa to Joe to Rob to Melissa, eliciting significant issues of leadership and responsibility set off because Lindsey dropped her dressing in the middle of service.

Then there's Art, small, slender, bespectacled, and absolutely unflappable on the line. Nothing fazes him. He's stonefaced on the line, never changes expression, and never stops moving. He's a great line cook.

Melissa can throw a dozen order-fires at him while he's picking up an eight-top and he just plows through it. She doesn't take it for granted. Yesterday when the twelve-top ordered and she read the ticket, she paused, stepped to the left side of the service shelf, Art's side, and caught his eye for the briefest moment, saying gently, "I've got a big one for you." She paused while he turned to grab a sauté pan behind him to plate a saltimbocca. "Three bass, four halibut, one scallop, one pappardelle, no shrimp on one of those halibuts." There's scarcely room on his station for all the plates on this ticket, let alone the time to cook them so they are all finished at the same time. Art doesn't flinch, working on a second saltimbocca, doesn't even call it back, just gives a barely perceptible nod. This allows Melissa to run back to pastry to help Alissa, who is all alone back there and getting her first rush of the night.

Unlike Art, Rob gets testy on big orders. "I'll hear it on the call back," Melissa says. "I've been managing people for thirteen years. I can see right through them. I know immediately what their strengths and weaknesses are."

Melissa could, of course, step into any of their stations at any moment and work it better than they themselves do. *That* is not part of being a cook; that is part of being a *real* chef. Melissa is an uncommonly elegant cook. It's not that she can handle ten pans at once, it's the ease and grace with which she does it. While guy cooks who are good, like Grant, like Art, are more athletic in their grace, Melissa is more like a dancer; there's a delicacy to the way she moves.

She's a cook's cook. She longs to be back on the line, but for now, as the expediter, the only tool she uses is a damp towel.

"Order: snapper, rouget," she says. "Order one tuna, order one grape leaves, soup, foie." Joe calls back "Tuna" and Chris says, "Grape leaves, soup, foie."

Chris Michet is taking over garde manger on Lindsey's day off. Chris is an extern from the CIA and has today recently returned from the emergency room. He put a boning knife deep into his left hand. Price got him fixed up, and now he's beginning service, hand bandaged. He's new to this station, and he says, "Chef, could you show me how you want these?"

Melissa strides around the line and demos the foie dish for him. She cuts poached peaches, mixes them with some greens, some spicy cress, and a little poaching liquid, sets them on the plate, sets down a piece of almond French toast topped by the foie, deglazing the foie pan with a little chicken jus, reducing it till it's thick on a portable gas burner at the station, and drizzling it on the salad. He plates the next one but the foie keeps tipping off the bread, which is perched on the salad. He sends it to the pass.

"He's all right," Melissa says to me. Then she smiles slyly toward Chris and says, "He's gonna get his ass kicked tonight."

—❦—

"*Amuse* for four," Bill, front-of-the-house expediter, says, which means that a four-top has just been seated. Melissa pours cold melon soup into four shot glasses, adds a flower garnish for tonight's *amuse-bouche,* the first taste for all guests tonight. She disappears to the walk-in for a moment, then returns with a fist full of thyme stems with thick purple flowers. She puts them in a cup on the mise en place tray on the woodblock surface that's the center of the brick-oven station, along with fennel-bread crumbs and tomato concassé for the oyster, oils, and vivid yellow and orange flower petals, calendula, that will finish some of the plates.

"Order two snapper, scallop, no vinaigrette. Order one rouget," Melissa calls, slipping the ticket into the top "ordered" section of the shelf.

She walks down to Chris's station and tells him to keep the lettuces in his lowboy cooler and to take them out with each order—don't leave them out. It's easier, but they get warm. Then she says, "Order two soup, order scallop, sword. I need that foie." Chris is already behind on his orders. He gets the foie up and Melissa carries it to a waiting server, this one tips as well. "We're having foie trouble tonight," she says. "Pick up one rouget. Order oyster, field. Pick up bolognese, saltimbocca, no potatoes, substitute beans, two scallops."

With a flurry, Natalie, a hostess tonight, bolts past the line and up the backstairs to the office, looking for Price. A six-top has walked in and she knows she can't make that call. Price trots down the stairs and heads to the dining room, checks the books, the tables, and makes his decision. He could have seated the walk-in six-top by asking one couple to move and putting a different table combination together in one of the rooms, but he can't justify that for a walk-in. If they'd had a reservation he'd have been forced to do it.

It proves to be a good decision because not long after they leave, the Porters, a four-top, arrive without a reservation. The Porters are regulars almost every Saturday night—they'd thought they had a standing reservation, and Price figured a way to squeeze them in. This would have been a problem had they taken the six-top, and a restaurant likes to take care of its regulars.

Price will go to great lengths to accommodate guests. Once in the middle of service, he went out back in his nice shirt and slacks, found a sheet of plywood, plugged in his circular saw, and cut a round tabletop big enough to seat a large group.

"Order mushroom pie, first course, order popover, crostada, tartlets. *Amuse* up."

It's 6:50 and twelve tickets representing between thirty and forty diners are impaled on a spike on the expediter's shelf, meaning entrées have gone out and eight more tickets flutter from the shelf.

She walks to Aaron, who's cooking in Art's spot tonight, and tells him she's eighty-sixing the scallops, which he's relieved to hear. There was so much water in them, they'd stick to the pan. To prevent the sticking, Aaron got the pan smoking hot, but this burned the scallops. It was an impossible situation. Melissa tells Bill, who will tell the servers no more scallops, then punches the eighty-six code into the computer. "Something's wrong," she says. "There was so much liquid in those scallops. The product's not good, it doesn't look good, it's not cooking right, it was driving me *crazy* to see it go out."

※

During the lull that follows the first push, she talks with Joe about his station, since Aaron, who has less experience on wood oven, will take it tomorrow, and she wants to get a jump on prep. But since he's hardly sold anything off his station during the first turn, the station's mise is still in pretty good shape. A few oysters, a couple of pies, a tuna, a couple of octopus salads, done with an orange nage, which is simply OJ, butter, and salt, with orange-marinated grilled octopus reheated in the wood oven, served with shaved fennel and mint.

The Pemaquid oysters are roasted with fennel-parsley sauce, the glaçage, and an excellent concoction of bread crumbs and toasted fennel seeds. Melissa almost always has a roasted-oyster dish on the menu. She serves them with shallot butter and fried shallot on top, or other flavored butters, puts a variation of James Beard's deviled crab on top, and has even done an oysters Rockefeller, but with the spinach-béchamel on the bottom and a fried oyster on top, because she doesn't like the traditional dish. When I'd eaten there two summers earlier, I'd been served oysters three ways—fried, roasted, and raw—and she always has available raw oysters at the bar.

Chris is cleaning and straightening his station after the first push and preparing for the second.

"How did your first turn go?" I ask.

"I got my ass kicked," he says. Melissa calls two fields, and he pulls some endive to slice. "I'm getting better though."

Price enters the kitchen and says to Melissa, "It's so quiet in the dining room."

Melissa counts the tickets. "We just did fifty-seven," she responds, "and we've already sent out a lot of desserts."

The printer chatters.

"Ordering three oysters, antipasti, four soup"—she steps to the other side of the line, combining each station—"order six saltimbocca, two rouget, one sword."

❧

At 8:00, the kitchen is still quiet, no orders are in, and Melissa, standing around nervously, says, "Where is everybody?"

I head out to the dining room to have a look. Is the place empty? I have no idea.

No. It's full. I see Price at the bar. He says, "*Whammo.* I just sat five fours, two sixes, and another five. And that table's about to get up. I'm not going back in *that* kitchen." Then he rethinks. "I better go tell Melissa to tighten up." He takes the back hall and staircase down to the kitchen.

With a big crunch coming, I'll only be in the way back there. Furthermore, I owe it to my craft to eat some of this food and wash it down with some good wine. It's one thing to be a cook and put out all that food—the last thing you want to do when you're working the line is eat—it's quite another to be standing still for hours watching and taking notes about the great food going out. You can eat with your eyes for only so long, then it drives you mad.

I'd been wanting to try Primo's saltimbocca, the one dish that never leaves the menu in honor of Melissa's granddad. Sautéed pork loin on mashed potatoes with a Madeira sauce, shiitakes, and some Parma ham on top. It's simple and delicious, do-at-home food, Primo's personal favorite.

Later, I say good night to Price and descend the staircase, exiting through the front door of the house. My footsteps on the wood porch floor echo softly in the quiet night, nothing now but crickets and muted sounds of a lot of people inside eating and drinking, like a great dinner party is going on in there. A lovely, starry, summer night. From the parking lot I can see the silhouette of the lush garden. The pigs will be asleep in their shelter. I turn back to look at the house. The back door to the kitchen is open and through the screen door I can hear the sounds of cooking.

Melissa had told me she'd never really intended to get into cooking. "When I was a kid I wanted to be a vet," she said. "This just kind of happened. I don't know how it happened."

"I think she's obsessive," Melissa's mom told me. Melissa's mom is shorter and rounder than Melissa but seems to have the same steady energy. "But this is her life, she loves what she does." She shook her head. "To cook every day for all these people! Why would anybody want to do that?"

On the other hand, she's not surprised by what Melissa's doing and the restaurant itself. "The way she is with this place is the way I was a mother. That was my passion." What she does here, her mom said proudly, is simply a reflection of the way Melissa was raised. Melissa is transferring who she is immediately to this place, to the food, of course, but more, she's putting the whole sense of family as she knows it into every part of the business.

Me, I saw the epitome of Melissa Kelly in the sheep's-milk ricotta, or rather in how she served it. The way she smiled and said exactly how she most wanted to eat it herself—it was seductive the way she said it. She was conveying with her every cell, her love of this fresh sheep's-milk cheese. I could see it and feel it. And later she served it to me, and after that, she decided to give the exact same thing to anyone who wanted it, garnished with a little arugula from the garden and a ripe Mission fig. But the importance of this to me, the lesson of it, was that she wanted to serve this perfect, fresh cheese to her customers in exactly the way she'd most want to eat it herself. Nothing fancy. No elaborate sauce or garnish. She didn't put it on a pedestal; she didn't dress it up or try to show off with it. She put it with some good olive oil on a bit of baguette that Michael Florence had baked that day. How could she fail to make people happy?

In a chef world increasingly giving itself over to branding and multiple restaurants and TV shows, chefs trying to cash in on their fame, I had been completely happy and at ease to be hanging out at this uniquely American restaurant with the garden, with all the cooks and their many advanced degrees abandoned for cooking, with Price and Melissa, who run a little restaurant in an old house on the coast of Maine.

PART FOUR

The Power of the Branded Chef

CHAPTER I

⭢·⭠

One Thing Leads to Another

When I wasn't on the road, or hanging out in other people's kitchens, or watching the continuing evolution of Keller or the trajectory of two driven but very different CIA graduates or the CIA itself, I was at home in Cleveland, writing. Happily, the booming interest in chefs and cooking ensured steady work, an indication of how fertile the food territory was. There seemed to be an endlessly expanding interest in food and cooking and chefs and restaurants.

Lives were changing rapidly for everyone inside this business, not just for Keller, though his life had changed dramatically since his days as French Laundry chef. At his least busiest he was, to choose one example, glazing vegetables for me for the Bouchon cookbook I was writing with him and his staff (glazing was badly misunderstood, he thought, a lost craft); the book work was the result of the popularity of *The French Laundry Cookbook,* and his being able to open a second very different restaurant, a bistro, the result of his general fame; earlier in the day, before the glazing demo, he'd been discussing chlorophyll molecules with Harold McGee, the food science expert and author of the 1984 classic *On Food and Cooking,* who also happened to be hanging out in the French Laundry kitchen when I was there; Keller was many months away from opening the Vegas Bouchon, the Bouchon bakery in New York, and the Inn in Yountville, and, of course, his then-unnamed Manhattan restaurant. (He'd considered "Point" as a possible name, a reference to his favorite chef, Fernand Point of La Pyramide, who died in 1955, the year Keller was born. He'd considered calling it "Aloysius," his middle name, but he was afraid people requesting the number or address wouldn't know how to spell it. In the end, it was Keller's answer to the most frequent question asked while the restaurant was under construction that gave him the name he was looking for: "Well, it's not going to be the French Laundry, per se.") He'd still be running the pass at tonight's service, and spoke hopefully of the time that he could return more permanently to just cooking.

Harold McGee, amazingly, was nearing the end of a massive rewrite of *On Food and Cooking.* Here was a book that most in the food industry considered a masterwork, the first comprehensive reference on why food behaves as it does, and McGee had chucked about 90 percent of it and was rewriting it. The revision would be published on the original's twentieth anniversary and had been ten years in the making. When that was done, McGee planned to begin another book, somehow utilizing the abundant material he'd had no room for in this new edition of *On Food and Cooking.* He'd gotten into food more or less by accident. A trained scientist with a degree from Cal Tech and a doctorate in English literature from Yale, he had hoped to write more generally about the science of everyday life. That had not happened. He'd gotten caught in the pull of the food industry vortex. He was not likely to free himself and had now begun to accept that writing about the science of food was simply his lot, which was OK, he noted with a shrug, because he enjoyed it and he was good at it.

Brian Polcyn, the Michigan chef I'd written about in *The Soul of a Chef* and with whom I was working on a cookbook about charcuterie, had managed to achieve something that was almost unheard of in the life of a chef-owner: balance. He was the father of five kids, still coached soc-

cer, had a fantastic wife he adored, and ran a thriving business called
Five Lakes Grill. When a chef has good balance in his life, it's typical
that his MO will be to pursue more work. Brian took on a second job—
full-time chef-instructor for nine months of the year at Schoolcraft College, his alma mater. And he also began taping a weekly cooking spot for
the local ABC affiliate's evening news, collaborated on our cookbook,
and continued his self-imposed obligatory charity work with groups such
as Taste of the NFL and Share Our Strength. In his few spare moments,
he earned his pilot's license.

"If you don't keep growing and evolving, you die," he said, speaking
of both himself and his restaurant. He'd given his ten-year-old establishment a $250,000 renovation and the next year bought $25,000 worth
of new china and glassware. "A restaurant is like a baby," he said. "You
gotta keep nurturing it."

He still worked the line and freely admitted he wasn't as fast as he used
to be. The other night, while working sauté and expediting, he realized
that it was taking him so long to read the tickets—he had to squint and
lean in to make them out—that the younger cooks just read the tickets
themselves from where they were on the line and cooked past him. As
a surgeon once said to me, there inevitably comes a point at which experience can no longer compensate for diminishing speed. Cooking is
no different from surgery in that physical way—it's *physical* work, like
professional sports. All chefs, if they continue to actually cook the food
they serve, reach this point.

Another chef I'd written about in *The Soul of a Chef* was Michael Symon,
in Cleveland. When I was home, I could head down to his neighborhood,
say hello to the staff I'd gotten to know years ago—Rebecca and Frankie
behind the bar; Chatty and Frank Rogers behind the range; Doug, the
suave server who now ran the front of the house, a remarkable circumstance in this itinerant business—and eat Michael's excellent food. He not
only remained a quintessential example of the working chef-owner, but
his course was also emblematic of chefs taking advantage of the new
opportunities available in the food industry, opportunities that now

abounded not only for high-profile chef superstars and celebrities but for those who chose for whatever reasons to remain in smaller markets.

Business at Lola, his funky bistro that served high-end food in a casual environment, remained strong, so strong, in fact, that he was able to buy the second floor of his two-story building and turn it into a private dining area with two rooms and an open demo kitchen for cooking classes. He was asked to be on a Food Network show, *Melting Pot,* which paired ten chefs who would cook ethnic cuisine, a different duo cooking each day. The show was cancelled, but he liked TV, had been nominated for a Beard award for a show he did with Bobby Flay, and he was developing a cooking and lifestyle show that he described as "Martha Stewart gone bad." He was so well known locally, he was able to hire a company to make, jar, and distribute a line of sauces he created. He did occasional special events and cooking demos for various organizations representing trade groups in the food industry, such as the National Pork Producers Council and the Wisconsin Dairy Council. A day with them could net him as much as ten grand. Admittedly, this kind of work was sporadic, but it was good money for a chef-owner who paid himself a salary of just five times that amount. And he did fifteen to twenty benefits a year, the bane of every well-known chef's existence, which cost him money and time.

He was a spokesman for Calphalon, the cookware manufacturer an hour and a half west of Cleveland, which featured him in a splashy double-page ad that opened *Bon Appétit* and paid him for appearances. When the company brought out a line of pans, they might package it with Symon's sauces, and Symon would sell thousands of units at a single pop. The sauce line earned him another ten grand a year, and this was sweet because it required no work on his part. He was also the spokesman for Vita-Mix blenders, the high-performance series designed for home use, for which he did an hour-long instructional DVD and made appearances, most recently four hours' worth of cooking demos featuring the appliance at a convention in Las Vegas.

How all this TV and national spokesman business got rolling from his relatively tiny outpost in a decrepit neighborhood in Cleveland is illustrative of the dynamics of chefs in the media. In 1998 he won a *Food & Wine* Best New Chefs award, given to ten chefs each year. That award, he says, was the catalyst. It led to the attention of the Food Network, which gave him a guest spot on Sara Moulton's show, which led to a couple of appearances on *Ready Set Cook,* the deceased cooking game show (in fact, the place where Ming Tsai got his start on television). His lively personality on these shows brought the *Melting Pot* offer. These appearances led to the spokesman jobs for two high-profile companies and their nationally marketed products. An offer from restaurateurs to open a place in the heart of Manhattan was soon to come. One thing leads to another.

On April 30, 2005, I headed down to Lola to watch the restaurant's last night of service. After more than eight years, Michael and his wife and partner, Liz, were closing Lola. For one month the space would be under redesign and reconstruction, including the installation of a huge wood-burning oven. In June it would reopen as Lolita, a restaurant serving more casual food than Lola. Michael and Liz would move Lola to Cleveland's downtown on a redeveloped East Fourth Street. His Lola had been a major force in the rebirth of the once sketchy Tremont neighborhood. There was every reason Lola could be a big part of the uplifting of another downtrodden piece of the city. To support the growth, he and Liz partnered with his friend Doug Petkovic, who'd opened a competing restaurant across the street from Lola (one of many that had come to the area in the wake of Lola's success) and who would now oversee general operations as Michael worked in all areas back of the house and Liz in all areas pertaining to front of the house for all three restaurants.

Symon was successful and busy, but for all the work, he wasn't getting rich. He chuckled at the idea that he was raking in the dough—as many in town simply assumed, given his renown and packed restaurant. "I didn't get into this business to make money, to get rich, but I do want to make a decent living," he said. And perhaps the varied endeavors will bring that in, eventually. Till then, "I'm just a bald guy in Cleveland trying to make a buck!" he said, laughing.

Few outside the industry realize how little money chef-owners make. Michael and Liz, for instance, paid themselves fifty grand apiece out of profits. Additional profits went back into the business, toward everything from new purchases and repairs to renovating the entire upstairs into a demo kitchen, offices, and private dining rooms. Michael and Liz also bought health insurance, including dental, for their cooks, all of whom are salaried, and many servers, some of whom are—almost unheard of in small chef-owned restaurants. They sent sous-chef Matt "Chatty" Harlan to California for an eight-month stage at the French Laundry. Chatty will be one of the opening chefs at the new Lola. The additional revenue from spokesperson gigs and demos for the Pork Council, a total of about $75,000, came in handy: They bought their first house in 1998, and he occasionally splurged (bought himself a Harley, enjoyed his golf, got himself a really elaborate tattoo from back to shoulder to chest, an Asian-inspired representation of his family, and then, on a whim, had some flying pigs tattooed on the other side of his chest with the ebullient and emphatic words "Got Pork"). But he and Liz didn't want for anything, and they wouldn't have a lot of time to spend money even if they suddenly had a lot of it. The reason he was successful in the first place, the reason he got that *Food & Wine* award, was at least in part because he was at the restaurant *all* the time.

For Polcyn the situation was not dissimilar, though he paid himself more, 10 percent of sales, which were currently in the $1.5 million range (pretty standard as far as chef compensation goes, and hardly extravagant, especially considering the two college tuitions under way and an expected three more during the next ten years). The breakdown of business expenses at Five Lakes Grill was similar to that of most restaurants and was difficult to change.

Cost of goods, food, and wine at restaurants generally runs 30 to 35 percent of sales, labor is 35 percent, overhead (rent, utilities, linens, maintenance, et cetera) is 20 percent, which leaves a profit of about 10 percent. And that profit almost always has to go right back into the business. The chef-owner increases profit by keeping a tight control on overhead, and/or increasing sales without raising overhead and labor. The cost of goods would always be proportionate to sales. Labor costs fluctuate but only incrementally. And that, in a nutshell, is the restaurant's profit-and-loss scenario. It varies according to type of restaurant. High-volume places with low food cost have a higher percentage of profits relative to sales. Low-volume places, with high food and overhead costs—the Manhattan four-star restaurant, for instance—can expect considerably less profit for higher sales. But generally, the basic model is difficult to change.

At Lola, Michael Symon had higher food costs than was normal for a restaurant, as much as 37 percent. This was because in his market, he could sell his food for only so much. This wasn't Chicago. In Chicago, at Blackbird, for instance, a restaurant comparable to Lola, chef Paul Kahan charged up to $16 for an appetizer and $32 for an entrée. Symon's highest prices were $13 and $28. But Symon paid the same prices for the products he used as Kahan did for his. What compensated for this higher food cost was a lower overhead—Cleveland was a lot cheaper to live in, so things like rent and utilities and services were less expensive.

In the last year it was open, Lola did nearly $2 million in sales, taking in an average of $55 per customer. Opening as Lolita, a much more casual place, he expected to average $35 per person, but he figured its more casual menu would allow for more covers, which would make revenue about the same. When he opened Lola in downtown Cleveland, he would face higher overhead than he'd had at the old Lola, but the restaurant was bigger and so could seat more people (105 seats rather than the current 65) than he could at the original location, which was typically booked six to eight weeks in advance. After eight years, he'd begun to grow the business. He and Liz could expect to double their revenue once the debts taken on for the restaurant had been paid.

What are you to do, though, if you're Melissa Kelly in Maine and know you're going to *lose* money by staying open January, February, and March just to keep your staff? While I was at Primo, she'd gotten a call from Tom Gutow, chef-owner of the Castine Inn, a B&B in nearby Castine, with the news that he couldn't afford to keep the restaurant going. Forget about the work—work was hard no matter where you were—the restaurant wasn't making it financially.

Consider Melissa's personal situation again, in terms of work versus compensation. She arrives at the restaurant at nine A.M. She works all day on her feet, prepping for that night's dinner, dealing with staff issues, making up a menu, taking calls from the press, running her daily meetings—what most people consider a normal working day. At dinnertime, she really begins to work, works really hard, from six P.M. to eleven P.M., expediting and often cooking as well. For the following hour and a half, she'll finish up dinner service and clean the kitchen with her staff. Then she'll head up to the office for an hour, and with any luck be home by two A.M., in bed with a couple of books and a notepad. This is her schedule seven days a week, from Memorial Day through Labor Day, with only July 4th off, and beyond, till the restaurant slows to a five-day service.

For this, the business pays her about $50,000. Price takes the same. Primo had about the same number of seats as Lola and the same check average. In 2004 Primo did $1,325,000 in sales, 70 percent of it from June through October. Their food cost is normal, 32 percent, and their labor is a little high, 38 percent, though Melissa's and Price's salaries are included here, as is the gardener's. What kills them is their overhead, about 28 percent—that's the garden, the mortgage on the house, taxes on the land, and three months of very slow business. (In 2004 they lost $140,000 during the slow months—by staying open; in 2005 they closed for three months and lost only $90,000. "We saved fifty thousand dollars by going on vacation!" says Price.) Add up those percentages and you see that they're left with a 2 percent profit. Moreover, food costs are rising, but they don't feel they can raise their prices—that is, expenses are increasing, but sales are staying the same—further cutting into that sliver of profit.

"What we need is twenty more seats," Price says. That would change the whole picture considerably. It would give them thirty more covers a night without substantially raising labor. That would amount to as much as $150,000 more in sales during their peak months. But putting on an addition to the house to create those seats would cost them $300,000, and Price doesn't need that kind of anxiety—they're working hard enough as it is.

And forget about saving money for their future.

"That's the scary part about this business," Melissa said. "We don't have a 401(k) plan. That's why we did the partnership with Marriott."

In 2002 the Marriott International contacted Melissa and Price to ask them to open a Primo in the Orlando hotel the corporation was opening the following year in conjunction with the Ritz-Carlton, which would include in its space a Norman's, an outpost of the well-known Miami restaurant created by Norman Van Aken, regarded as the father of New World cuisine.

Hotel chains across the country had begun taking a lesson from Vegas, the country's megalopolis of celebrity-chef outposts, a movement likely started when a man named Sheldon Gordon lured Wolfgang Puck into the Forum Shops at Caesars Palace in 1992. Emeril Lagasse was not long behind Puck. Then a bona fide French fine-dining guy, the late Jean-Louis Palladin, opened Napa in the Rio, and pushing the boulder over the crest of the hill was Steve Wynn, who brought multiple chefs into the Bellagio, and Rob Goldstein, who lured them into the Venetian (Emeril's Delmonico Steakhouse there did a staggering $18 million last year). The avalanche of chefs, from TV stars to French three-stars, is still pouring in.

It happened in Vegas, so hotel executives no doubt asked why not in Orlando, Seattle, Santa Fe, Atlanta? These cities didn't have the tourist concentration that Vegas had, but Vegas proved that people wanted to go to name-brand chefs' restaurants. Todd English is a big name in several cities—he has his signature Boston restaurant, Olives, in the W Hotel in Manhattan, the St. Regis in Aspen, the Bellagio in Vegas, and elsewhere. He opened a restaurant in a Seattle Marriott called the Fish Club. Marriott then asked him to open a place in the new Orlando hotel. But the timing and the place weren't right. With English out, the Marriott executive chef brought Melissa's name to the table as the hotel searched for a well-known. Why? He was from Maine and knew her from there. She was a viable contender to the hotel suits because of her frequent appearances in the national food press.

So they called her, Melissa explained to me, told her they wanted her to open a restaurant for them, told her they'd make it worth her while. She told them she didn't like the idea but had to admit the extra income was appealing. Well then, they said, sensing victory, why don't you come on down and cook for us, just tell us what you want to cook and we'll have it here for you.

It rubbed Melissa the wrong way. *Look,* she said, *I don't even know if I want to do this. Why do you want me to cook for you if you already know you want me to open a restaurant, and if I do cook for you, I'll bring my own food, how do I know what you'll get me—my* food *is the whole* point.

She's a pretty, petite thing—just don't fuck with her.

She and Price talked it over. She didn't want to do this—she was working hard enough as it was—but they sure could use that *cash*. The two restaurants did have alternating seasons—that was a positive. She was worried about losing control, diminishing her reputation, but thinking ahead, they both knew they had no plan for the future. She flew to Orlando, cooked the executives ten courses, and they loved her food. She would ultimately give in to their offer, which was fairly standard for a chef such as Melissa. The big corporation pays the chef a onetime licensing fee for the use of the restaurant name and her name, and for her to set up and staff a restaurant and get it up and running. They also pay her a monthly management fee, which is a percentage of that month's sales.

But—she would agree to do this only if they agreed to her requests: They had to put in a garden (she was known for her garden), she had to be allowed to purchase as much organic product as she wanted (and not be restricted by Marriott's protocols, a common gripe among independent chefs within hotels, forced to buy specific products), and the hotel had to have a recycling program.

They agreed, and Melissa was able to install one of her trusted chefs as chef de cuisine, a mother of four who needed the stability of a corporate-controlled restaurant. (I'd worked for a Marriott, and the health insurance alone was almost worth the job.)

"It's for our retirement," she explained to me, almost apologetically, it seemed.

Two years after opening, the relationship had proven to be productive. Yes, it was more work, and she was forced to fly down and do cooking benefits, which was especially annoying during the summer months in Maine. But it gave her staff new opportunities for advancement, and she felt good about being the cause of the Marriott's recycling program and their increasing use of organic farmers. Moreover, it promised some financial security for her and Price's future. Indeed, the experience proved so good that the following winter, she gave in to Price's wishes and closed Primo for three months. During this time, they worked in Orlando a bit, then moved to the Southwest, to open a third Primo, this one at JW Marriott's Starr Pass Resort and Spa in Arizona's Tucson Valley. And when they reopened in Maine in April 2005, she found that her fears of losing her staff were for naught. She had been able to keep the key players in her kitchen, all but Art, who'd married and returned to his hometown of Rochester, New York. Joe moved into Art's spot, Aaron became sous-chef, the fair Lindsey had moved up to wood oven, and even Chris, the CIA extern, had graduated and returned to a full-time position, taking Lindsey's spot on garde manger.

⋙⋘

These were all good stories about hard-working chefs in small markets, but what were the broader ramifications of what was happening here? Certainly Michael Symon's deciding to partner with a friend to run three restaurants in his hometown, to reopen his flagship restaurant in a new location, the owners of which had, in his words, thrown him a bag of cash to build and outfit the restaurant he wanted, requiring him and Liz to take on a personal loan but no investors. They owned their own businesses. His devoted sous-chefs Chatty and Frank could, after eight years, get a much-needed break and change of venue, a brand-new kitchen. Others at Lola would move up to take over for Chatty and Frank. Frankie would move from bartender to beverage manager for the operations. The business was growing—a good thing. Likewise for Melissa and Price. And for Thomas Keller, yes? Growth was hard but good if you did it right—three new restaurants, a bakery, two books, a line of silver, a line of porcelain, and more. Grant Achatz, at age thirty-one, was about to open his own restaurant. Assuming this restaurant is successful, what will the business climate be for him when *he's* ready to grow, when his Alinea becomes not just his restaurant but the flagship? Will he want to open clones of his four-star edge cuisine? Will he open more casual restaurants that don't require his continuous time and attention, ones that he might be able to replicate easily? Would he design products for his unusual style of cooking, unusual serving pieces, for instance? Would he do books? Would he—*BAM!*—find his way onto TV? Will he . . . *open in Vegas?*

The food world had changed and was changing still, maybe faster now than ever. Opportunities abounded. Who knew where it was going? Often it seemed the possibilities were limited only by a chef's imagination. This was exactly why Tim Ryan at the CIA all but insisted that incoming students plan to stay for four years, learn how to perform in the business world as well as how to sauté and braise. They weren't just training broiler cooks anymore—the industry was much bigger than that. The CIA wanted to prepare its graduates for the uncertain, possibility-rich future and to nurture the next Wolfgang Puck, the next culinary innovator, the young man or woman who was not just going to open up the next great American restaurant but who was going to anticipate the next new trend in food and culture, and give her or him all the tools they'd need to ride that wave to the land of milk and honey, fame and fortune, and a place in culinary lore.

In order to guess where that place might be, it's necessary to understand where the best chefs are now in our culture, what is available to the most successful of them, and what they are choosing to do, given a wealth of ideas (ranging from innovative to harebrained), given an abundance of offers (ranging from noble to lucrative to sketchy), and given their own personal tangle of unarticulated, poorly understood, ghost-itch goals and hungers.

CHAPTER 2

❧

The Branded Chef

Just as the cultural role of the chef has grown and evolved, so have the chefs themselves. Those who are defining what it means to be a chef today began working in the 1970s, the end of the culinary dark ages in America, illuminated only in spots by a few distinctive lights. They are now about fifty years old, give or take a few years. They are mainly too old to work a line or to want to. They've done that. They've worked their asses off. They've built successful businesses. They want to enjoy the fruits of their labors. But where are the fruits? You can't hang in St. Bart's on renown alone, or buy a little stone house on Majorca on a single famous restaurant. Celebrity is not a commodity. They're thinking, *Show me the money.* But they don't know exactly who to say it to.

Here they toil in an America obsessed with food, an America so hungry for their restaurants they're paying as much as $100 for a single entrée in Vegas, or $350 simply to take a seat at the bar at Masa in Manhattan so the chef can feed them not what they want but what he feels like. They go to group signings of their own books and see the line for Emeril looking like the one for the most popular ride at Disney World during spring vacation and think, *I want a line like that.* They feel the power of themselves when they put on a chef's coat and walk into a room. They are adored. They are famous. Now: How can they exchange that adoration and fame for the cash it must be worth?

Keller had a telling premonition many years ago when he was only the chef-owner of the French Laundry. He was part of a multichef benefit outside California and was in the fitness center of the hotel when he ran into Norman Van Aken, the Miami chef. They began talking about their various prospects—restaurants, books, endorsements, licensing agreements, the media—and Keller realized there was no real formula for making decisions or a good model for proceeding once you got to their level, nationally recognized chef-owners ready to expand and diversify. "We should get a group of us together and invite Wolfgang Puck to discuss the issues we're facing," he said to Van Aken.

Nothing ever came of their treadmill discussion, but it was a prescient idea. Keller recognized that there was no consistent precedent for growth—who better than the biggest chef brand in the business to help lead the way for others, to discuss good decisions and bad decisions he'd made along the way. Puck had surely made both. He had opened multiple fine-dining restaurants, "fast casuals" as they're called, high-end fast food. Grocery stores sold his pizzas and soup. He'd authored a half dozen cookbooks and had a television show. His chef brand was the broadest and arguably the most successful in terms of venues and total sales.

There were others out there expanding, too. Todd English was expanding in restaurants, but there were signs of undercapitalization, not enough infrastructure to support the growth. Michael Chiarello, chef at Tra Vigne, in St. Helena, was moving out of restaurants altogether and toward products and lifestyle entertainment with the company Napa-Style. Chefs smelled opportunity everywhere—the soil was fertile but what to grow?

They all knew that single restaurants can't do it, no matter how famous—it's simply never going to generate the cash. A single book won't likely do it, nor a TV show, nor a set of pans. It's got to be multiple restaurants, or multiple books and shows, or, more precisely, a unique combination of all these things—restaurants, books, products, and media presence.

In order for that to happen—indeed, even before "celebrity" happens—something else, something more elusive and hard to define and distinctly American, has to happen: a brand must take shape. The brand is the key to the money box.

"There's always a brand before there's celebrity—always," says Adam Block, an adviser to scores of the country's most successful chefs on contracts and financial issues. "Not everybody likes a brand, but everybody likes a celebrity," he says. "You become a celebrity because everybody likes your brand."

Once you have a brand you have the critical lever to roll that hefty log of fame into cash. If you have a good, strong brand, it scarcely matters how you're using that brand, it seems. As long as it's not diminishing itself, that brand can work toward more restaurants, more products, media, now, amazingly, even things unrelated to food and cooking—skin-care products, toothpaste, golf clubs.

Eric Ripert, chef and co-owner of Manhattan's revered Le Bernardin, one of the city's five four-star restaurants, has over the past year or so thought seriously about the branding issue. "It's what I'm trying to do," he told me. "My goal is to be able to retire in ten years." That would be before he's fifty.

In addition to running the New York flagship, Ripert has several consultant contracts and opened Blue by Eric Ripert in the winter of 2005 at the Ritz-Carlton in the Cayman Islands. In the fall of 2005 he partnered with restaurateur Stephen Hanson to open a tapas joint, Barca 18. With the help of Fred Siegel, partner of Antsnpants, a brand-development company based in Philadelphia and Chicago, he is exercising another branding strategy—producing culinary products, including, he hopes, a line of organic baby food.

"Eric is at a great point to start a brand in terms of public awareness, the amount of ink he's generating, and personal appearances," says

Siegel. "Also, the trend toward organic is building, so he's very much on-trend."

"The bread and butter of this," says Scott Feldman, who created the Manhattan-based Two Twelve Management and Marketing ("Building brands to their boiling point"), "is if you can build an entire brand strategy that has multiple diverse components, including all parameters of having a restaurant—having a consumer base, having a product line, having a book, having a TV show—those are all the things that allow someone to have a fruitful and financially successful business. They all feed each other."

What's perhaps even more interesting than the superstars' developing restaurants and products to capitalize on the success of their high-end food or mass appeal—Keller and Trotter, Flay and Batali, et al., not to mention Puck (considered to be the originator of the branded chef) or Emeril (the first restaurant chef to combine entertainment and cooking on television)—is that lesser-known chefs are entering the arena as well. These chefs are kicking the one-thing-leads-to-another up a notch: They're not waiting for it to happen naturally; they're aggressively pursuing it, trying to crank that gear faster.

How many people outside the New York food world know Geoffrey Zakarian? I don't know, but he's not yet a household word (you really need a TV show for that). Nevertheless, working with both Feldman and Block, Zakarian has opened a second Manhattan restaurant, Country (his current restaurant, Town, is highly regarded and has three stars from the *Times*), and plans to publish a book, launch not one but two restaurants in Vegas, and produce a line of food-based skin-care products.

"We have our talent and our integrity," Zakarian said, while slicing foie gras terrines for a Beard benefit dinner at Lola last fall. "To solidify that, you develop a brand that replicates who you are."

Michael Chiarello created a name for himself with the restaurant Tra Vigne in the Napa Valley town of St. Helena and made the unusual choice to leave restaurants altogether.

He began as the restaurant's twenty-four-year-old chef in 1987 and slaved away during the 1980s like most other young chefs. Featuring Italian cuisine, the restaurant went through tons of olive oil, more than fifty gallons a week. He and his partners decided to make their own and contracted for the fruit and the production of it. It now went out on the tables as a condiment for bread, a relatively new idea in American restaurants at the time. One diner at the restaurant was Chuck Williams, founder of Williams-Sonoma. He loved the oil so much, Chiarello recalls, that Williams said, "God, Michael, you've got to bottle this and I'll sell it at my stores."

After two years at the restaurant, Chiarello was in the olive oil business. It became Williams-Sonoma's biggest-selling food item. The infused-oil business didn't exist, and Chiarello set to work creating a line of oil specialties, with things like basil and porcini mushrooms. "The specialty market was so different then," he said. "It was wide open." The business grew to the point at which they could move into grocery stores. Next he did vinegars. Chiarello did a book on cooking with the product he was selling, *Flavored Oils,* followed by a book called *Flavored Vinegars.*

The Napa Valley became hot, and life began to speed up for Chiarello. He opened more restaurants, with partners, in Aspen and in Walnut Creek, California. He did a TV show for the Food Network. And with all these new ventures, his professional life and his personal life became more complicated.

"You begin to say, 'Who am I, what am I doing?' I've used about every good idea I have. I'm not able to spend the twelve hours in the kitchen I need for my food to really evolve. You have hundreds of employees, a couple of bakeries—it was just more like giving profit-and-loss meetings rather than inspiring your team to create. It was time to hit the reset button. I control-alt-deleted my life. Which is really scary. . . . But it was a culmination of a bunch of things I wanted."

He left the restaurant world completely and embraced the retail world in 2000 by creating a company called NapaStyle. "Could you bring a point of view to life on air," he recalled wondering, "and then support it with product?" That point of view was The Good Life in the

Napa Valley—blue skies, crisp nights, dry days, mountain vistas, amazing wine, golden vineyards—the rustic, upscale life enjoyed by the most sophisticated agricultural community in the country. The first catalog came out in 2001, just when the economy "went into a nosedive," he says. "Certainly we had to fight our way through to today. . . . It wasn't an easy haul."

On its Web site, NapaStyle calls itself a "media company" that produces books and television shows—on both the Food Network and the Living Channel—designed to portray a specific perception of Napa Valley life. NapaStyle has a catalog containing more than four hundred diverse products—books and knives, plates and bowls and baskets, vinegars and oils, bedroom furniture and panini grills—everything pertaining to the "lifestyle."

"I'm the host of the brand," Chiarello says. "I'm not the brand. . . . One of the things we're superconscious of is that the brand's not me. Napa's much, much bigger than I am. And all we get is a chance to represent a style of life that we're blessed to be able to enjoy. . . . But it's not about me. It's: 'We're going on this trip together and I'll steer the bus for now.'"

This, by his own admission, had not been an easy road, even for an established chef of a popular restaurant who had a success in olive oil, infused oils, and vinegars. He may not yet have succeeded in his bid to become the Martha Stewart of the Napa Valley, but he does have a company—he owns it, he notes, along with other investors—two TV shows, books, and products in a country hungry for just this kind of stuff.

⇒⋅⇐

Even chefs with less behind them are looking for the branding key to the cash box.

Tanya Holland is a forty-year-old chef, currently working on financing for a restaurant of her own in Oakland. Holland, who grew up in upstate New York, worked front of the house for seven years before deciding to learn how to cook at Peter Kump's in New York and La Varenne,

Anne Willan's cooking school in Burgundy, France. After graduation in 1992, she did the rounds as a cook, an expected progression, working the line at a lot of good restaurants, including Hamersley's Bistro in Boston and Bobby Flay's Mesa Grill in New York. In 2000 she was in New York waiting tables at El Teddy's (she'd left a recent chef job in TriBeCa and was searching for the right kitchen) when she got a call from the director of the career services office at Peter Kump's—she'd stayed in touch and asked him to keep her in mind if he heard of any opportunities that might be available to her. The Food Network was looking for a young female, African American, to take part in a hip, multicultural show, *Melting Pot*. She contacted the network, they arranged for what they called a "talent test," and she did well. Exciting as this was, she was also skeptical.

"When I first got it," Holland says, "I was like, ya know, I trained in France, I worked at Mesa, I worked at Hamersley's Bistro, I worked at Verbena—and they want me to cook *soul food*? *What*? It just seemed a little ridiculous. But then I realized I did have the freedom to give it my own interpretation. And *then* I realized there really was no African American voice in food that people could really relate to."

The more she thought about it, the more the idea seemed to make sense to her—there was a niche to be filled. How many African American chefs under forty could you name? Indeed, the professional kitchen is one of the great multicultural petri dishes, where immigrants and ethnicities of every stripe can thrive—except, apparently, for American blacks. They are vastly underrepresented in the professional restaurant kitchen. Here was a great opportunity to be an African American voice in what was virtually a vacuum, especially in New York City restaurant kitchens. Holland never really had a role model, never had a chef she became close enough to call a mentor, and she wishes she had.

Her appearance on *Melting Pot* led to a cookbook, *New Soul Cooking*, in 2003. Meanwhile, she kept cooking at a restaurant in Berkeley called Le Théâtre until leaving to pursue her own restaurant, and she hoped more.

She wants an iconic design for her restaurant, she says, "so that I could translate it into product design or signature pieces, a line of cookware. . . . Now in this industry, there's so much potential to brand yourself. You don't have to be just a chef."

And she'd like to be a mentor. "I see there are a lot of young people," she says, "especially women, especially of color, they latch on to me—'Oh wow, someone who looks like me who I can relate to.' I want to achieve this thing. I feel I'm able to and I want to let people know they can do it.

"I want to have a far-reaching brand so I can, I don't know, get people to experience better flavor—a lot of people in this country eat mediocre food. . . . I feel like it's a no-brainer, I've got such a niche that I can fill. I just feel like it's a great opportunity."

Her first priority is her restaurant, and from there to branch out into other venues—cookware, books, television, culinary spokesperson.

"Bobby interprets Southwestern food; Mario, Italian; all these people take these other cuisines, that were peasant cuisines, and elevated them. Why can't I do that for soul food?"

And yet it's not that easy. She may be able to cook, she may have a real niche to fill, she may have great ideas for excellent products, but she's missing that lever that's going to make these gears engage and move her forward. What is it, where's that magic key?

I sent an e-mail to ask what had happened in the time since we'd spoken, which had been nearly a year.

"Much has happened in the past year," she wrote back.

Opportunities come and go. At the moment, I'm focusing on getting a new TV gig. This exposure always gives leverage to negotiate new deals. I have since been introduced to a woman with a branding and licensing background. . . . Very sharp, but I haven't seen anything tangible just yet. . . . I've continued to look for restaurant spaces and make contacts with developers and landlords. I've brainstormed about my next book and a way to tie it into building products and a brand. Personally, I think I'd be a great candidate for spokesperson gigs, but nothing has happened just yet. I continue to teach at recreational cooking schools (promoting my book, *New Soul Cooking*) and to demonstrate recipes at special events. I cater private events. I've done several television appearances, starred in the trailer for the San Francisco Black Film Festival. I've also become engaged and purchased a condo with my fiancé. Life has been interesting to say the least.

❧

Cat Cora is perhaps the model example of the new American chef, the one who's completely bypassing the traditional route to celebrity chef-dom, which for thirty years has meant establishing oneself as the chef-owner of a nationally renowned restaurant. She may represent the next generation of star chefs. Cora went to the CIA after college, then spent about a decade in restaurant kitchens (including a stint under Melissa Kelly at Old Chatham) before moving full-throttle into television, setting up a company called 3 Street Media and The Cat Cora Show, LLC. Her television concept is an hour-long talk show about food and living issues, and until she gets that off the ground, she's got a slot on *Kitchen Accomplished,* a kitchen-renovation show on the Food Network. She was featured in a documentary called *Cat's in the Kitchen,* and has one book out, *Cat Cora's Kitchens,* and another in the works. And, notably, she became the first woman to become an Iron Chef America, a hugely hyped production of the Food Network well covered by the major food media.

When I called her at home in Northern California for an article on chef branding, she seemed eager to talk about it. "You go to bed one day and you're the chef, and you wake up the next day and you've got an agent, a manager, and a publicist—how does this happen?" she said. "It's been wild.

"It's something I've wanted all my life," she continued. "To have the fame. Without beating around the bush, that's the bottom line. . . . When I was going to culinary school, chefs weren't the celebrity chefs they are today." Her dream in culinary school was to cook for the best chefs in America, and to be the best chef she could be, but the chef world has changed in a way that seems to suit her disposition.

"For me it started at a young age. I wanted to be famous since I can remember. I knew that I had a bigger calling from a young age, that I had something big to offer. . . . How can I combine what I love to do with also the celebrity of it or becoming well known throughout the country, throughout the world—how can I branch those together?

"I have to be on television—I got the bug."

Toward that end, she put together a team that includes a Hollywood manager (she's a member of the Screen Actors Guild), an agent, and a publicist—"a branding team," she calls it, "a team that is helping me go from the food industry, crossing over into the entertainment industry, to build me as a household name. That is my ultimate goal, not only to have a syndicated show but eventually products, a signature restaurant, . . . a clothing line that I'm working on right now. The world is our oyster. We can do a lot of what actors and actresses have done today, what singers have done today. Chefs can do the same thing. It's really an endless opportunity for marketing, so that's what our ultimate goal is, to build a brand, the Cat Cora brand."

Look out, Martha Stewart Living Omnimedia Inc.!

Or not. That kind of growth is not easy. On the other hand, Martha did it, why not Cat Cora? It is a catchy name. There's no reason she *can't* achieve that household-name status. Rachael Ray did it from her beginnings as a salesperson at a gourmet market in Albany. Emeril opened up the door for food-entertainment TV. Why not take it to the next level, and why not Cat Cora?

A year after we spoke, the indomitable Cat Cora, in customary fashion, responded to an e-mail asking how her career had progressed: "Things are fantastic!" she wrote. "I am the new Sears spokesperson, working on a second book, endorsements, a restaurant project, of course, I am now an Iron Chef, which is huge, and I am working with the same production company that shoots *Iron Chef* to develop my own show."

She'd signed with the William Morris Agency and had decided on her branding tag, or theme: "From the Hip," also the title of her second book, and had even hooked up with Adam Block to help set up her restaurant deal. She was rushing out the door, practically, heading for a cruise on which she'd be featured as a celebrity chef and monthlong travel in Europe with her partner and her twenty-month-old son. Life was exciting.

CHAPTER 3

❦

The Outpost and the Rollout

"Man, opening day is fuckin' hard," says Bobby Flay, celebrity chef and television personality, to Bradley Ogden. They're standing in the kitchen of the new restaurant Flay is opening in ninety minutes. The place looks like most restaurants do just before opening the doors for the first time. The kitchen is buzzing, and a swarm of guys with tool belts are pounding and drilling and fastening as though opening day were weeks away, not an hour and a half. A fellow celebrity chef, Ogden has left his restaurant and threaded his way through the banks of *binging*, *beeping* slot machines and clouds of cigarette smoke in Caesars Palace to say hello. A line of plump, dowdy, middle America, eager to be the first to eat at Flay's Vegas outpost of Mesa Grill, has formed hours before the place opens.

"The rotisserie, man, it's like eight hundred and ninety degrees," Flay tells Ogden. The giant rotisserie on a second level above the kitchen and on view to the whole restaurant appears to be on fire. "You can't even work near it. Those chickens would go up in flames."

"You'll be *poêléeing* those chickens," Ogden chuckles—that is, cooking them in their own juices in a covered pot in the oven, not crackling, crispy-skinned, and juicy off the spit for everyone to see.

Flay shakes his head over the gigantic rotisserie snafu. "You see it on paper, you think, 'Oh yeah, put it on the second floor, it'll look great, make the room smell great." He jerks his head. "Fuckin' pain in the ass."

But the doors will open, and the bar will fill up with margarita drinkers who sample the shrimp with sweet corn tamale and the blue corn pancake with duck and habanero chili sauce, and talk about their favorite food TV shows, as the latest celebrity chef opens another Vegas brandname restaurant. The Vegas strip, once a culinary embarrassment, is now accomplishing the unbelievable: luring Michelin three-star chefs Alain Ducasse, Joël Robuchon, and Guy Savoy, in addition to celebrity chefs, such as Flay and Manhattan's famed Daniel Boulud and their outposts.

"Other than New York," says Tom Colicchio, executive chef of New York's Craft and Gramercy Tavern who opened Craftsteak and 'wichcraft in the MGM Grand, "it's the number one dining spot in the country."

Las Vegas is the epicenter of the latest issue burning through the chef world—the multiple-unit concept, the ability of a chef to open branches of his or her flagship restaurant. The wily Bourdain curls his lip at the movement, calls the Vegas phenomenon "the final cash-out strategy for the inarticulate chef," but for better or worse, it's an avalanche that shows no sign of stopping. Steve Wynn, the man who upped the ante in Vegas with his Wynn resorts, lured not just outposts but the chefs themselves. Of the chefs of the eleven showcase-chef restaurants, all but Daniel Boulud will be uprooting from home base and moving to Vegas. Wynn and his lieutenant in restaurants, Elizabeth Blau, wanted the artist in the kitchen.

"It's the pivotal difference," says Blau, executive VP of restaurant development for Wynn but who also has her own restaurant-consulting business and is a partner with Kerry Simon in his Vegas restaurant. "Because no matter what, when Thomas is at the French Laundry overseeing a sixteen-course meal, or you've sat at David Burke's tasting table, or Jean-Georges', it's the artist creating the experience for you. There's no way to replicate that. He's the artist, he's the master. Every real estate developer, every hotel or land developer, is looking for a celebrity-chef deal, and when you think about it, you can count them on two hands. It's not like there's a hundred of these guys.

"Chefs have become personalities, as well as being the chefs, and people enjoy the interaction, they like seeing them. It's a big deal and it really adds to the experience. My start in the industry was working for Sirio Maccioni in a non-chef-driven restaurant [Le Cirque], but Sirio was always there. And I know one of the big reasons people would go to the restaurant was to see him. You have to look at restaurants as a global experience, not just a dining experience. It's a whole entertainment experience, and part of that is having a chef."

You might say, given Wynn's formidable track record of innovation, that he was bucking the trend, which has been one of well-known chefs throughout the country opening outposts but spending little time if any in the outpost's kitchen. But then again, perhaps Wynn's demanding that the chef be at his restaurant was little more than a quaint throwback to a more romantic era in the American restaurant kitchen.

The truth is, a chef who becomes very successful can't open a second restaurant and be in both places. So what did you expect him or her to do? Be André Soltner, alone in his single world-renowned kitchen, but now, long since retired, practically unknown among young cooks walking onto the hot line?

"There are chefs in New York right now who should know who André Soltner is and they don't, and that's astounding to me, and they're working in nice restaurants in New York City," says restaurant adviser Adam Block, who helps chefs to expand their businesses.

Chefs are by nature unusually driven people—the work is simply too hard for anyone who's not driven. The not-driven get driven out or into the ground. And that's just to exist—they have to be unusually driven *just to stay alive*. To succeed, you've got to have more than just infinite energy and stamina. One of those qualities a chef must have is massive ambition. You have to have ambition to succeed at your first restaurant.

Then what? Do you turn off your ambition switch? No, that's who you are. Do you shut down and move to Vegas and open there? Only a chef between certain levels will do what Wynn has asked—one who's at a level high enough to be asked, but not so high as to be a national brand or overly worked in other areas. This is why Takashi Yagihashi, of the well-known and highly praised restaurant Tribute, outside Detroit, has left his Farmington Hills kitchen and moved to Vegas, but Daniel Boulud has not. The reason Boulud can do this and not Yagihashi—what Wynn knows—is that Boulud's brand is strong enough to support the restaurant. Also, these chefs on the cusp of celebrity are probably of a certain age, they've been around, know their limitations, have goals beyond working 120 hours a week, maybe spending time with their kids or wife. They'll be paid well, surely earning solid six-figure incomes, but they're not going to make the *real* money.

No, the chef whose goal it is to make *real* money is going to have to grow his business by opening more of them. Thus, chefs who have worked so hard to build their flagship have begun to open outposts of their restaurants, and we have now a country filling up with restaurants bearing the names of our top culinary artists. Vegas is by no means alone. Cities and tourist hot spots across the country are seeing the opening of name-brand venues. Jasper White, who earned fame in Boston for his fine-dining establishment that bore his name, now runs a small cluster of lobster houses also with his namesake, Jasper White's Summer Shack, in Boston, Cambridge, and at Logan Airport and the Mohegan Sun casino in Connecticut. Melissa and Price are doing it in Orlando and Tucson; and Todd English, a bluezoo at the request of Disney World. Norman Van Aken, who made his fame at Norman's in Miami, opened another Norman's on the opposite coast, in Los Angeles. Jean-Georges Vongerichten planned to open a restaurant in Minneapolis.

Putting aside, for the moment, the question of whether these restaurants are any good, let's simply look at it from a business standpoint. From this vantage, it seems to be a very good idea for the chef.

The paradigm of this phenomenon is simple: An unknown, talented

chef creates an outstanding one-of-a-kind restaurant that is quickly recognized throughout the country by the press, its quality conveyed by
word of mouth and the difficulty in getting a reservation. It becomes
successful. The philosophy and quality of this flagship restaurant is the
"brand." The chef then creates a midlevel fine-dining restaurant, one
that doesn't require his or her daily presence. Daniel Boulud has his
four-star Daniel, but he also has upscale cafés in Manhattan, Palm Beach,
and now Las Vegas. People go there because the brand of the flagship is
the same, but the chef doesn't have to be there and, more to the point,
isn't *expected* to be there. And, because the food and the environment at
the establishment are not chef dependent, they can thus be replicated
over and over again. *Voilà!*—a chain is born, appearing in many con-
figurations, such as the French bistro (Bouchon by Thomas Keller), the
Californian bistro (Spago by Wolfgang Puck), the Italian bistro (Olives
by Todd English). No one, of course, wants to call the creation of our
culinary artists "chains"—chains connote "cheap" and "mass produced,"
plastic rather than authentic. "Rollout" seems to be the preferred term.

❧❧

Again, let's reiterate that we've relinquished our sweet but outdated notions of the marquee chef personally preparing our food. Emeril Lagasse
doesn't cook at Emeril's; Wolfgang Puck doesn't cook at his Spago, his
Chinois, his Lupo, his Postrio, or even at his Wolfgang Puck Bar and
Grill; Todd English doesn't cook at Olives; Michael Mina doesn't cook at
Michael Mina. While most of these chefs have some sort of management
contract that guarantees his presence at the outpost for a few days or
more each month, his presence in the kitchen is not the point, nor
should it be. The point is, that the chef's celebrity now drives his businesses. Wolfgang or Emeril doesn't have to be there—just his name.

The successful outposts in Vegas underscore the power of this national phenomenon: As the chef moves out of his revered cultural role
of artist-monk—a position that used to be an end in itself—and into the
realm of celebrity, he passes through the branding process and thus puts

himself in the position to make far more money than he ever could with just one restaurant.

Michael Symon's Lola, the most popular restaurant in its midsized American city, generates $2 million in sales. The French Laundry, the most famous four-star restaurant in the country, generates more than $7.5 million in sales. Wolfgang Puck generates $80 million at his fine-dining restaurants alone, and he doesn't even have to cook anymore.

That $80 million is why in the chef's argot, "demi-glace" and "confit" have been replaced by "rollout" and "exit strategy." Discussion among chefs themselves concerns not farm-raised versus wild, but rather management contract versus equity partner. A meeting with the chef's lieutenant can now mean not the sous-chef but rather the brand consultant.

All of which begs the questions: Are chef's merely creating high-end versions of the very fast-food chains reviled among the culinary intelligentsia? Are our culinary artists selling out, betraying us with ersatz gourmet? Is Vegas, which created themed malls of ancient Rome and a Venice complete with indoor canals and gondola rides, now creating theme-park versions of the country's best restaurants? Don't need to be in Manhattan or L.A. or Napa—just go to Vegas and dine at New York's Mesa Grill, L.A.'s Spago, Napa's Bouchon! Tastes just like chicken!

❧

"[Successful chefs] create a brand that they can roll out, that has their proprietary mark associated with it, but doesn't require them to be in the kitchen," explains Block, whose clients include Thomas Keller, Eric Ripert, and Charlie Trotter. "It's the only way they will ever make a lot of money. They're going to have to grow their concepts up to multiunit levels and have somebody buy them out."

The magic number, Block says, seems to be five or six. When a chef has that many viable outposts of a single restaurant, bigger companies find them attractive, buy them out, and grow them big.

Joachim Splichal, for instance, created a series of high-end restaurants in Los Angeles, beginning with Patina in 1989. In 1999 he sold his company, the Patina Group, which consisted of eight restaurants and three catering units, to Restaurant Associates for $40 million, while retaining control of the business.

The important distinction here is ownership versus management contract. Almost all celebrity chefs have a management contract (rather than a lease agreement that implies ownership). This means they run the restaurant and earn a percentage of sales and/or profits. But they're essentially employees, not owners. This is the deal Flay has, just like Melissa Kelly and the Primos in Florida and Arizona. Keller leases his space from the Venetian, in effect maintaining ownership of the Vegas Bouchon. If he were to open a few more Bouchons, they might become attractive to a big company to whom he could sell. You can't sell a management contract. The downside, of course, is that the business might lose money and you'd be the owner of a loser rather than an employee.

Is there a difference in quality? It likely depends on the chef. Ownership can result in a greater "sense of ownership" translating into extreme care or concern from the celebrity chef, resulting in a better restaurant. On the other hand, a chef with a management contract still has a huge stake in the success of his or her outpost both financially and also in terms of his or her brand. If the outpost is crappy, everyone will begin to think the flagship is too.

Most chefs in the industry embrace the multiunit phenomenon. Mario Batali (with books, TV credentials, and numerous critically acclaimed restaurants in Manhattan) notes the increased opportunities for his staff. Emeril Lagasse said one reason he opened his second restaurant, long before he appeared on television, was to keep his first restaurant from being a "revolving door"—training chefs only to have them leave didn't make sense to him. He's since opened a total of nine restaurants in five cities.

While the media's knee-jerk response to rollouts is to wail "crass commercialism"—Emeril's Atlanta was trashed by the local paper in much the way Larry Forgione's Miami outpost of An American Place was—journalists who cover the industry deeply seem to be on the fence about the issue, applauding the increased availability of innovative cuisine but remaining skeptical that chefs can work their magic by cell phone and occasional visits.

"It's complicated," explained Russ Parsons of the *Los Angeles Times.* "Joachim Splichal is probably one of the two or three best chefs in L.A. . . . when he wants to be. . . . The Patina flagship for years was at the north end of Hancock Park—very old money, pricey neighborhood. [Quality] went up and down, depending on who was cooking and what their commitment was. Few chefs lasted more than a couple of years."

Ultimately, the success of a rollout depends on how well the branded chef is able to train his chefs de cuisine. As is the case with any category of product in our sprawling commercial culture, there are good restaurants and there are bad restaurants. Provided the dining public is aware of the distinction between a restaurant where the chef is actually on premises and a restaurant that is a representation of that chef's brand, that public can make a considered opinion and vote yes or no with their wallets.

"They hate whenever you write that they have a chain," says Juliette Rossant, author of *Super Chef: The Making of the Great Modern Restaurant Empires.* "They don't actually give you an alternative. And frankly, what is the difference between their chains and McDonald's? I mean they are chains—they're structured like chains.

"The way you create wealth," says Rossant, who notes Splichal's success story in her book, "is by creating clones of it, creating other opportunities for yourself in pots and pans, in food products, consulting, in starring roles in movies and TV. Are they cashing in on their celebrity? Of course they are. . . . But I don't know if that's such a negative thing."

Rossant and others have drawn a parallel between two worlds that are increasingly linked—restaurants and fashion—observing that "like fine dining, haute couture is necessary to establish quality and reputation, but that the money is in prêt-à-porter for fashion and in casual dining for food." Or to use the industry buzzword, the "fast casual," exemplified in the Wolfgang Puck Expresses, quality fast-food spots in malls and airports.

This capacity to open culinary prêt-à-porter is not limited to name-brand chefs with books and TV shows to help drive the brand. Robert Del Grande, who for many years has been the culinary talent behind Cafe Annie in Houston, Texas, well known in his area and respected among chefs but not a national brand, opened Cafe Express in 1984, selling simple, contemporary American fare, handmade from fresh ingredients, in a fast-food environment. He and his partners now have nineteen Cafe Expresses throughout the state, and the player that allowed this small restaurant group to grow was, ironically, a fast-food giant, Wendy's International.

According to Del Grande, the company was looking to get into the next new wave of fast food, "high-quality, handmade food," he said. "So they became our major investor and are now helping run the operations, which is far beyond what I can possibly do." In a similar move, McDonald's bought out a fast-food chain called Chipotle, specializing in gourmet burritos and tacos and using naturally raised pork.

Common problems beyond greed and hubris (not unknown in a high-ego business) are undercapitalization and the taking on of huge debt, and lack of infrastructure and personnel to support growth.

Among the biggest conundrums for the small restaurant group is how to build infrastructure to support the growth before having the cash flow generated by the growth. For Todd English, whose Olives Group operates a dozen and a half restaurants, growth was erratic with false steps and restaurant closings. The main problem, English himself noted, was "not being fully capitalized at the beginning of my career."

A corporation such as Wendy's already has the marketing and support infrastructure, while the chef, such as Del Grande, can maintain control of food and menu development.

Adam Block stresses that chefs became celebrities by cooking food, not by earning degrees in business. Consequently, he observes, "They don't have a clue what they're getting into."

Block particularly likes the model set by Thomas Keller, who's famed in the industry for consistent four-star standards. Having opened two flagship fine-dining restaurants on each coast, he has also opened two Bouchon restaurants, urban French bistros, that don't require him to be there. Yet despite Keller's absence, the bistros still serve four-star cuisine, thanks to the day-to-day guidance of longtime French Laundry chefs Jeff Cerciello and Mark Hopper. Both Cerciello (executive chef of Bouchon) and Hopper (chef de cuisine at the Bouchon in Las Vegas) are thoroughly trained in, and able to replicate, Keller's famously fanatical standards.

Are we in danger, though, of creating a lot of McHighend restaurants or simply foisting more chains on the unsuspecting and often undifferentiating public?

"No," says Pamela Parseghian, executive food editor of *Nation's Restaurant News*. "I think that we have a future of bringing great food to the masses, that's the way I look at it. To have a Jasper White coming up with a menu and recipes that are affordable to most everybody is a wonderful thing. I'm excited by it. I started covering chain restaurants over twelve years ago, and you couldn't find a piece of fresh cilantro in a dish, and now it's everywhere, and a lot of other really lovely things you can get around the country, and most people can afford it. How can that be bad?"

If we're going to be obsessed by chefs and restaurants, it's important to recognize and acknowledge the different categories before we evaluate the experience and the food. To go to a P.F. Chang's China Bistro, a successful Arizona-based chain, in Cleveland, for instance, is different on many levels from going to Michael Symon's Lola Bistro or any of Cleveland's numerous and excellent independent restaurants. P.F. Chang's is a corporate-driven menu composed of decent but generic Asian food designed to appeal to people from California to Texas to Wisconsin to Alabama to New York. The ingredients used are available to all chefs all year round. An independent restaurant is more likely to serve regional specialties using seasonal ingredients. The menu will change more frequently and probably convey the particular tastes and eccentricities of the chef. On the other hand, these independents will be less consistent in quality—the first time in you don't know what you'll get. Among the biggest lessons we've learned in this gigantic dining industry is the primacy of consistency over quality (thank you, McDonald's!). But there's an impact consumers don't normally consider when figuring where to take their evening meal. All P.F. Chang's China Bistros are company owned, so some of the money spent there is going back to Arizona rather than into your own city's economy, which happens when you eat at an independent restaurant run by a chef who gets his or her food locally. Given the increasing prominence of higher-end chains, this can have a not-insubstantial impact on a midsized city's economy, not to mention on all the purveyors who grow or raise the ingredients in the area.

Recognizing such facts is good. Few in the industry doubt that one of the ultimate effects of the celebrity-chef phenomenon is in part an increased awareness among Americans of where their food comes from, an awareness that has resulted in an increased availability at our grocery stores of organic or sustainably farmed produce, farm-raised chickens, and grass-fed beef. Not to mention cilantro, shiitake mushrooms, gingerroot, and other ingredients we now take for granted.

❧

The secret to successful replication seems to be—*surprise!*—a good product, regardless of whether the venue is fast-casual or fine-dining: "If I'm doing something at Cafe Annie or Cafe Express or other places," Del Grande says, "I put my name on it. I'm involved in that and I would eat it myself. . . . That I think is what the idea of a strong brand would mean—that you're very strongly connected with the product going out."

The danger, it should go without saying, is an inconsistent or bad product that inevitably diminishes the brand. Rick Bayless, of Frontera

Grill and Topolobampo in Chicago, is a particularly vivid example of one such chef. Famed for his artisanal approach to Mexican cuisine and stellar restaurants, Bayless endorsed Burger King's low-fat chicken sandwiches. The product did not last long on the BK menu, and Bayless was widely seen by fellow chefs and adoring foodies as having sold out.

For years, Jean-Georges Vongerichten has been one of Manhattan's culinary shamans, with Vong, JoJo, and his flagship, the four-star Jean Georges. But with a slew of recent openings in New York, a steak house in Vegas, a three-star review of Spice Market tarnished by the asterisk of an editor's note in *The New York Times,* and a crushing one-star review also in the *Times* of V Steakhouse in the Time Warner Center, his brand is in danger of being diluted. His recent Perry Streest has received strong reviews, but as he reaches further, and with less success, from his core philosophy—cutting-edge food in hip rooms—he ignores the talent and diminishes the reputation that elevated him to brand-worthy prominence in the first place.

⬥⬥

All chefs admit that successful branding is a tricky balance of celebrity management and maintaining high-quality product. Each has a different response to being in the kitchen. Many, those hitting age fifty particularly, have had enough cooking and expediting and ninety-hour workweeks. They're happy to move into the world of the restaurateur. Yet for some big-name chefs, being in the kitchen is still the ultimate reward. David Burke, considered among chefs to be a creative genius of near-lunatic proportions, spent several years as corporate chef for a big steak chain. (Steak chains, which run on simple heat-and-serve menus, are no-brainers for chefs.) While Burke enjoyed the corporate hours and corporate salary (mid–six figures), he missed the kitchen. So he opened David Burke & Donatella in Manhattan, where he's in the kitchen cooking and will work on his own branded products. Bradley Ogden, who is an owner of numerous restaurants in the San Francisco Bay Area and whose place in Las Vegas won Best New Restaurant of 2004 at the Beard awards, put his name on his restaurant and so felt it was important to be there every day.

"People are amazed to see me walking around here," Ogden chuckles.

Even Flay, a TV personality who has never intended to spend time cooking at his Vegas restaurant, knows the importance of staying in the kitchen. "I hate the word 'branding,'" he says, the day after his successful Vegas opening. "I hate it. What's it mean? Whenever a chef becomes successful, the word 'branding' sort of seeps into their vocabulary. I have some good opportunities based on not only what I do in the kitchen but what I do on television, which is very helpful obviously. But when the word 'brand' comes to mind, I have the same reaction as I do to 'chain.' . . . When you try to become a brand that's a disaster.

"Look, just go to work every day, the opportunities come. You just put your head down and continue to work. That's been my philosophy. So the branding thing to me is overrated. There's very few people who can do it. I think that it's distracting. I know that it all begins and ends in the kitchen in my profession. The reason why I have success on television is because it's what I do in the kitchen. So whenever I feel like I'm getting away from what I love, I put my whites on and I stand in the kitchen."

❧·❧

While the power of Vegas is now undeniable, as recently as the mid-1990s it was still a tough sell. "If I'd called them in 1996," says Rob Goldstein, president of the Venetian, which opened in 1999 with Valentino, Emeril's Delmonico, Lutèce, one of Splichal's Pinots, and would later lure a Keller Bouchon and an Esca by Mario Batali, "they'd have said, 'No, I'm a serious chef. I don't do Vegas.' Now the risk is trying to keep the guys who come here honest"—that is, to do authentic restaurants and create great products. He added, "It's become almost like sport."

As Puck discovered in 1992, a time when the Vegas restaurant was nothing more than a casino amenity, there turned out to be a huge hunger for an individualistic restaurant by a chef of Puck's caliber. Spago in

Los Angeles, says Puck's business partner Tom Kaplan, was doing between $4 million and $5 million. When they opened Spago in the Caesars Palace mall, which was about the same size, they doubled sales.
Spago, which they'd only worked as a dinner-only restaurant serving
300 customers a night, became in Vegas a place open twelve hours a day
serving between 1,000 and 1,500 people a day and bringing in $10
million.

On the other hand, Charlie Trotter's opened in Vegas in the 1990s
and failed—people weren't ready for the three- to four-hour dinner in a
Vegas teeming with things to do. "I don't think it was Charlie's fault,"
says Goldstein. "It was the market's fault. A lot of people spend a hundred fifty, two hundred a head for a fine-dining experience. The problem is not money, it's time. It's the amount of things that Las Vegas offers.
People come here for three or four days, and they want to cram in a
thousand experiences. They don't have time to sit at Ducasse." It had
not, at the time, reached the culinary Dorado—or Dorado theme park,
rather—that it is now. Goldstein says, "Charlie Trotter today would be
able to succeed."

Vegas has yet to reach its restaurant saturation point, as Wynn's ability to lure chefs to the desert shows. Goldstein noted, "Last year, we did
one hundred and seventy-five million dollars in restaurant sales." Banquet and bar sales were $100 million. "I don't know another hotel in the
world that does three hundred million dollars in food and beverage," he
said. This in an operation that does approximately $1.5 billion in sales
overall—a hotel and casino that does *a billion and a half dollars*. It's no
wonder everyone's flocking to Vegas. And the celebrity-chef phenomenon is one of the forces propelling the Vegas cash vortex.

CHAPTER 4

❧·❧

Emeril and Rachael

Television is arguably the most powerful force shaping the culinary landscape today. More people are reached through television—entertained, educated, changed in some little or large food-related way—than through any other medium by far.

Television cooking began in 1946, when writer and food authority James Beard taped his first cooking show. He was chosen, authors Andrew Dornenburg and Karen Page note, "because of his experience as an actor and a cook," forecasting the ultimate need for cooks and chefs who appear on television to be entertaining, to *act*. Julia Child would follow, as would others, such as Martin Yan and the Frugal Gourmet Jeff Smith, almost exclusively in the domain of public broadcasting. Then in November 1993 the Food Network hit the air, at first with sparse offerings, mumbling chefs, Robin Leach, and food news, reaching 6.5 million subscribers. By 2005 the network had extended its reach to 87 million of a total of 109 million TV households, according to the network, comparable to the saturation of CNN (its creator, not surprisingly, was Reese Schonfeld, one of the creators of CNN). Its best prime-time shows are watched by a half million people each day, and ratings seem only to be growing.

These shows, unlike the best restaurants, are not ultimately about cooking, but about what the host conveys, an attitude. "Cooking shows will always be personality driven," Brooke Bailey Johnson, who became the network's president in 2004, said. How else to explain the popularity of the show *Two Fat Ladies,* featuring two eccentric Brits who adored just about everything Americans were taught to fear, notably lashings of butter and animal fat. They rejoiced in it.

I truly didn't appreciate the size and passion of the Food Network audience until four of its stars came to Cleveland. The Food Network, as part of a broader marketing effort, sent Rachael Ray, Mario Batali, Alton Brown, and Marc Summers to my fair city and others to Philadelphia for a weekend of demos and book signings, to be joined by scores of food and gadget booths and local chefs doing their own demos. I couldn't resist and forked over the twenty bucks for a ticket. I wanted to see who was here and why, and at least I'd be able to say hello to Michael Symon, who had demos planned, and Liz, who would man the Lola booth.

The event was held in the I-X Center, an enormous warehouse out by the airport that sometimes hosts entire carnivals, with Ferris wheels and roller coasters inside. The parking lot was a seemingly endless field of cars. Inside, thousands of people packed the place. It was unbelievable. I'd approach men and women, often they had equally starstruck kids in tow, who were stationary in one of the many lines available to stand in, and talk to them about their favorite shows and hosts and how they cooked at home. I found one line that was unique in that I couldn't see the beginning or the end—it must have gone on for miles. I struck up a conversation with a woman who told me it was the Rachael Ray booksigning line. There was no Rachael Ray in sight. The woman said she'd driven five hours from Indiana to be here, to see Ray live and get a book signed. Ray used to hawk her books in Albany grocery stores, where she did a good business. On her weekend in Cleveland, she signed thousands of books and had to sign programs and T-shirts when the books ran out. When her time for the space she was using ran out, organizers had to cut off the line, and there was an uproar by people who'd been waiting for hours. "They moved us to another area so we could continue sign-ing after our allotted time," Ray recalled. "Kids were crying and peo-ple were so upset at being cut off that the arena worked with the Food Network and got another whole area so we could keep on signing."

I hope my friend from Indiana got hers, I thought. Then I thought, *I don't sell thousands of books in a weekend in Cleveland and I've got a home field advantage—I gotta get a TV show.*

The Food Network was ahead of me, already devising a show pre-cisely for someone like me, who'd just got this bright idea. *The Next Food Network Star* is a reality cooking show, featuring nine people who wanted to do their own cooking show. The producers would ask these people to compete in tests uniquely designed to gauge their television-star qualities, and importantly, show the audience the specific skills required to be a good TV host. I watched most of it and thought it was both fascinating and entertaining, the mark of a successful food show.

Clearly there was no shortage of wannabe Emerils out there. And not just Aunt Jeannie who's been called by God to share her fruitcake fetish with America. A large number of young men and women currently work-ing in the chef world were hungry for a shot at TV cooking.

In addition to being a successful chef-restaurateur, Bobby Flay is a Food Network star. He gets the question all the time, and it drives him "fuckin' nuts," he says. When I'd stopped in at Mesa Grill in Vegas, it was one of the first things he brought up.

During the short time between when he had enough prestige to be asked to do demos at the French Culinary Institute, his alma mater, and now, the change has been astonishing, and to him, completely misguided. He can't even count how many culinary students tell him they want to be on TV. It used to be they'd ask him where could they get the best jobs, he said: "'How should I approach a chef? How do I get my foot in the door?'

"Now they ask, 'How do I get my own television show?'" he said. "I don't even answer the question. Look, you're in the wrong class—this is cooking school, learn to cook first. Before the Food Network, Emeril was just a great chef in New Orleans. He worked his ass off to get there, OK? He didn't just happen one day. . . . He spent a long time cooking a lot of Cajun food and using a lot of cayenne pepper, and he understands it like the back of his hand. I said, 'You guys think you're gonna go to culinary school, then get an interview with the Food Network and get your own cooking show? First of all, nobody will believe you because when you pick up a lemon, you're not going to pick it up with confidence, because you don't know what the fuckin' lemon is. You just know it's a lemon. And second of all, you need to learn how to cook first. This is a cooking class, this is a cooking school, it's about being a chef, not being a television star."

But he's resigned to the fact that as long as he and his TV colleagues keep doing what they're doing, the perception won't change, and it's not all bad: "We'll get some good people in the industry," he says. "And the rest will drop out because they want to be a star instead of a cook. There are no stars in this kitchen." He pointed to Larry, his fifty-three-year-old longtime line cook now opening the Vegas kitchen. "They're coming to work twelve hours every day."

Cooking *school,* ironically, is not the place to go if what you want is a cooking *show.*

When I'd spoken with Rachael Ray on the set of her show *30-Minute Meals,* I'd told her that at cooking schools today, a lot of the students enter hoping one day to have a TV show. As giggly and chatty off camera as on, though with a more natural edge off, Ray *snorted.* That was one of the most ridiculous things she'd ever heard, she said. If they want a TV show, they should go to a media training school or get a job at a local news station. That was how you learn to do television, she said.

"We're working harder to find chefs, our chef hosts, because that's proven much more of a challenge for us," says Bob Tuschman, a senior vice president at the network. Many have noted that of the hosts, fewer and fewer are restaurant chefs. "Our bar is raised very high now," Tusch-man continued. "It is hard in any case to find a chef who combines everything we need to host a cooking show. They have to have a tele-genic personality that's really capable of true star power. They have to be a passionate, entertaining teacher. And this next one is what's hard for restaurant chefs: They have to really be able to talk to home cooks about the kind of food and kind of cooking that home cooks care about, which is very different from restaurant food. And they also have to have a unique food point of view that our audience wants to hear about. When you put those together, it's hard in any case to find talent for our air."

In short, it's no rare skill to be able to cook simple food, but not ev-erybody can be a great TV host. What culinary students don't seem to know or want to acknowledge is that TV cooking shows aren't really about cooking. They're about entertainment and comfort. Cooking may be the vehicle for the entertainment, notions of pots simmering on the stovetop may be inherently appealing, but the quality of the cooking is all but irrelevant. How could it possibly be relevant—the audience can't smell it or taste it? Ray could be frying up rat shit and who would know? All she has to do is make it look good. Yes, she puts her food in the books and the backstage staff gets her recipes up on the Web site, so she's got to have decent workable ideas and recipes, but a lot of people have those. What they don't have is Rachael's gift for making the heart-land feel comfortable in the kitchen. Rachael inspires women to drive five hours from Indiana to get a glimpse of her and her signature. In 2004 Rachael Ray did the unimaginable: She beat the king—began to register higher ratings than Emeril himself, the man who took the idea of combining food with entertainment and ran with it, the entertainer-chef who is credited with carrying the Food Network to where it is today.

"He put the TV Food Network on the map," says Ming Tsai, who began on the Food Network, then moved to PBS, now with a show called *Simply Ming.* "Me, Bobby, Mario, Sara—we just had a seat on that train."

❧

In 1983 a twenty-three-year-old chef, recruited from a hotel chain in New England, expedited at one of New Orleans' premier restaurants, Commander's Palace, most esteemed gentry among restaurants there. The young man was skinny, of medium height, had thick curly dark hair, Groucho eyebrows, and a heavy working-class Massachusetts accent. He'd learned to be a screamer like the chefs he'd trained under. He'd spent his apprenticeship in cellar prep kitchens getting pans thrown at him. That's how this business worked. That's why he had no remorse, or worry, firing seven of his thirteen line cooks in a single night, just weeks into his new job. *During* service. *Get out, you're not good enough, I'll fucking do it myself.* He was the kind of kid chef (not unlike, perhaps, the twenty-four-year-old Melissa Kelly—"You like being a chef, little girl?" . . . "*FUCK* you, wait outside!") who would take the box of rank fish on ice and heave it into the street in front of the deliverer. Order *not* accepted. Don't bring me shit fish.

This was the new kid Ella Brennan, Commander's matriarch, had hired. Brunch service at the restaurant was typically packed, and in the middle of one of his early services, the young chef was screaming again, no one was moving fast enough, crazy busy and screaming. Brennan could see the kid going down in flames—he wasn't being tough, she knew, he was being a fool. *Listen to Mr. Big Bad Chef.* Which was a shame, because underneath the volume and the egotistical screaming, he had serious talent. She shook her head and thought *He is too good to be doing something so asinine.* So in the middle of this service, having had enough from her new hire (who continued to scream at his *sorry-ass hung-over line rats who can't cook their way out of a fucking paper bag at eleven o'clock on a Sunday morning! You want me to do it for you?!*—just look at him!), she scratched out an angry note and gave it to the boy. What else could she do? There were customers waiting for their eggs Benedict. Middle of service!

The chef read it to himself—Brennan had written, she said, "You're too damn smart to be so damn stupid." *Huh,* the young chef thought, annoyed, and he carried on with service. What else could he do? He's in the middle of service—not exactly a time for reflection.

This was a pivotal moment in Emeril Lagasse's career. Lagasse remembers going home and reading the inscrutable note from his boss—whom he liked, whom he admired, who was one of the most prominent members of New Orleans, a woman who could fire him if she felt like it. He read the note and read it again.

"The next morning," Lagasse says today, "when I got up, I thought, *I'm gonna leave my ego at home and I'm gonna bring my professionalism and talent to work.*"

He did, and he distinguished himself there, updating the classic dishes, introducing a new commitment to fresh, excellent ingredients and innovative dishes. He stayed at Commander's for seven years before hanging his own shingle. Emeril's was an immediate success. Two years later, he opened another restaurant, Nola, which became another success, with his own energetic take on the Cajun-Creole food of Loooz-iana. The food revolution was on a roll, and Lagasse was one of scores of talented young chefs opening hot restaurants throughout the country. Ben Barker in Durham, Rick Bayless in Chicago, Lydia Shire in Boston, Susan Spicer just around the corner from his Nola—the list could go on and on. He was in the middle of a pack of talented American chefs.

❈

On May 18, 2005, Lagasse breaks from backstage into the center of the *Emeril Live* set, stops, and raises evangelical palms to the people, who bolt up out of their seats clapping, whooping, and cheering. A young girl in the front row opens her mouth in disbelief—*It's actually him.* Emeril works the audience, pressing flesh, stopping to hug an elderly woman using an oxygen tank. He halts before the camera with the teleprompter and welcomes the audience to his fifteen-hundredth show for the Food Network, on which he'll cook some of his most adored recipes—the signature barbecue shrimp, a seafood boil, the Boston cream pie. "Welcome, everybody! Welcome!" he says. "Emeril Lagasse here, welcome to *Emeril Live!*"

Twenty-two years after his debut at Commander's Palace and the note from Ella Brennan, Emeril Lagasse had left the pack of hot American chefs and had transformed himself into not only the most popular chef on television but arguably the most influential chef in America—*ever.*

Emeril Lagasse, the most influential chef *of all time.*

Name another *chef* who's touched or influenced more people. Julia Child? Not a chef—and anyway, she didn't do near the numbers Lagasse does. Escoffier—hard to gauge the cumulative effect of the century since he published *Le Guide Culinaire.* I don't think anyone comes close from a numbers standpoint. Jacques Pépin? Thomas Keller? Not even close. Keller himself remembers going to a book signing in Philadelphia to autograph copies of his *French Laundry Cookbook,* a huge seller in its own right. He sat behind a table in the store shaking hands and smiling and nodding and signing *"It's all about finesse"* in book after book. And when he was done, when the last in line had gotten his signature, the line for Emeril still snaked endlessly through the store. Emeril himself was on a stage. Keller wanted to shake the guy's hand and say hello, but he couldn't get through the crowd. He penned a greeting on a business card and asked one of Emeril's entourage to give it to the most influential chef ever.

Emeril did not get to this unique position through cooking. A lot of people can cook—Thomas Keller can cook, Ben Barker, Susan Spicer, they can all cook. He got that way through television. But why him? Why not Norman Van Aken, who also taped shows in the early Food Network days, who remembers watching his friend: "I saw *How to Boil Water* the first time, and I just felt so bad for him. You didn't see Emeril at all, he was hunched over the table, you could see the top of his head, it was like we were all wincing."

Emeril, at the time of his launching, was a young man, thirty-four, a respected chef and restaurateur who happened to be in the right place at the right time—or, more exactly, he happened to be *the right kind of person* in the right place at the right time.

The right time was the spring of 1993 and the right place was Nashville, Tennessee. It was here that Emeril stopped midway through a tour promoting his first cookbook, *Emeril's New New Orleans Cooking.* There he was met by a television producer named Allen Reid, who taped him as a guest on a local daily cooking channel. Then Reid taped what he called a ten-minute pilot.

Reid was close friends with a man named Reese Schonfeld. Schonfeld had become well known in television as one of the men responsible for starting CNN with Ted Turner (recounted in his memoir, *Me and Ted Against the World*). Schonfeld was busy at work on a new network, one devoted completely to food, and he was looking for chefs to put on TV in the same way that, in 1980, he was looking for journalists to put on TV (Katie Couric and Bernard Shaw, for example). He asked Reid to be on the lookout, to make some pilots of chefs coming through Nashville who were promising hosts. In July 1993, Reid flew to New York with tapes of the best of those he'd collected: Debbie Fields, Curtis Aiken, Bobby Flay, Norman Van Aken, and Emeril Lagasse.

Schonfeld's office was stacked floor to ceiling with tapes, so Reid and his wife and partner, Mady Land, viewed the tapes along with Schonfeld. He had hoped a chef named Jasper White might host the show they called *How to Boil Water,* but Schonfeld didn't feel he had the screen personality for it. In fact, he didn't see anyone who truly thrilled him. Reid couldn't believe Schonfeld didn't love Emeril. "This guy's terrific," he told Schonfeld. "This guy's a star."

Schonfeld still wasn't sure, but, because he'd promised to give his old friend two shows to produce, and because Reid was so high on Emeril, he said, OK, go with Emeril.

⇥·⇤

Emeril began filming *How to Boil Water* in Reid's Nashville studio soon after—Emeril, Reid, and a couple of cameramen (Emeril used to shout *"Bam!"* to keep the cameramen awake, Emeril says). I've seen clips from some of these early shows. Emeril is stiff and awkward. He's stiff and awkward on the next show too, *Emeril and Friends*. Neither show did well. What on earth had Reid seen in this guy that made him so good?

"What you see now," Reid responded from his offices in New York. Emeril being Emeril, a chef filled with energy and enthusiasm. The Food Network had made a mistake in forcing him into the role of host of a show on how to boil water and cook grilled-cheese sandwiches. Even here, Reid said he was told to tone Emeril down, that Emeril had too much energy, so rein him in. The shows were so lackluster it amazes Reid today that anyone agreed to do a third show with Emeril, but that's what did it. In *The Essence of Emeril,* the New Orleans chef could be himself and cook the food that he loved.

It, along with a handful of other chef-driven shows, did fine. And then better. Ratings began to rise. Emeril continued to commute to New York to do shows at three hundred bucks apiece. He could do seven in a day, a staggering number. Soon his ratings were twice that of any other Food Network show.

With that show succeeding, Emeril said to his producers, he recalls, "Somebody should do a Leno-style food show that was entertaining, that had music—music is certainly a connection that I had in my heart and soul—but it's real cooking. They said 'You're nuts.'"

Now the first thing you have to understand about Emeril to begin to see how he got to be *Emeril* is that the man is a savvy marketer. Or as his buddy, celeb chef and restaurateur Mario Batali, says, "He's not just a good marketing guy, he's an *amazing* marketing guy."

Yes, Emeril was savvy and aggressive in pursuing partners with good companies: All-Clad (pots and pans), Wüsthof (knives), Waterford Wedgwood (glasses and plates), Pride of San Juan (produce), B&G Foods (grocery-store-shelf foods, "shelf-stable" in industry parlance, seventy of them, spices, sauces, et cetera), William Morrow/Harper-

Collins (more than 4 million books sold), New Orleans Fish House (shrimp), Monogram Foods (coffee), Sanita Clogs (kitchen clogs), Sara Lee Foods (sausage). He licenses his name, rents it to them, so they can sell a product that he's involved with, and he takes part of the sales. "The consumer wanted something representing Emeril," he says. "You either give it to him or they're gonna get it somewhere else."

But marketing is more than putting your name on products. Batali's talking about a sensibility.

Here's the perfect example I learned from Alain Joseph, Emeril's culinary assistant and writer, who began as a cook at Emeril's: It was a pretty normal restaurant kitchen, and Emeril was a normal chef, which suprised Alain (he was by then on the Food Network and considered a celebrity). The next thing that surprised Alain was a detail. Big kitchens often have big table-mounted can openers that make the work very quick and easy. This kitchen had none. In fact, this kitchen didn't have any can openers at all. Alain eventually understood that Emeril didn't want them to be seen in the open kitchen by the customer—if the customer sees can openers that means *not fresh;* if they see can openers, that means *the kitchen is opening a lot of cans.* It wasn't that they didn't open any cans (Alain remembers all the cooks had to bring in their own hand-held openers from home in order to open cans), it was the impression they gave to the customer.

That, my friends, is marketing. That describes a chef who is thinking about the detail, thinking about the customer, thinking about the *impression* of appearances. But—that is not the secret element that turned Emeril into *Emeril.*

In 1996, with his show topping the list at Food Network, Emeril, who has for a while wanted to merge the *Tonight Show* format with food and cooking, gets to thinking. Chefs cook in front of live audiences all the time—they just haven't done it on TV before. He's got his second book coming out, *Louisiana Real & Rustic.* He wants it to sell, obviously. He also is aching to put this new "You're nuts" idea into action. But to do that he needed to convince the network it was worth a shot—and even if they did like the idea, they'd still ask him, "What's the show?" Well, now, the show is *Real & Rustic,* based on the cookbook. The show will promote the book. The book will give a theme and reason for the show. With the *Essence* audience growing, the network agreed. And there Emeril hit his trifecta: a way to promote the book to his audience, a good show built around the book, and at last, a live audience in a *Late Show* format in which he'd stride out from backstage à la David Letterman, but instead of tell jokes, he'd cook and talk about food.

In July 1996, the first live audience was ushered into a Manhattan studio. Emeril rushed out in a T-shirt and jeans, and the crowd cheered. Unleashed from the isolation of the private studio, Emeril screamed and began making a chicken clap its drumsticks while whooping himself. This was television history. Maybe not Beatles-on-Ed-Sullivan history, but a small bit of history nonetheless, and a seminal moment in the culinary shaping of America. Cooking as entertainment television had arrived.

Erica Gruen, then president and CEO of the network, was in the control room during the taping, watching the monitors. A chill went up her spine when Emeril appeared—she knew instantly Emeril was on to something. "It was one of those great moments in show business," she recalled later. When it aired in October, it did the unthinkable for the struggling foodie cable network: It registered the company's first Nielsen rating. Within months, they got *Emeril Live* on the air, and it was an instant success that has only increased every year.

❧

Now, here is the bit of information that makes the pieces fit together, in the big-picture puzzle, of seeing how this working-class kid from Fall River, Massachusetts, this energetic and likable young man who had become an experienced chef and successful restaurateur, how and why he became the most influential chef ever. I mean, yes, he's a good cook, food's terrific, restaurants are popular—but you could say the same of countless chefs doing great food in hip rooms across the country. Why this guy?

Part of this piece can be glimpsed in the young chef who'd excelled at Commander's Palace after Brennan's note. He'd begun by managing the kitchen, but by the end, he managed front-of-the-house staff as well, including general managers and sommeliers, 170 people in all, he says. He instituted "management summits"—motivational meetings for his staff—"a Dale Carnegie thing," he calls it. Once he even hired the coach of the New Orleans Saints to pump up the staff. Then he opened his own restaurant but not under the best of circumstances. He did it in a part of town so barren and beat up that no one thought he'd survive. But success was immediate, and he'd never doubted it. His pre-service meetings became famous for their energy and enthusiasm. When he saw that his cooks were lackluster, he'd tell them to put down their knives and follow him—they were going on a jog through the warehouse district. Success was all about attitude.

Receiving that note from Miss Ella, he said, was the second pivotal moment in his career. The first, though, is the key to understanding Emeril's extraordinary appeal to the masses of America: He read a book, *The Magic of Thinking Big,* written in 1959 by David Schwartz. That was it—reading that book was the key pivotal moment of his career, he says. He was in his early twenties, working as a chef for a New England hotel chain, and he read this bestselling motivational book from the 1950s, and it changed his life.

"It was the first thing that made me realize what life was all about," Emeril says today. "That you could look inside yourself and see who you are and knowing who you are, you could see that anything was possible."

He carried it with him in his heart, put it into place in Commander's Palace, and it kept growing from there.

Food is the medium, not the message. The message is: You can do it, too, and have fun. The message is empowerment. In our Internetted, overbusy, disconnected lives, food is a way back to the things that matter, and Emeril can show us the way—*"Oh yeah, babe."* Emeril is the tent-revival preacher, calling his people into the kitchen! He doesn't shout, "Praise the Lord!" He shouts, "Add more garlic!" but the resulting

"Amen!" is the same. You won't see a laying on of hands here, but Emeril does toss food into the audience. He calls ganache what it really is—chocolate sauce—and the people cherish him for it. He's one of them.

Ten million viewers a week, rock star–sized crowds in every city he visits—it ain't because they love his barbecued shrimp. It's because they love his message.

We the people have the power, and Emeril can show us the way. Emeril inspires the masses. You, too, can return to the kitchen, you, too, can cook good food and connect with your family! You, too, can live the good life! You can know yourself. All you have to do is *kick it up a notch.* Through Emeril, anything is possible.

⋟⋞

Ironically, it is exactly at this moment when Emeril begins to inspire a bristling among his colleagues. When he was a chef with a show, that was fine, respectable, good for you. But the moment he moves from chef to entertainer, the moment the throbbing middle classes embrace him, the moment he becomes America's culinary Dale Carnegie, is when his own industry turns on him, reviles him for bad cooking technique, derides him for turning the culinary arts into a circus of late-night talk-show shtick, with costumes, a live band, and jokey banter.

"He seemed to have the same relationship to real cooking as the Brady Bunch did to real families," says Bourdain, trying to explain the response among working chefs. "I genuinely hated—and still hate—the show. . . . And, to be honest, he provided a cheap, quick, and easy laugh, as I knew many—if not most—working chefs felt instinctively as I did."

"It cheapens the industry to me," says a public relations veteran, of Emeril's seminal television show. "It's like *The Price Is Right.*"

Melissa Kelly commented, "[Chefs] have seen him as a little bit too much of a clown. . . . But to a home audience, that captures their attention."

One need watch only a few *Emeril Live* episodes, complete with late show–style repartee with the Emeril Live band and the audience, to understand what chefs saw. In a holiday-themed show recently, I watched Emeril make an eggnog so laden with whipped egg whites that it looked like mashed potatoes. His expression seemed to suggest he knew full well that this was really quite a bit thicker than he'd intended, not something you could really *drink*. He didn't taste it that I saw (what did *that* matter?). He *thwapped* a serving into a mug, leaving a nice peak, offered it to a woman in the audience, and encouraged the woman to respond favorably. Go on, he said, tell 80 million people how good that is! A bald-faced reminder how many might be watching her, an exaggerated figure, but still a dare to give his eggnog a negative review. (Maybe it was me, but I thought I saw a grimace of irony in his expression—he knew exactly what was happening here.) The poor woman took a mouthful and nodded, eyebrows raised, as the show moved into a commercial break.

"I think I do remember that," he said when I asked him about it many months later. "I think there were too many egg whites. See, some of the times what happens, too, the recipe that you do, it doesn't look camera-friendly, so they take it upon themselves to double it or triple it so that it is camera-friendly. And I'm not making any excuses, but I know that that recipe came from *Creole Christmas,* I've been making it for twenty years.

"Everybody's so critical today," he continued. "Nobody criticized Julia for dropping swordfish on the floor and then picking it up, brushing it, and continuing. She wasn't in the media the next day, people going 'Oh my god, what are you doing?' These days you've got the chicken police, the frogs legs police, hamster police, they're coming at you."

No one seems to realize that taste is not the point.

In November 1998, Amanda Hesser, a food reporter for *The New York Times* (now the food editor of the paper's Sunday magazine), wrote a 2,500-word article mercilessly thrashing Emeril. Hesser was particularly ruthless in her description of the food and the cooking, attending the show and critiquing the food as if it were a restaurant's and grading Lagasse's cooking techniques as if she were his skills instructor. She tasted the food and it was bad, "very bad." Some of the recipes in his books are "ghastly," even "suicidal," she wrote. His Essence, a patented spice blend, she calls "a bitter mixture of garlic powder, onion powder, dried thyme, dried oregano, cayenne, sweet paprika, salt and pepper." "A 'panzanella' he made on one recent show looked disturbingly like a heap of food headed for the garbage disposal," she wrote. Emeril, she decided, was "more jester than cook."

She begins the story by quoting a remark that makes him sound like a simpleton, then describes how captivated the audience is by the man. She ends with a report card announcing "bad cooking skills," "mangled tradition," "a façade of accessibility," and "sloppy presentation."

This was more than a surprised and innocent Dorothy witnessing Toto exposing a benevolent Wizard as mere flesh and bones. Hesser spotted a fraud and went out to hunt him down.

I think even Emeril-bashers were surprised by the intensity of her blows—one thing to post it on a blog, another thing entirely to make it permanent in the nation's paper of record. Some chefs, bitter about Emeril's success within the burgeoning foodie rabble of America's heartland, surely rubbed their hands with glee. But Emeril has many friends as well as detractors, so plenty of people were likely pissed off. I asked Bourdain for his recollection of the article and his response to it: "I recall it as an early shot from a heavyweight—on a previously untouched sacred cow. Over the top? Mean-spirited? Sure. But not entirely undeserved. . . . I kinda admired [Hesser] for the piece—however mean it was. Took balls."

Hesser's something of a lightning rod for charged opinions, and the article, I understand, generated a lot of angry mail—to the point where Hesser may well have been unnerved by it. It remains her most notorious piece. That's a rare thing, a newspaper article several years old that's well remembered and still discussed. I don't know how she feels about it—when I reached her by e-mail to ask, she said she preferred to let the article speak for itself and declined to comment.

What really dismayed Hesser, it seems to me, and to so many others in the cooking profession, and what still dismays people in the industry, perhaps, is not the fact that the guy's cooking technique can be spotty. (I haven't met a single chef who didn't have a blind spot. Lagasse got a show in the first place because he ran very good restaurants and was an excellent restaurant cook, a fact no one disputes.) It was rather the fact that Lagasse wasn't any better or any worse than any one of the growing legion of young chefs, yet he had become the most influential chef in America.

On another level, the disdain for Emeril is the pundits' knee-jerk response to the tastes of the middle class. Some intellectuals and cultural critics have long made a business of deriding the tastes of the masses. But instead of being mean in the very permanent format of *The New York Times*—Hesser is a great writer, but I really wanted to ask her if she regretted her harshness—she might instead have turned the opportunity into an analysis of why TV cooking and restaurant cooking are different species altogether, apples and oranges. Ask most chefs today their opinion of Emeril, nine out of ten will say they don't agree with his cooking techniques or like the jokey style of the show, but that his impact on this country from a culinary standpoint is huge and undeniable. If they've met him, they'll usually tell you what a nice guy he is in person. He has popularized cooking on an unprecedented scale. He's lured people into the kitchen, he's gotten them cooking, and that, chefs believe, no matter how you look at it, is a good thing for America. Few seem to begrudge him anymore—he's too embedded in our culture.

"Just because we may not agree with the way he delivers his information, therefore it's not good?" says Thomas Keller. "The delivery he's using is one that relates to a large group of people. So am I going to be a snob and say, that's not a good thing? No, I'm going to be a realist and say it's a great thing, because at the end of the day, people are starting to learn about food at a higher level than I ever did when I was a kid."

Even Bourdain has been softened by Lagasse's magnanimity toward him, and displayed a glimpse of wisdom and perspective, amazing as that may sound. I e-mailed Bourdain, who happened to be in Kuala Lumpur for his own television show *Anthony Bourdain: No Reservations*—I be-

lieve he said he was preparing to go blowgun hunting with the natives—
and he responded with an unusually long explanation that verges almost
on apology:

After years of book tours, interviews and television, it's become more
difficult to separate myself from what Emeril does. Or to take a superior attitude. Of course, all along, chefs who I respected like Eric Ripert
and Norman Van Aken would take me aside and say, "You know, actually, he's not such a bad guy. He's really nice." And in my time on the
road—I met a number of chefs and cooks who work for—or worked
for—Emeril—and had nothing but nice things to say about him—and
about their experiences. I began to examine, I guess, myself—and the
fact that Emeril had—like me—worked his way up from lowly positions in Massachusetts eateries. That he'd in fact, accomplished far, far
more than I ever had—as a chef and restaurateur (the TV thing aside)—
and that was worthy of a lot more respect than I'd acknowledged. I was
tired of making cracks about the guy as well—as people seemed to
expect it—and I—to a less and less degree—found myself not really
having the stomach for it. Beating up on Emeril regularly seemed just
as bad as having a catchphrase like BAM. And as Food Network became populated by more and more dipshit "personalities" with no professional cooking experience or ability whatsoever, Emeril began to
look increasingly like Escoffier by comparison.

Next to final straw was meeting the guy at Eric Ripert's birthday
party. He shook hands, showed enormous good grace—and a sense of
humor about all the mean shit I'd been saying. You have to like a guy
who can take a ball busting.

Last straw was he fed me and Mario at his Miami store—again showing tremendous generosity of spirit. His wife joined us—a tough, funny
lady with strong opinions—who I also immediately liked. And the food
wasn't bad. Frankly, I don't know how he does it. I'm beginning to respect him simply for his endurance as a public figure. It's an impressive
empire he's built. And the fact that after all these years he's still crap on

TV—still unpolished, awkward, his diction awful, posture terrible . . . I'm beginning—in a perverse but admiring way—to respect that too.

❧•❧

At the after party celebrating fifteen hundred shows, Kenneth Lowe, CEO and president of the E.W. Scripps Company, which owns the Food Network, said it bluntly to the crowd of staff and crew: "Without Emeril, there would be no Food Network."

Emeril combined cooking with fun and not only changed the face of food television but helped to shape the culinary landscape in America, educating and entertaining millions and luring countless people, most notably men, into the kitchen.

❧•❧

"OK, guys, rolling tape," says Jen Messina, stage manager for *30-Minute Meals* with Rachael Ray. Two handheld cameras and two jib cameras are trained on Ray, who stands behind a peanut-shaped island in what appears to be an everywhere suburban kitchen, ready to begin her cold open, the intro to the show. "Let's go, eight, seven, six, five, four, three." Jen raises two fingers in the air, then one. Mark Dissin, the show's executive producer, says, "Cue" from the control room, delivered to Ray's earpiece.

"Hi there. I'm Rachael Ray and I make thirty minute meals." She halts and says, "I'm sorry, I've got to start again. I've got a real tickle." Ray presses fingers to her throat and asks if anyone has some water. No one responds. "I'll take anybody's water—I don't have cooties," she calls out to the open black space beyond the set. Lesli Baker, her hair and makeup stylist, comes through with some water, and Ray's again off after that rare stutter into the production of the first of four shows she'll tape today, one of thirty-nine shows over the course of twelve days of shooting, the last of which is a double, an hour-long Thanksgiving special. The show is, says Dissin, "a business-school model"—very low cost, very efficient to shoot, and incredibly popular. Indeed, it's the most watched show on the network, averaging about 750,000 viewers for her six P.M.–weekdays show.

Her other show is also geared toward the typical Food Network fan, a travel series called *$40 a Day,* and she had already begun taping a third, *Inside Dish with Rachael Ray,* which combines travel and celebrity as she ventures inside the homes and kitchens of movie and television actors. By the following summer, the network announced a new talk show called *Day to Day with Rachael Ray,* featuring, according to the network, "food and fashion, fitness, and lifestyle, plus amazing special guests with expert advice."

The week I'd arrived to watch the production of her show, an article in the *Los Angeles Times* about the growing popularity of cooking shows led with the suggestion that Ray had become one of the highest-paid cookbook authors in the country as she'd signed "a multimillion-dollar, multibook deal that is one of the largest in cookbook history." Judging from the line of fans in Cleveland alone, that doesn't surprise me.

She and the network have begun partnering with the companies whose products she uses. Evidently, people who want to cook like Rachael will buy Rachael-endorsed knives, so there can be no excuse why you, too, can't make a decent meal in thirty minutes—just go to the Food Network Web site and click the SHOP BY HOST tab.

And the following spring, *Reader's Digest* would announce its partnership with Ray to produce a magazine called *Every Day with Rachael Ray.* If there is a potential personality to eclipse Martha Stewart and her Omnimedia company, it's undoubtedly the thirtysomething gal from Albany. She surpassed Emeril in ratings. With a few aggressive business moves, she could conceivably dethrone queen Martha.

But for now, she's muscling through this four-shows-a-day grind. It's exactly this kind of television that gave her such power in the first place—and the resultant money generated through media and licensing, not to mention the substantial salary for the show itself. All good reasons why scads of culinary students have their sights set on television.

Hi there. I'm Rachael Ray and I make thirty-minute meals. Look how easy that is!

⟨⟩

Born in 1968, Ray is invariably described as "perky" by journalists who don't want to be snotty about her unstoppable, air-filling giggles and unfaltering gift of gab. What they don't say is that she is actually more beautiful in person than she is on television. She has oversized features, large deep brown eyes, brunette hair that seems never to have had a bad day, a huge mouth and dazzling teeth that might seem a caricature on anyone with a smaller personality. But television's effects tone that dazzle down so that on screen Ray comes across as simply pretty, the unintimidating girl-next-door figure. When I saw a "normal" person on the network recently—Bob Tuschman, on *The Next Food Network Star*—he seemed positively dweeby. That couldn't possibly be the same guy I'd met when I'd visited the studio several months earlier. When Tuschman appears next to Gordon Elliott, a fellow judge on that show, himself an accomplished host with a big frame, distinguished air, and commanding voice, the reducing effect of television became vivid. You've got to have bigness, whether in personality or in looks, to be effective on TV. You don't have to be beautiful (look at Charles Kuralt!), only big.

Ray has both forms of big, and in addition to an easy manner in front of the camera and a message of empowerment not dissimilar to Emeril's, she has captured an enormous audience.

Today that bigness is presenting what Rachael calls a "meatza," a dish that uses a corn bread–muffin mix to make the pizzalike crust and a chili taco–style ground-beef concoction to go on top. The idea for this show is not just a normal-quick meal, but a superfast normal-quick meal, for when you're really busy, when thirty minutes is too much to ask.

After Ray has the corn bread in the oven and the ground beef browning, Jen says, "Good, we're out! Good act two," and Rachael thanks the crew, as the core team converges on the peanut island to discuss actions and topics of the third of four acts. Mark Dissin and director Michael

Schear traverse the catwalk and descend the stairs from the control room. Dissin is impressive to me because he left television in 1995 at age forty to pursue a culinary education at the French Culinary Institute. He graduated in six months, then worked the line at Follonico, a small Tuscan restaurant in the Flatiron District for more than a year, and then was part of the launch of Eleven Madison Park. He then freelanced for the Food Network, was ultimately hired, and was soon after promoted to VP of Production. I admired people in the food media who had a bona fide culinary education and had done actual time on the hot line—I knew that it gave them a credibility and perspective that other food-media types lacked. Dissin, tall and lanky in jeans and fashionably untucked shirt, balding head shaved close, brings a laconic ease to the ensemble here.

Emily Rieger, the culinary producer, graduated from the CIA in 1991 and was for years a cook and chef before being hired by the network, after a series of part-time jobs in the network kitchen. She takes a seat at the island, and Andrea Steinberg, the "culinary stylist," the woman in the chef's coat, a Johnson & Wales graduate (like Emeril) in charge of off-camera cooking for the show, lowers the heat on the ground beef and gives it a stir. Emily begins a run-through of act three.

"We'll come back," she says, "and Rachael will be messing with the ground beef, then she'll go to the pantry"—typically Ray acts out what Emily describes as she's saying it, taking big, slow, exaggerated steps to the pantry, to the fridge, repeating the ingredients aloud—"get the chili and ground cumin . . ."

Ray says, "Spice up the meat. . . ."

Emily continues, "Go back to the fridge . . ."

Meanwhile, Dissin is looking at the ground beef, which is only half-cooked. He wants all the pink out of it when they start the third act, he says, so Andrea turns up the heat.

When Emily and Rachael have moved through all the steps of the act, every action and every ingredient, Dissin and Schear return to the control room, and Dissin runs through "traffic" with the guys up there—where all the music, graphics, and video are originating from, alerting the various technicians. During the show he'll watch each moment carefully, directing when the graphics should appear and staying in touch with Ray—*Stir the pasta,* he'll instruct her as she's about to go to break, or, *Don't forget the nutmeg.* And a moment later, on cue, Ray dips down to retrieve the spices—*Whoops, almost forgot the nutmeg and cinnamon for the baked apples, but I can add them now and they'll melt down with the sugar.* Perfectly seamless, efficient. Once when she tasted a soup that was so hot Dissin could hear her tongue sizzle, Ray heard his sympathetic "*Ooooh*" in her ear. She smiles through it all—cut hand, burned tongue—she almost never stops.

Emily and Rachael continue talking as Dissin and Schear get ready in the control room. There seems to be some concern with the fact that this meal is so easy, she has a lot of time to talk. "No one can suck wind like me," she says. "Chatty Cathy comes to town. Oh! I can explain how this can be vegetarian, that's good!"

"Didn't you say this was a good college kids' meal?" Emily asks.

"No, good dorm-room meal. You can use both your pots." Sometimes Ray will speak as if answering an invisible questioner—but it's actually Dissin in the control room talking into her earpiece and watching her on a screen. "Emily, you know what I'm going to do? I'm going to taste the meat for seasoning!"

"You're the smartest person in this room," Emily deadpans.

By the end of this act, which in the control room is an intense flurry of Schear's "ready camera two . . . camera two, ready camera one . . . camera one," Ray is already chopping the cilantro.

"I'm sorry I started chopping the cilantro," she says to the approaching Emily. "There was truly nothing else to do."

In fact, she's completely finished, she did her whole meal in three acts instead of four—what will they do with the fourth? They stand around the island talking. Andrea, the chef here, suggests a mango sorbet. But Ray says, "Oh, my mom used to make Mexican ice cream sundaes—coffee ice cream, chocolate sauce, and Mexican salted peanuts. We've got all that." Mark and Emily confer and there's their dessert. "My mom will be so happy," Ray says. "We could put whipped cream and a little cinnamon. That will be *awesome*."

Dissin and Schear head back to the control room while the new ingredients and serving dish are brought onto the set. Andrea checks the progress of the meatza, finishing in the oven. Ray sees it, "*Mmm*, doesn't that look good!" and picks a tomato chunk from the top to taste.

She goes back to the island, observes the sundae dish, looks into the air, and says, "Mark, this is going to be friggin' gorgeous."

They open on the fourth act cold, meaning there's no graphic opener, just a brief snippet of her music. She gets her cue, moves through the very short act, little more than two minutes, serving up and reviewing the meal, concluding with "I got a minute left, so let me show you a quick dessert." She serves and presents the Mexican sundae in less than sixty seconds, then concludes with "This is quicker than calling the pizza man!" and her signature sign off: "Remember, a great meal is never more than thirty minutes away."

The entire show has been filmed in one hour, an especially quick one. While Andrea and her assistants clean up and wipe down, Dissin discusses the show in the control room, instructs any editing fixes to be done in a nearby room, and the finished show is on tape and ready to air before they begin the next show.

⁂

It's true—Ray really can do these meals in thirty minutes. When she first started demonstrating them in grocery stores, people would actually bring a stopwatch. For the show, the biggest food hurdle is the fact that they have to slow the cooking down. During another show, after the second act, having begun to sauté her nut-crusted chicken breasts, she'd had to say to Andrea, "Drea, I totally scorched these nuts, I'm sorry. I turned it up really high to get the Hollywood sizzle and I burned the nuts." Andrea nods and takes the burned ones away and heads to the spacious network kitchen to cook some more. This, too, is relatively rare. Virtually all the dishes on the show appear pretty much as Ray cooks them in her suburban-deco kitchen set. The chicken breasts are just a little bit burned, not inedible, but she wants to present food that's friendly, "not something that's going to make them cry," she says.

"But you got the Hollywood sizzle," Emily says, taking a seat at the island to block out the third act.

"See, that's what's hard about this, we had to stop the cooking," Ray tells me. "Other shows they have to swap out. We have to slow things down. These really are thirty-minute meals."

On other occasions the group around the yellow peanut island discusses various talking points—how to describe the flavor of dill, for instance, or how to deal with the anchovies she puts in her osso buco soup, which much of her core audience may be afraid of. (During discussion she says: "You can leave the anchovies out, but you'd be a dumb ass to do that." On the show she says, "You can omit the anchovies if you don't groove on anchovies.") And Dissin will wonder about how the soup, which uses veal meatballs, will look cooking. "Won't the meatballs release scum?" he asks. "No, they don't," Ray responds. "I've made this a lot. John loves this soup." John Cusimano, then her fiancé; they married the following fall.

And this is all there is to it—the biggest hit on the Food Network. Osso Buco Soup, a Meatza with Corn Bread–Mix Crust, a Mexican Sundae—the foundation of a dynasty in the making—shows, books, licensing deals, magazines.

❧

Just as, in Flay's words, Emeril "didn't just happen," neither did Ray. She grew up on Cape Cod, where her family owned a restaurant. In the late 1970s, the gas crisis cut into business enough for the family to move to upstate New York, and her mom, first-generation American-born of Sicilian parents, separated from her husband. Her mom from then on worked in restaurants, as did Ray. Ray makes a big point of the fact that she's not a chef—which is true, but she has cooked in restaurants, in addition to washing dishes, waiting tables, and tending bar.

She worked for a short time in food retail in Manhattan but ultimately returned upstate, where she got a job as a food buyer for a gourmet market in Albany called Cowan & Lobel. As this was the state capital, many of the customers were state employees and working several jobs, she says. But they weren't buying the specialty ingredients she was purchasing for the store. So she ventured into the aisles to talk to the customers to find out why they weren't buying her food. "They said they never learned to cook and they had no time," she discovered.

When Christmastime rolled around, Ray, clearly a savvy marketer, like Lagasse, came up with an idea to sell cooking classes. People were interested in learning to cook, and she needed them to learn how to use the food so they'd buy it. She sold four classes and called them "30-Minute Mediterranean Meals," because people were buying Italian products. Next, she went around to local chefs and asked them to teach these classes. They wanted to charge her so much money that she wouldn't even break even, so she said, "Screw it, I'll just teach it myself."

The first classes were three hours long. She taught six base recipes and gave five variations on each. "So you got one recipe pack," Ray says, "and we made six things in class, so you'd know how to make thirty different things. So then you really had no excuse not to be cooking."

The classes became so popular that she had to start offering more. There were twenty-five to a class. Everyone would bring an apron and a sharp knife, and she'd start with the basics—how to hold that knife. Football teams, Girl Scout troops, seniors—all signed up. When a local television station wanted to do a story on Cowan & Lobel's bestselling item, the manager said, "The cooking classes." So that's what was featured. The news director loved the segment and asked Ray to do a weekly thirty-minute-meals piece for him.

Ray told him, "I think I gotta pass on that one. I'm not really a TV kind of person." The director said, "Oh no, trust me. You are."

They began airing every Thursday night and soon became more popular than the weather segment. The audience began to write to Ray, complaining that they couldn't keep track of all the recipes—would she please publish them in a book. She thought that was a good idea, took her stack of notes and recipes and computer printouts to a small publisher whose name she got from her dad, who'd been in publishing, and "begged myself into her office."

After three hours with the small, skeptical publisher, Hiroko Kiiffner, at Lake Isle Press, she left with a book deal.

Ray knew she could sell the books at her classes, and she did demos at a local grocery-store chain. They agreed to let her hawk her books in-store. "We sold three thousand books in four days, and ten thousand books before Christmas," Ray explained.

Those numbers would be low but not unrespectable for any cookbook by a relative unknown over the course of a *year,* but to sell like that, in only a local market, and do so so quickly, is significant. So was the royalty check: $17,000. "I thought it was like all the money in the free world," Ray recalls. "My mother and I, we didn't even cash it right away, we just stared at it." She made seventy grand off that book that first year, 1999, and she thought to herself, *Shit, man, this is something.*

Meanwhile, she continued to teach her classes and tape her local news segments. A new news director at the station loved her show and asked what else she could do. "Well," she said, "I'm poor and I eat well. And I happen to travel really well, too." She offered a travel segment in which she'd do any kind of recreation or vacation if it was within one hundred miles and cost less than one hundred dollars. She was now beginning to understand how TV worked, how to write for it, how to edit tapes and use the equipment.

She did another book, *Comfort Foods,* continued giving her classes, teaching at grocery stores, and doing her news segments (they'd finally started paying her: a hundred bucks a segment). When the *Today* show called, she thought it was joke, a prank by friends in the city. She called the number; an NBC receptionist answered and Ray slammed the phone down. Al Roker, she would soon learn, had gotten a copy of her book and wanted her on the show.

At about the same time, a friend of hers, Joe Donahue, who hosted a call-in talk show called *Vox Pop* on public radio, contacted her, explaining that he'd had a cancellation and begging her to come on the show to do a thirty-minute meal. Ray said, "It's radio, dude." He said, "We'll talk about what you're doing, just bring a hot plate and make me lunch, *please.*"

She agreed. That day, a man named Lou Ekus, a chef media trainer, was lecturing at the CIA in the Hudson Valley and heard the WAMC program. Ekus called his friend Bob Tuschman, a producer at the Food Network. Tuschman called Ray's publisher. Kiiffner was delighted to be able to say to Tuschman, according to Ray, "If you want to see what she looks like on TV, she'll be on the *Today* show on Monday." He watched the segment and invited her up for a meeting with network executives.

Ray recalls, "The first thing I said when I went to that meeting was 'I don't belong here. I'm not a chef, I can't wear a chef coat, I won't tell people I'm a chef, I don't know how to do fancy stuff. I don't belong here.'"

They said, she recalls, "'Let us be the judge. We don't care that you're not a chef, that's kind of what we like.'

"I left that meeting with two television shows," Ray says. They were simply half-hour versions of what she'd already been doing for a couple years now, her thirty-minute-meal segments and her travel segment, which would become the *$40 a Day* show. (She's never watched her *Today* show segment—she thinks she'd throw up from residual nerves.)

"I'm a very lucky girl," she says, sitting in her dressing room during lunch. She'd agreed to chat, rather than do her usual lunchtime thing—pedicures, shopping, "girl stuff," she explains. "The fact that you can get paid to chat and make food amazes me." Of her success and the speed of it (the first show aired in 2001), she says, "It's mind-boggling to me.

"I can't believe the Food Network was brave enough to do it," she continues. "Because I clearly don't know what I'm doing half the time. I cook the way real people cook. I make mistakes, my things don't look as pretty as fancy chefs', and I'm out there in street clothes. . . . They let me do my own thing—they didn't try to gussy me up, and I think that's what people responded to. Not necessarily me, but the fact that they could see themselves in the show. There was nothing there to distance them.

"You watch a show done by someone in a chef coat, you have a different perspective," she says. She used to watch Julia Child and Graham Kerr as a kid. "When I think about it now it's like, 'That's why, it's because they wore regular clothes.' They're telling funny stories. Julia would stick her finger in the pot, she'd drink wine, she'd throw in a handful of salt, not measure. Normal clothing, she wasn't in a fancy coat. Graham Kerr—same thing, cracking jokes, making food that appealed to all your senses, and there was nothing there to put you off. I watch a lot of cooking shows. Emeril, he kind of overcomes the coat thing because he's got such a big, wonderful personality." (Conversely, she points to Martha Stewart: "She was always dressed in street clothes, and yet I never thought I could do anything that she did.")

"But a lot of times," she continued, "I'd watch those [chef] shows and it was more like a kid looking through a candy-shop window. I just wanted to look at them because they were pretty and made pretty things. But I never thought I could do those things. I just thought, *Oh that's lovely and fancy but who has time for that crap,* ya know?

"I grew up in the hospitality industry and I consider that I'm still in it," she continues. "We're very customer-oriented on these shows—what makes a viewer feel good about themselves, not what makes a viewer feel good about me, or how good I can be at whatever. . . . We're there to make people at home feel good about themselves.

"People are excited to tell me about themselves, not to tell me what they think about me, and that to me means I'm doing my job correctly. I have been a waitress, a bartender, a grocery-store person. I am a hospitality person. My job is to make other people feel good, to give other people what they want and what they need. And I'm doing the exact same thing here. I'm just doing it for a lot more people."

❧❧

"At most, I think you tend to get one or two celebrity chefs a generation at most," says Schear, who also directs *Emeril Live*.

This will be a disappointment to the legions who see their future on the tube, at least if they had the dreams of multimillion-dollar book contracts. There does seem to be plenty of room, though, for new talent as hours of food programming continue to go up (for people I should say who truly want to do television because they love to do television rather than because it's a means to fame and riches). What is it, then, that makes Rachael so popular? While her ratings are tops at the network—which makes no bones about trying to appeal to the broadest base of consumers—her television personality is widely loathed by those in the foodie community, who see the Rachael Ray phenomenon as representing a dumbing down of food television.

To pick a random comment from the foodie Web site eGullet.org, filled with Rachael and Emeril animosity: "I first thought Ms. Ray was annoying," writes one eGulleter, "then I watched her show ('30 Minute Meals') a couple more times. Now I'm positive she's annoying. Her show is like a train wreck waiting to happen. I anxiously await the day she drops her mise en place after haphazardly piling it up in her arms."

Those less harsh critics see Ray as an emblem of pandering to the marketplace as opposed to an example of truly excellent food television (whatever that might be)—again, this comes from the pundits' camp, the same ones who love to deride Emeril. I have to confess that I'm in this camp to some degree. I can't watch Ray's shows without grinding my teeth. I feel as though she's talking to me as if I were an especially dim-witted and clueless four-year-old—and I kind of resent that. Does she really want me to believe that she's actually like this in real life? (In fact, she's pretty close! Replace half the sugar with lime juice and stir.)

But part of the strength of my reaction is that I do feel she's talking directly to me, which of course is the source of her enormous power, whether you like her or not.

"I totally come from a snobby food background," says Emily, the show's culinary producer, "and it all of a sudden dawned on me when we started to do the show, there's just so much good from this show. . . . It touches people's lives. It puts them at home so they spend more time together. There's a sense of pride when you make a meal for people you love. And I think she has a way of doing that, of creating meals that are fun, flavors people can wrap their heads around, and really enjoy and actually make."

Emily notes that Ray does food everybody can use—she doesn't use any food that you can't find in the supermarket. "That's really important."

During one of the powwows between acts at the peanut island, Rachael was making a bid for using fresh bay leaves. Emily didn't think they were easily available and told Rachael she needed to be cognizant of the people.

"I'm cognizant of the people," she responded, miffed. "I *am* the people. And I can get fresh bay leaves." Ray's basic rule is if she can get it in Glen Falls, four hours north of the city where she was born and where she lives with her cat and her pit bull, it's fair game.

Ray is very good at coming up with recipes, says Dissin, and she's easy to work with. "We understand the brand," he says, "and she understands the brand. And whenever she goes off brand, it's easy to pull her back. She's very good at deconstructing food to fit her brand."

"What's off brand?" I ask.

"Truffle oil," he says. "Every now and then truffle oil sneaks in there."

He's produced hundreds of these shows. They are now doing about one hundred twenty *30-Minute Meals* a year. "I can write six hundred recipes a year and not break a sweat," Ray says. "I've gotten to the point where I can virtual cook. In my head, playing with food."

❧

We, the audience, see none of this. We see only how easy it looks—*Hi there. I'm Rachael Ray and I make thirty-minute meals.* But talk to Schear and Dissin, guys who work on numerous shows, and they shake their heads at how good she is, how easy she makes their work. Sometimes she screws something up—sure. Burning toast is her Achilles' heel, says one technician. Then they'll have to stop shooting, redo the toast, and Ray will have to perform what's called a live pickup, start filming exactly where she'd been moments before discovering the error. To conclude the first act of one such show, she said, "I'm going to check my toast, which I hope I didn't burn." She opened the broiler of the 1950s-era Chambers range and said, "Which I did." And she shook her head with a smile of hilarity but didn't stop the act. Instead, she said, "I'm gonna get cracking my eggs and cutting some more slices of toast!"

In the control room, producer Mark Dissin sighs. They watched the tape again and he said, "It's kind of cute. But I don't know if you want to have your host burning toast."

So in the finished show, you now hear her say, ". . . which I hope I didn't burn," followed by her opening the broiler to behold . . . *perfect toast!* Ray picked it up live and finished the final minute of that act.

"That pickup," Dissin says, "of three-hundred-odd shows"—1,200 acts—"that happens maybe fifty times. She is flawless at the live pickup."

The girl with the giggle is a pro, an artisan in her own right, and part of that craft is making the hard stuff look easy.

"It's easy to watch," says Schear. "It's *got* to be easy to watch because it's too easily turned off. . . . . It's really hard to do."

Ease is an illusion. Same with four-star service at a great restaurant—you don't even notice it. No one sees the manipulation—that's the magic.

That's television. And I suppose it should be no surprise, then, that the professional chef, for a time the reigning figure in ratings at the Food Network, has now been eclipsed by the self-taught home-style cook. The television chef may be fading away as we return to the origins of food television and the personalities of James Beard and Julia Child.

PART FIVE

❧

The Chefs at 10 Columbus Circle

CHAPTER I

⋖∙⋗

Per Se

The night I happened into Per Se, November 18, 2004, to find not a finely tuned machine in action but a chaos of media and strangers and an executive chef who'd lost his shoes, was to me to be a kind of peak in my experience of reporting from within the restaurant kitchen, an uneasy awkward apex in the life of the chef. The lost-shoes business seemed the perfect metaphor for the changing role of the chef, and for the chef who didn't quite know who he was supposed to be anymore.

But the literal fact of the shoes, too, was surprising. How do you lose your shoes when they never leave the place? How does Thomas Keller lose his shoes? The Per Se kitchen and offices were big but not that big. The kitchen is cleaned thoroughly, continually, throughout the day. A pair of kitchen clogs on the floor would be equally noticeable in the small administrative warren. Certainly Keller's clogs (occasionally cryovacked as a joke), which would have an almost talismanic effect among the staff, would be noticed.

Clearly this was not what Keller had expected in January 2000 when he handed Adam Block the prospectus for the Time Warner property. There appeared to be little finesse in this. Keller seeks refinement and

271

luxury, not the entertainment of a carnival midway. And yet that's what it felt like on the night of the *60 Minutes Wednesday* shoot in his massively expensive, meticulously planned, and carefully built kitchen. The network news show had homed in on the man Bourdain called, with customary frankness, "the chef many consider the best and most respected in the world."

And look where he was? The best and most respected in the world was in a Manhattan mall derided by urbanists as an ominous encroachment of evil suburbia on the great metropolis. Foodies in particular lamented the fact of what might be one of America's great restaurants bunched in with a Borders, a grocery store, a hotel, and a dozen boutiques. Four stories off the ground, no less. Keller couldn't find his shoes, there was madness in his kitchen, and he was in the heart of an enormous mall in New York City, like Kurtz in the Darkness.

The order of this world, the world of professional cooking, was changing, but for better or for worse? Was this progress or the point at which the velocity of The Chef, this cultural juggernaut, becomes too great to maintain—it wobbles, and it's moving too fast to right itself, then spins out of control, flames out, and crashes to the ground?

Certainly November 18 provided a handy moment for a writer prone to metaphor. The moment was true but, of course, it was *momentary*. The night ended, the dining-room tables were cleared, the kitchen cleaned, the lights extinguished, and the next day would begin as every day begins, with the first of the brigade and bakers arriving at dawn, followed at midmorning by chefs (who would work the line and run the pass till after midnight), followed by the team of young men and women in T-shirts and black trousers who would buff the glasses, fold the napkins, then transform themselves into the evening servers. And the steady, heads-down ethos of the watchmaker's shop would return. It had been a crazy night, that's all, in a business that has more crazy nights than could possibly be recorded.

If it was more momentary than metaphor, then, what to make of *this*:

Long after that night, with the restaurant returned to its daily example of elegance and finesse, in the spring of 2005, in fact, the day after Per Se won the James Beard award for the country's Best New Restaurant, I arranged for a few minutes with Keller to find out how he was and where he was in this fascinating evolution that I'd been invited seven years ago to watch. He sat on the corner couch facing the small bar of Per Se, dressed in a white dress shirt and black jacket, late morning, having just spent a half hour reviewing some new plates and saucers to be purchased for the Bouchons.

"It's something that I've just realized recently," he said of Per Se and where he was. "I only need to do things once. I don't need to do things twice. I didn't need to do this." The lives of a hundred employees, the media, the labor on the part of countless people, his own workhorse input included, and many millions of dollars—he didn't need to do it.

"I'm not a chef anymore," he said moments later. "And it breaks my heart."

❧

In 2001, just after the New Year, Keller had lunch with Adam Block, the business adviser on contracts and financial issues within the restaurant industry who counts dozens of celebrity chefs as his clients. Block is one of a small circle of advisers Keller relies on for business decisions. He is five-eight, fit, handsome, with a narrow face, sharp features, and frizzy hair cut short and neat with prominent sideburns. His confident manner, dapper attire, aggressive posture, and energetic intensity always made me think of him as a professional baseball player off season, though, at the age of forty, he'd been in the restaurant business his whole professional life. Because the French Laundry was closed for its annual two-week winter break, Keller and Block enjoyed a long casual lunch at Bistro Jeanty in Yountville, which allowed Keller to reflect on where he was and where he and his growing business ought to be headed. The first Bouchon was currently being built and would open later in the year. If that proved successful, then they'd move on their intent to open others. There were plans to build a bakery next to it, and he had hopes of opening a Relais & Châteaux–caliber inn across the street from the French Laundry, to accommodate guests of the restaurant in the manner of some of the European Michelin three-stars, such as Georges Blanc and Michel Bras.

At the moment, though, he was still a chef with one restaurant and one coffee-table cookbook.

And he was *itching* to open another fine-dining restaurant. He'd been frustrated that he'd found no acceptable venues where he might make that happen. He wasn't sure what he wanted to do, but he knew he didn't want to be an André Soltner or a Frédy Giradet, famous chefs synonymous with their solo restaurant, who more or less faded away once they left their kitchens, as a chef inevitably must. He'd seen a number of properties and considered several offers, but no place enticed him. He'd looked as far as Tokyo. Nothing was good enough. He wondered aloud that day whether or not he'd ever find another place.

"Am I being unrealistic?" he asked Block.

Block replied, "Thomas, you shouldn't have to sacrifice. You shouldn't think that, in order to diversify, you have to lower your standards."

They settled the bill and strolled up Washington Street toward the French Laundry. As they were passing the building that would become Bouchon, Keller handed Block a brochure for a major new construction in Manhattan called the AOL Time Warner Center. It had been sent to him by Ken Himmel, the CEO of Related Urban Development, the company managing it and filling it, and the man in charge of all Related's mixed-use developments. The $1.7 billion double-barreled skyscraper would include several levels of retail space, a Mandarin Oriental Hotel, a performing-arts complex for Jazz at Lincoln Center, a Whole Foods Market, and condos. Its fourth level would house restaurants.

Block nodded. He knew about the project already. He'd been asked to consider it for another of his clients, Gray Kunz, and immediately said, "Fourth floor? Forget it." Himmel spoke carefully to Block, urging him not to dismiss it. Not an easy sell, to say the least. Not even easy to avoid having it dismissed out of hand. It was common knowledge that to open a Manhattan restaurant that didn't have immediate street access was crazy. New Yorkers wanted to be able to walk into and out of a restaurant in a snap. They needed the immediacy of the street. A long walk through hushed corridors to the silent interior of a hotel restaurant made people here uncomfortable—they simply wouldn't go. In the case of the Time Warner Center, the restaurants would be several floors above street level in what amounted to a mall. You couldn't walk right in; you'd need to take escalators. Furthermore, Himmel was wooing chain restaurants, such as Houston's, to fill the space, which would further diminish the cachet of the fine-dining restaurants Block trafficked in.

But—Thomas *Keller's* entering this project . . . now this was something different. Adam Block has a shrewd imagination. He didn't dismiss it out of hand. He did imagine it. Thomas Keller's moving in was different from Gray Kunz's moving in. Kunz, a European chef raised in Singapore who was heavily influenced by his work in the Far East, had last led Lespinasse to four *New York Times* stars but hadn't been in the kitchen for several years. He was a New York chef, considered to be among the best, but mostly locally familiar—news, but not big news.

A dozen chefs in America could reasonably lay claim to best chef in the country on any given night, and Kunz was in that echelon along with Keller. But Keller was different from the others, different from Daniel Boulud and Jean-Georges Vongerichten, Frenchmen who had created their own four-star Manhattan temples, different from Alain Ducasse, the Michelin three-star phenomenon who'd opened a controversial restaurant in the Essex Hotel (at the time the most expensive, and many said, the most pretentious, restaurant in New York; it had been mercilessly lambasted in the press). Keller was an American, but he somehow enjoyed the mystique typically given to the Michelin three-star chefs. Indeed, it had been Michel Richard, another Frenchman with a big reputation working in the United States, who told me, in a whisper that mixed respect with astonishment, "Thomas Keller is the best *French* chef in America."

There were others, Charlie Trotter, the Chicago perfectionist, and

Patrick O'Connell, of the Inn at Little Washington, Americans who had created restaurants of great quality and refinement on the level of the French Laundry. But there was something about Keller. Somehow, for reasons that weren't identifiable, he'd remained in a league of his own. Why, for instance, had Keller's cookbook sold hundreds of thousands of copies, more than any single book by any of these other chefs? Adam Block didn't need to know the answer to recognize that Thomas Keller's world-renown would lure the New York crowd at least once, that his return to Manhattan would be an event large enough to generate a big media interest. He saw too that traffic through the Time Warner Center and the affluent clientele of the Mandarin Oriental Hotel and those purchasing the expensive condos would ensure the critical mass of people, if it were done right, to make a success of a wannabe-four-star in the toughest, most competitive, most media-snarky city in the world. And Keller was clearly ready to make a move. If Block could work out the right kind of deal with the Related Companies, it just might work. He knew that to have Thomas Keller on board in the Time Warner Center would be an amazing coup that would alter the shape of the center itself.

Thomas Keller's mystique was based on integrity and excellence—and that integrity and excellence, Block knew, was so pronounced and distinctive that it had become the Thomas Keller *brand*. If the Related Companies wanted that brand badly enough, saw the power of that brand, Block could engineer a sweetheart deal, enough to make the colossal risk and strain of opening a fine-dining restaurant, on the fourth floor of a mall in New York City, worth taking.

❧

Block indeed brokered such a deal over five relatively sleepless days in his offices in Ross, California, north of San Francisco, in the spring of 2001, as construction of the behemoth Time Warner Center was begun. With many late-night calls to Himmel for an answer on a make-or-break question, both sides had an operating agreement, a lease agreement, a personal guarantee from Keller, and a loan agreement.

If there was a moment when Keller recognized the magnitude of what he was about to do, or felt a tiny tremor run along the ground before the avalanche could be seen, it was likely the day Adam Block met him with the five agreements that composed the Time Warner deal and all the paperwork involved. They met at Jamba Juice. Block recalls arriving with "a stack of paper two feet high." It spelled out everything Keller was getting himself into.

Keller looked at Adam and said, "Remind me again. *Why* are we doing this?"

Block later told me why, or at least part of the reason. Keller's failure to make money in New York at Rakel, and his humbling departure in 1991 for a hotel kitchen in Los Angeles, left him with some unfinished business: "He hasn't slain the father yet," Block said. "That's kind of what New York is to him."

There's enough to do in just trying to open a restaurant in Manhattan. But he was still working at the French Laundry, had opened Bouchon, and was opening a Bouchon in Las Vegas, while planning the New York restaurant. Everything seemed to be happening at once. He'd been flying to Limoges, France, with his lead designer to finish a line of porcelain with the prestigious Raynaud porcelain company. It marked the first time a chef had designed an entire line of serving vessels that would accommodate the vision of the chef and the way he wanted to serve his food—special eggcups for his famous truffle custard served in the shell, a bowl-plate hybrid for serving risotto loose, the way he liked it, soup boxes that came with tops, so that they appeared at the table like small precious gifts. Then it was off to Paris to work on the line of Christofle silver with designer Adam Tihany. And then a stopover in England where the Duchess of York, Sarah Ferguson, would present him with Wedgwood's best chef in the world award. Then back to California and up early to cook for Diane Sawyer on *Good Morning America.* And then work on the Bouchon cookbook and design plans for the Bouchon bakery. Then to Vegas, and then back to New York.

The New York venture, though, with the enormous amounts of

money involved and the huge personal stake he was investing in time and reputation, was stressful. He began to have a nightmare—in it he ran and ran; Ken Himmel and the CEO of the parent company, Steve Ross, were actual giants pursuing him.

A year before Keller would open Per Se, I traveled to Napa to work on the Bouchon cookbook. It was harder and harder to speak with him by phone because of his schedule—it usually happened when he was in cars to airports or waiting to board a plane—so the concentrated time here was productive. I remember his sighing heavily in the afternoon sun, resting on the stone wall in front of the restaurant, wishing that all of this *stuff* would come to completion so that he could get back in the kitchen and just cook.

—*·*—

On January 1, 2004, Keller shut down the French Laundry, not for its biannual two-week respite, but for four whole months, while he moved forty staffers to Manhattan and let the bulldozers onto French Laundry ground to begin a major renovation of the entire facility surrounding the kitchen, breezeway, and dining rooms.

Shutting down the French Laundry had not been his idea, but when he heard it, he knew immediately it was a good one. He kept it quiet for a while from his investors before he made it known. Closing down a restaurant with annual revenues of $7.5 million is no small reduction in cash flow and profit. But it included bigger advantages: It would allow for the improvement of his flagship, it would free up his core staff (who knew his standards, obviating the need to find and train an entire new staff quickly), and not least in his mind in order of importance, or at least what he referred to continually as his goal, it showed New York and the media that he was truly and entirely committed to this restaurant. He did not want to be lampooned for his ambitions to open another potential four-star restaurant, this one in one of the world's cultural capitals.

So, at great expense (including lodgings for his staff at various Manhattan hotels), he welcomed the French Laundry family into the 15,000-

square-foot restaurant, with half of that space devoted to the kitchen. What a kitchen it was—or kitchens, rather. It included the Per Se kitchen, a separate kitchen for private parties (the business plan hoped for $2 million in revenues from such functions), a small refrigerated butchering room, a back prep kitchen. Beyond these luxurious spaces were dry storage areas, a laundry station, a staff bathroom, and a corridor leading to the offices. Beyond the offices was a small cool, enclosed patisserie station, and, finally, the small bakery.

Again, Bourdain, this from an e-mail after Keller gave him a tour of the place:

Jesus, Ruhlman!

The Per Se kitchen is NOT just a dream kitchen. It's positively fucking revolutionary! I was just gob-smacked amazed. . . . Thomas explained, for instance, the "transitional" breezeway for the waiters . . . the individual knife drawers for the cooks, the individual sous-chef drawers, the sight-lines for chefs and sous-chefs (and the thinking behind it all) . . . the centralized compressors for ALL the refrigeration units . . . the specific-use walk-ins, separate party/a la carte facilities. All figured by sq. foot vs. anticipated revenue generation. Just amazing. Amazing. If he wasn't already a genius, he'd be considered a visionary in kitchen design.

Bourdain may be a bit smitten by Keller, but this was especially valuable as comment because Bourdain had spent years as a chef in New York City kitchens and knew what was out there and what mattered in terms of design.

One of the amazing features he didn't mention in his e-mail was the ultraviolet light fixtures above the range that vaporized the airborne particles of grease that are the cook's postservice drudgery, those cleaning the hoods anyway. No more laborious hood scrubbing.

Still, Keller wasn't completely content. The spaces weren't completely right. He wanted one wall moved a few inches back. The window from the poissonnier's station into the pot room could have been better placed. The cooks' drawers, in which each kept his or her tools, needed a half inch more depth. The dishwashing station wasn't level, so water pooled in places that should drain.

"I had the chance to design a perfect kitchen," he said. "It's not perfect." A moment later, thinking about it, he said, "I think perfection is an accident. The thing is to recognize when it happens," and "I'm learning to tolerate a certain level of imperfection."

Later, watching the cooks at work, he would say of the kitchen, "You know what the other problem is—the kitchen is too big. Chris has to go all the way over there and he's going to get distracted." Chris L'Hommedieu, a sous-chef, indeed got distracted on his trek to dry storage and was nowhere in sight when Keller wanted him.

⋇

I'd returned to New York about a week before Per Se was scheduled to open, mid-February 2004. Keller and Laura Cunningham planned to have several services of only family and friends to try to ensure a smooth opening night. (Also toward this end, Keller was flying his key dishwasher, Juan Venegas, in from Vegas, where he was training the dishwashers at Bouchon. Keller often called Juan the most important man in the kitchen, or sometimes he called him "Juan the Great.") There were several media events planned around not only the restaurant's opening but the opening of the Time Warner Center.

The kitchen bustled. Fascinating food was everywhere. A five-gallon plastic stock container filled with chicken feet. A cook butchering a fish I'd never seen, called a *yagara,* he said, a long eel-like fish whose hard snout had been removed. The cook sliced open the belly and found various small fish and an undigested squid. Sous-chef Corey Lee removed large cod fillets out of salt. This fish, like many items in this kitchen, gets a brief but heavy salt cure. It would then be placed in 150-degree olive oil to cook gently.

There were familiar sights, such as a commis standing before a huge pile of raw favas, carefully removing the skin from each hard bean. The pervasive use of rolling things in plastic wrap, everything from foie gras butter (foie and butter whipped smooth and creamy in a Robot Coupe) to pig's head—when chilled and set up, the roulades could be sliced into small elegant disks.

And I saw changes, too. The restaurant, for instance, would no longer poach lobster tails in butter as had been done at the French Laundry. Instead, single portions of lobster tails were placed in a plastic pouch with some butter, vacuum-sealed, and would be dropped into a specially built water bath kept at 51.5 degrees Celsius (about 125 degrees Fahrenheit; as in all of Keller's kitchens, everything here is measured in metrics, a far more practical system for cooking). The lobster can be held in water that temperature, ready to serve in a snap.

There was the same fanatical attention to detail, such as the careful cleaning of bones that would be used for stock. All the fat was removed from them by hand for the cleanest possible final result. And with this fanatical attention to detail was the pervasive tone of place: organized efficiency, vivid cooks in blue aprons working out of deli cups.

Eric Ziebold, the longtime French Laundry sous-chef, had the previous September given his notice to Keller, intending to leave after nine years when the restaurant shut down in January. Keller had asked Ziebold to stay on to help open Per Se, and he'd agreed. I'd known Eric as long as I'd known Grant Achatz and loved to talk with him about food and cooking.

Ziebold, thirty-two at the time, from Iowa, had a dozen small beets in a pan, ready to be cooked.

"What are the beets for?" I asked.

"Borscht," he said.

"What's going to make it special?"

"The beef stock." This would give the soup an extraordinary depth of flavor. He paused and grinned. "And the truffle sandwich that goes with it."

He was working with a younger cook. When he sprinkled sugar into the beet water, the cook tasted the sugar to make sure he knew what it was. Ziebold said, "Don't be afraid to cook with sugar." Then he added some sturdy, five-finger pinches of salt.

"With simple food," he added, "any imperfection is glaring. You've got to hit it exactly or it sucks."

Later I watched him work with what he called *shirako,* the sperm sac of Japanese cod. "It's better than brandade," he said. "It's *really* good. If you can get over it spiritually." He would blend it with milk that had been infused with aromatic vegetables and cooked potatoes, then strain and cook it very gently so that the proteins would thicken the sauce without breaking apart from it. It tasted like a brandade milkshake, very fine and elegant, and would be the sauce for a cod dish.

This was a perfect example of Keller's food—the intense focusing of flavors, the fish combined with sauce made from that same fish. Keller had become famous not for experimentation, noted Joshua Schwartz, chef de cuisine for the private-function kitchen and longtime French Laundry veteran, but "for doing innovative interpretations of classical dishes with the best possible ingredients."

Even classics that were pretty tired to begin with, such as duck à l'orange. His, of course, were scarcely recognizable as the classics that informed them. His duck à l'orange comprised chunks of duck breast sautéed and served with baby leeks, duck gizzard, a juniper-scented reduction, and a marmalade made from navel oranges.

But he was also well known for his love of less familiar items.

On Friday, February 13, after the kitchen had served one of its "friends and family" meals, he says to his sous-chefs Ziebold, Corey Lee, and Devin Knell, "Monday's coming up and it's time to start thinking about VIPs." Monday was the official opening day. "Corey, do we have any cock's combs?" Corey shakes his head. "Can we get some?" Keller asks. "Call D'Artagnan. Do we have any pig's ears? Any brains? Any veal hearts?"

Corey, a native New Yorker whose family emigrated from Korea, shakes his head inscrutably but will make sure these items go on the order list tonight.

"Devin?" Keller asks. "Do we have any pop tarts?" Devin Knell created these items—a shortbread dough, filled with chopped black truffle and coated with a truffle glaze—they looked exactly like mini Pop-Tarts. They'd been one of the canapés for a media party the day before.

"No," he said.

"None?"

"I cooked off three hundred for the party. I can make some more."

Service had slowly been improving. The "friends" meals were critical for getting all the cooks up to speed, an element of which is handling what's not expected, such as when Paolo Novello, a manager, follows a server in and says, "Two no truffles."

The truffle custard canapés (served with chopped truffle in an egg-shell with a potato chip sticking out of it, a signature French Laundry dish) were to be sent to the table. Keller is at the pass expediting early in the service along with Corey Lee. Keller calls "Two no truffles" to the canapé station. Then to Paolo, "No truffle *oil?*" The oil is in the custard itself.

"No."

"What do we have for canapé?" Keller calls. "Two canapé salads, let's go."

"Yes, chef."

"I need those now, chef," Keller says.

"Yes, chef."

Two canapé chefs each make a salad on the fly. One dips into the curried butternut squash and mango *appareil* (for a vegetarian dish that's still in development) on a square of roasted red pepper, topped with baby arugula. The other makes a shaved fennel salad with herbs, baby artichokes, and fennel tops.

Service feels confusing with a lot of voices and an unusual noise level.

Keller says, "Who's running the pass? Are you, Corey?" Corey says nothing and takes a step back. Keller does not want to be in there and says, "No, no, I'll step out." This kitchen has to run without him.

Lee is in the SAS station tonight. At the French Laundry, Keller had added a second chef behind the expediter to assist when things got busy. But this position wasn't always busy and got the informal name among staff as the "Standing Around Station," or SAS. When Keller asked what *S-A-S* stood for, though, a nervous cook replied "Sous-chef assistant." Keller liked the name and it stuck—SAS is now on the work assignment sheet posted on the wall.

Keller steps away, but the two canapé salads still haven't come up, and he says, "Pick up two salads, come on, pay attention."

Corey is assisting Jonathan Benno, Per Se's chef de cuisine, the one Keller will rely on to run this kitchen. Benno is a quiet, somewhat brooding chef with a shaved head and years of experience with Keller and a few of the city's top chefs. A CIA graduate, Benno began at the French Laundry in 1994, left to do a year with Daniel Boulud, then a year with Christian Delouvrier, followed by four years at Tom Colicchio's Gramercy Tavern, before returning to the French Laundry.

"That first year at the French Laundry set the bar, set the standard," Benno said, when I'd spoken with him earlier in the day. "I've never met a chef who'd go to the ends of the earth to find . . ." Benno looked up to see where Keller was. Keller happened to be near the dish station removing bubble wrap from an ornate wooden box, a new acquisition that had just arrived. Benno smiled and said, ". . . the perfect box for truffles."

Keller is now off to the side, watching service, rubbing his chin. Laura Cunningham is there as well, watching front staff. There seems to be a lot of activity without enough getting done, servers are bunching up at the pass before the food is ready to go. The nature of the "friends" meal is a predetermined timing and seating, so a lot of the same dishes are picking up simultaneously, like private-party dining.

"Let's go, gentlemen," Keller says. "Gotta go, pick this up like a banquet. Pick up food. I'm not sure where we forgot how to do it. It's twenty minutes to ten, come on, we gotta go quicker."

The servers begin to hurry as well and one, taking a plate in each hand, whips around to leave the kitchen. Laura is on him like a hawk. *"Whoa whoa whoa,"* she says, stopping him. "Never ever carry a plate like that." The food could slide all over the plate, or even fly off it. She removes a towel that is draped over his arm, makes sure his hands are positioned correctly, and sends him out.

The agnolotti course, Keller's pillow-like ravioli, here filled with a rich celery-root puree, served with Vermont cheese, shaved Virginia ham, and butter a farmer makes especially for him, took twenty minutes to pick up, which is too long. Keller scratches out notes on a white legal pad:

Too long for p/u

No sense of urgency

Need to engage people

He wants his trainees on the line acting autonomously, calling back the orders, which they aren't doing. The cooks aren't in sync.

One voice in the kitchen

While the staff is progressing, Keller on opening day still says, "I'm nervous." Small glitches continue to pop up—the ticket printer is malfunctioning, some people smell smoke from the fireplace in the dining room, a toilet backfired on a hapless gentleman customer.

When I see Cunningham, she has a big grin on her face, and I comment on it. The smile not diminishing a watt, she said, "It's fear," and the grave intensity of her eyes says she's not kidding.

But ultimately the opening would scarcely feel like an opening, at least back in the kitchen, because everything was already begun. Keller and Cunningham had now opened four restaurants and knew what they were doing. Keller gave speeches to front of the house and back of the house before service on Monday, February 16, fairly standard words of encouragement and gratitude.

"I hope it's an extraordinary experience," he told the servers, standing above them on the raised section of the dining room. "I have no doubt it will be every night. We want to give our guests an experience they can remember. . . . Our goal is to have an impact on everybody we come into contact with. . . . Thank you for your hard work and dedication. Thank you." He begins a round of applause and departs.

Cunningham has noted he's gotten awfully chatty and speechifying of late.

Keller heads into the kitchen and gathers the cooks. "Can I get everybody in here at the pass?" The cooks are slow to gather—cooks don't normally do pregame motivational huddles. Michael Swenton, another Laundry veteran, starts to sauté off some cèpes in a very hot pan, and they smoke and sizzle loudly. Keller, annoyed, says, "What are you doing? Are you hungry?" Michael, having already got them in the pan, says, "Cooking mushrooms, chef." What could he do? Swenton shakes his head. I imagine the cooks thinking, *What's with this meeting? We've got things to do, it's almost service, and he wants to get sentimental?*

"This is it," Keller says, "this is the beginning. We have guests coming tonight. This is our big debut. It's a great moment when you open a restaurant." He tells them that the success of it hasn't come from him. People have been spellbound by the room, by the food, he says, "but also by the quality of the people in this room. You have made the standards here very high."

He thanks Benno, Ziebold, Swenton, Knell, and numerous others by name for all their work both here and at the French Laundry.

"Look around you," he concludes. "Look around and remember this. I don't want you to forget it. Thanks."

He claps to signal the end of the speech and all applaud, and then, at last, they can get back to their work, setting up the pass, wiping down stations, checking mise en place one more time, Knell and Swenton going over order-fire-pickup instructions with the line cooks they're training.

Soon Benno calls out, "Ordering for two! One lango, one foie gras, one sturgeon, one mackerel, one duck, one pork," and the restaurant is up and running.

"Nobody can remember a better opening," Keller would say the next day.

The entire week leading up to the opening had been celebratory, filled with the top food journalists and celebrities, such as Bruce Springsteen and Sarah Jessica Parker, wandering through the kitchen. All of Keller's meticulous planning had paid off. And his decision to shut down the French Laundry had been a masterful stroke, giving him the time to focus his attention on Per Se and to prove to New York that he was as committed to this place as to any. And they seemed to be buying it. There was none of the lampooning Ducasse received on his entry into New York. All the proper sacrifices had been made. The gods, apparently, were pleased.

As if to underscore the grace of the opening, the first paying customers at Per Se delivered Keller to his cooking roots and brought to this opening night a circular element that delighted him. Their names were Art Sherin and Sue Horsey, and when they finished their meal—he had a nine-course chef's tasting and she a vegetarian tasting—they asked that their menu be signed by the chef. The server took away their menu but returned and told the couple that the chef had invited them back to the kitchen—he'd like to meet them and thank them as the restaurant's first customers. They were thrilled.

A short couple in their late fifties, Sherin and Horsey were led back to the kitchen, where Keller remained off to the side observing service and taking notes. He's already got the first dollar bill the restaurant has earned, and he wants the couple who paid it to sign the first ticket, which he intended to frame.

They entered the bright kitchen smiling and chuckling nervously, apparently thrilled and surprised by this invitation. Keller beamed and greeted them warmly.

"It's an honor," Sue Horsey said, shaking Keller's hand. "We knew you from La Rive. That's how we knew about you, that's why we came."

La Rive! This had been Keller's idyll.

A remote restaurant outside Catskill, New York, run by René and Paulette Macary, a French couple, La Rive was a simple country place in the European tradition. Paulette wrote out the menu daily, Keller cooked French country fare in the small kitchen with no other help than Paulette's octogenarian mom, who peeled his shallots and picked his beans. Keller lived in a cabin behind the restaurant. He built a smokehouse for his meats. For the first time, he developed relationships with his purveyors, the Hudson Valley farmers who sold him their food. Here he taught himself to skin and to butcher rabbits, and learned the importance of treating his food with the intense care he would become famous for. It was here that he received his first attention from the New York media (Gael Greene and Raymond Sokolov, who wrote a survey of Hudson River Valley restaurants). And it was here that he learned to cook and appreciate offal, which the Macarys loved, despite the fact that American restaurant goers in the early 1980s weren't exactly familiar with roasted veal kidney, calf's brain, pig's ears, and braised tripe. This, too, would become another facet of Keller's renown.

La Rive was truly where Keller the young man, age twenty-five, began his transformation into the Thomas Keller of the French Laundry. At La Rive he cooked alone, experimenting and studying, teaching himself. And here now in this new Mecca were two people, greeting the world-famous chef, who with a handshake returned him to that period of his life on Per Se's opening day.

They live in Freeport, Long Island, Horsey explained, but they used to live in Woodstock. "There weren't a lot of places to eat up there back then," she said.

Keller signed their menu, and they each signed their order ticket. Keller shook their hands again, still grinning like a boy, and said, "Thank you! Thank you for coming. I really appreciate your being here."

Sherin and Horsey were led back to the dining room, still chuckling and shaking their heads happily.

Cunningham had watched the encounter. Keller turned to her and said, "The last time they had my food was at La Rive." She smiled and returned to the dining room. Keller still can't believe it. "Wow," he says. "That was twenty years ago. Full circle."

⇥⇤

The following Sunday, hours before the restaurant began the final service of its first week, the hoods seemed to be malfunctioning. The kitchen had begun to fill with smoke. Joshua Schwartz was in his kitchen, behind the Per Se kitchen, which was also filling with smoke. It became eerie, Schwartz said, because he, and others, quickly realized that nobody was cooking anything.

The entire staff was evacuated from the restaurant, and when Keller next returned he saw that the wall separating the two kitchens had been smashed in and New York City firefighters were dumping heavy gushes of water from their hoses down into the broken wall and all through that section of the restaurant—including the Bonnet range, a Rolls-Royce of cooking tools—to extinguish the fire burning within the wall.

The beautiful kitchen and brand-new Manhattan restaurant would be shut down by an electrical fire before it had been open a week. The closing of the French Laundry, the work of all these people, all the planning, all the celebrations leading up to its opening, the successful wooing of the New York media, all of it came to a soggy, smoking halt.

The next morning, February 23, on the front page of *The New York Times,* the headline read: "Chef's Lofty Dream Is Set Back by Fire at Columbus Circle."

※

To all those who had worked toward the opening of this restaurant, most of all to Keller and Cunningham, the electrical fire felt like a tragedy. To just stop like that. It seemed impossible. How could this be? But as Monday wore on, it was clear that Per Se would be shut down for weeks.

And yet, after the inevitable sense of dismay and disbelief and crushing discouragement had begun not to hurt so much, once a week or so had passed and everyone got used to the facts and the staff made plans for other work, travel, and stages, even this setback, though costly and frustrating, had its benefits: a chance to perfect the kitchen and the food, and more media coverage. A writer for *New York* magazine named Alex Williams contacted me for a story he was writing about Keller. The magazine had already written one about him and Gray Kunz, who was also eventually to open on the third floor of the building. When I asked why another article on Keller, Williams responded in an e-mail:

I can't think of another instance in which a minor kitchen fire in which no one was hurt made A1 of the Times. So far what's striking is that the buzz (another word I'm not fond of) has been tremendous, but there's been no even slightly snarky subtext, which you'd sort of expect with any place that's "the" place to be yet no one, essentially, can get into. That's pretty un-New York. Also, no one seems dubious of the scale of Per Se's ambitions, however you choose to define those. When Alain Ducasse opened, all that basically anyone could talk about were the prices; it was the same sort of resentment people back then reserved for dot-com multi-millionaires. In contrast, I haven't heard a negative word about Thomas or Per Se. I think people are genuinely curious and, in an odd way, feel privileged that Thomas is going to be giving them a chance to experience his mastery without making them plan a summer vacation in Napa.

I spoke with Eric Ripert about Keller and the mood among chefs regarding his opening a restaurant so self-consciously bucking for four stars. Among themselves are they quietly resentful of his ambitions, I wondered, which arguably could be construed as arrogant, and does Ripert personally worry about what it might do to his business eight blocks south? "It would be politically incorrect" to say anything negative about Keller and his restaurant, Ripert said, even if you wanted to be snarky. Ripert may need to do something to generate more press for his four-star restaurant, Le Bernardin, he said, but "we all want Thomas to succeed. If he succeeds, we succeed." And if Keller doesn't succeed, Ripert concluded, then that theoretically prevents others from raising the bar for themselves. Keller's being there only raises the standards for everyone else, and that was a good thing.

Keller was able to reopen Per Se on May 1 with considerably less hoopla than the first time, but he had to fly out shortly thereafter back to Yountville, where the French Laundry was reopening after a four-month overhaul. But he couldn't even be at that! He was obligated to be on the set of James L. Brooks's new movie *Spanglish,* about a chef of

Keller's prominence, for which Keller had been hired as a consultant. I'd spoken with him that night by chance—it was almost the only time to reach him, when he was in transit to or from an airport. Here he was in a car bound for the San Francisco airport as his restaurant, his baby, was celebrating its reopening. It killed him. But life was irrevocably sped up by now—no going back, not with Bouchon and Bouchon Vegas, the second book in the works, plans for the inn across from the French Laundry under way, and the Bouchon bakeries in the works, both next to Bouchon Yountville and one in the Time Warner Center, the four-star California restaurant to run, as well as the new restaurant, for which he desperately wanted four stars.

On Sunday, May 30, before Per Se had been open a full month, Cunningham spotted Frank Bruni, the new restaurant critic for *The New York Times,* seated with three other people. It was possible and perhaps likely that this was not his first visit. "I'm sure he dined at Per Se before that or after that, but wasn't recognized," she said. Two weeks later, she saw him at the French Laundry. In the second week in July, she saw him again at Per Se. After three confirmed sightings, it was obvious that Bruni would be reviewing the restaurant sooner rather than later.

The power of *The New York Times* review cannot be overstated. That at least is the feeling of Manhattan chefs, especially those who run high-end restaurants. And it's the reason that, when Bruni began reviewing (his first column, for Babbo, three stars, appeared on June 9, 2004), his photograph was quickly circulated via the Internet and shared by restaurants. The media gossip site, gawker.com, posted his picture on April 8 below these words: "For all our maître d' friends here on the isla bonita of Manhattan, a few photos of Frank Bruni, the *NYT*'s new restaurant critic. No one likes to be surprised by a food critic, right?" Bruni's mugshot is likely as frequent in restaurants as signs reminding employees to wash their hands.

The higher the high-end restaurant is, the more damage the *Times* critic can do. Eric Ripert, for instance, said as far as he was concerned, the matter couldn't be more straightforward: "If we lose a star, we go out of business." ("Only the Four Stars Remain Constant," the headline would read over Bruni's four-star review of Le Bernardin.)

Bruni has short, straight dark hair, dark eyes, and a lively, engaged manner, hyper-alert to nuance and detail. He's apparently lost quite a bit of weight since his days as a political reporter—photos from the *Columbia Journalism Review* show a man with a healthy appetite. He's quite trim now, and young-looking. Born in 1964, he could still pass for an eager-eyed grad-school student. Bruni seemed to me on the two occasions I'd met him to be very smart, and also very thoughtful, even sweet (which I mention because it contrasts the jaundiced, snarky, one-upsmanship common in New York media circles, not to mention the arrogance that can result when a reporter becomes overly accustomed to the power conveyed by *The New York Times*). Bruni never reveals how many times he visits a restaurant, though surely it varies depending on what he feels he needs in order to review a place properly. I asked him about Ruth Reichl's recent book about her career reviewing for the *Times,* which is loosely structured on the various costumes she's used to conceal her identity, and he seemed slightly annoyed by the pressure of expectation that might put on him. He doesn't wear wigs and doesn't intend to. Mimi Sheraton, a former *Times* restaurant critic, also had a recent memoir out and felt strongly that anonymity was critical to reviewing restaurants well. Other critics take the stance that a kitchen can either cook or it can't, and if it can't there's very little that a restaurant can do to change that fact, whether they know the *Times* is in the house or not. Reichl agrees with this, but she also makes an excellent case for the former position with her well-known review taking away one of Le Cirque's four stars for shabby treatment when she was disguised as a helpless nobody and star treatment when she went as *The New York Times* Restaurant Critic.

The job cannot be an easy one. Reichl notes that she was physically ill in the days leading up to the publication of her Le Cirque review, so nervous was she about potential uncaught errors and general fallout. It's among the most visible posts in New York journalism. Bruni seemed to be unnerved by the Web site devoted to making fun of him (who wouldn't be unnerved by an anonymous amateur taking potshots at your prose style?).

Russ Parsons, at the *Los Angeles Times,* furthermore noted how hard life seems to be *after* you turn in your guns of Navarone and stop being the critic for *The New York Times:* "It's amazing how that one job seems to be a dead end for so many talented people: Craig Claiborne, John Hess, Mimi Sheraton, Bryan Miller. Ruth is the only one so far who has been able to enjoy a strong second act. It remains to be seen what Bill Grimes [Bruni's predecessor] will do, though the book-review job sounds pretty sweet."

They all surely are aware of the power of their review and so write with considerable care. How does Bruni award stars? (Always a contentious subject among critics, that is—to use stars or not?) Ultimately, he said, what you need is "a solid impression in your gut—what is this restaurant? . . . How happy am I?"

For Keller the wait was nerve-racking. It's one thing to feel the anticipation of the review at each Bruni sighting. It's another emotion when the fact-checkers call and the photography department requests a photo shoot. Keller tried to downplay the importance of the review. He kept saying to himself and to the staff, according to Cunningham: "A newspaper doesn't define us, doesn't define who we are." But he was obviously bracing himself for a disappointment. Four stars matter to him. He put stars on the main stove hood above the pass at the French Laundry, where everyone who entered the kitchen would see it, a symbol the servers faced when they picked up food at the pass. He wanted that constant reminder to maintain four-star standards. How could he possibly ask his chefs and his servers to maintain four-star standards at Per Se if the paper of record deemed them worthy of three, or fewer. Jean-Georges Vongerichten, one of Manhattan's most cutting-edge chefs, chef-owner of the four-star Jean Georges, opened a high-end steak house on the opposite end of the fourth floor from Per Se, and Bruni had a month earlier given the restaurant a single humiliating star. And simply because your restaurant was ultra-expensive high-haute French with great pedigree and refinement didn't grant it automatic four-star status, either. Bruni was soon to remove the fourth star from Alain Ducasse at the Essex House, opened by the chef famed for his Michelin stars. You couldn't know what Bruni might think of Per Se.

Keller made plane reservations to arrive September 7, the day before the review would appear. It was an especially influential Wednesday because it was the first day after Labor Day, when all of New York City returns from summer vacationing and gets back to the work of living in New York City. A big review was warranted to open the fall season, a review of the most hyped, the most ambitious, the most written-about restaurant in the controversial Time Warner Center.

Keller had wanted to be there when the news actually arrived. But by the time he walked in the back of the kitchen, the review was on the Internet and a copy had been printed out and was handed to him immediately. The headline read, "The Magic of Napa With Urban Polish," and the piece concluded, "But this restaurant shoots straight for the stars. And it soars high—and often—enough to grab four of them."

Was the decision to give the restaurant four stars even close? Apparently not. Nearly a year later, Bruni confessed: "I was really, really bummed when I knew it was my last meal at Per Se."

Keller and Cunningham and their staff had done it. Keller had returned to Manhattan and had earned four stars from the *Times*. He now led four-star restaurants on both coasts.

CHAPTER 2

❧❧

Masa

Per Se was the first new four-star restaurant in Manhattan since Alain Ducasse at the Essex House received its ranking from William Grimes in 2001, three years earlier, bringing the total to five. Amazingly, New York's next new four-star restaurant was named just a few months later. Notably, it was not French, or French-based, as all the others were; it was Japanese and specialized in sushi, the first Japanese restaurant to earn four stars in more than twenty years. But perhaps most amazing of all, this restaurant, Masa, was right next door to Per Se, its equal in ranking but its antithesis in spirit. In a city of thousands of full-service restaurants—*Zagat* surveys nearly 2,000 of them, and says 174 "noteworthy" restaurants *opened* that year—two of New York's four-stars were side by side, four stories and three escalator rides from the street in a retail mall.

Regardless of place—this unusual mall situation—just the idea of this particular restaurant, Masa, was controversial. It was rumored to be the most expensive in the United States—you had to fork over four bills just to sit down at the bar. The place demanding this sum was not Alain Ducasse or Le Bernardin or Per Se, promising the elaborate preparations and expensive ingredients haute French cuisine was famous for, but rather raw fish and sauces often no more elaborate than a really good soy or a squeeze of a limelike fruit called *sudachi*. Moreover, the chef-owner, Masayoshi Takayama, had been in the States more than twenty years, but his English was limited, and so it was hard for the public to get to know him—profiles and interviews of the man were hardly revealing of why his skills as a chef were worth the astonishing prices. The two restaurants where he'd made his reputation in Los Angeles sat ten people at the bar (and twelve more at three tables), so his business was physically restrictive in addition to being financially exclusionary. And last, the chef didn't *want* to be known outside his restaurant, shunned attention, couldn't care less about reviews. In the age of the celebrity chef, Masa Takayama, age fifty, was an anomaly.

Solidifying the controversy over this chef and restaurant in the mall was, as it happened, the most controversial of the food writers at the *Times,* Amanda Hesser. In her final column as an interim reviewer before Bruni took over, a tumultuous term marked by infuriated restaurateurs and chefs and one "Editor's Note," Hesser did not give any stars to Masa. Instead, she, and the *Times,* did the unprecedented: She gave the restaurant four question marks. This was a surprising thing to read on Wednesday morning in the conservative and fiercely edited *New York Times.* In much the same way that Reichl had said that Le Cirque was two different restaurants depending on who you were, Hesser explained that Masa was two different experiences depending on where you sat. If you sat at the bar to be served by Masa himself, it was four stars. If you sat away from the bar at one of the four tables to Masa's left, it was three stars. She would not commit to either, and left it to Mr. Bruni to be decisive in the paper of record.

At the end of the year, he was:

Masa, despite its chosen peculiarities and pitiless expense, belongs in the thinly populated pantheon of New York's most stellar restaurants. Simply put, Masa engineers discrete moments of pure elation that few if any other restaurants can match. If you appreciate sushi, Masa will take you to the frontier of how expansively good a single (and singular) bite of it can make you feel.

The chef and owner, Masayoshi Takayama, who operated Ginza Sushiko in Beverly Hills before relocating to Manhattan, does not present you with a menu or choices. You are fed what he elects to feed you, most of it sushi, in the sequence and according to the rhythm he decrees. You do not seize control at Masa. You surrender it. You pay to be putty. And you pay dearly. . . . Lunch or dinner for two can easily exceed $1,000.

Justifiable? I leave that question to accountants and ethicists. Worth it? The answer depends on your budget and priorities. But in my experience, the silky, melting quality of Masa's toro and uni and sea bream, coupled with the serenity of its ambience, does not exist in New York at a lower price.

Concluding not lightly but seriously, he wrote: "Masa is divine."

❧

You enter Masa off the polished marble floors of the mall, pass through a dark curtain into a small black vestibule, and through a large wood door, a huge rough piece of cedar, twenty-five hundred years old, and feel immediately that it is an alternate universe from the one you've just left.

The restaurant is boxy and small, its walls painted black, but it does not feel claustrophobic; instead, it feels open and comfortable. The long, thick slab of *hinoki*—the bar, a soft, pale, fragrant cypress wood—seems to glow in the spotlights, and runs almost the length of the main room. Beside this room, separated by small bamboo curtains, are four tables seating four each. With ten seats at the bar, one night's capacity seating is twenty-six. Across the bar are some low cases that will hold fish during service, but not much, and they are not so tall as to block the view of Masa's workstation. Masa has a large round, shaved head, a solid athletic build, and an easy smile. He always wears a loose Japanese shirt, loose cotton pants beneath his long apron, and on his feet he wears either clogs or sandals. Behind Masa's station is a large floral arrangement he creates with seasonal plants—viburnum, forsythia, pussy willow, maple— and scattered bamboo in a pot in a shallow pool of water just inches deep. The sound of trickling water is distinct and peaceful. On each side of where Masa stands for service are stations that will be worked by Keinosuke Kawakami, age thirty-two, and Nick Kim, twenty-nine. Nick is from Korea but grew up in Los Angeles. Kei is from Fukuoka, Japan, and has been in the States for eight years, four of them with Masa, his only chef's job. Nick and Kei do most of the prepping and will also cut and serve sushi during busy services. There is a small grill behind them, called *okudo-san,* burning wood charcoal, for beef and mushrooms and for toasting the Ariake seaweed. There are two gas burners there for cooking as well. And in the far corner a discreet grill station, now manned by Ryan Becze, twenty-nine. Ryan, from Iowa, attended the New England Culinary Institute, but his compulsion to learn Japanese cuisine was kindled during two years in Japan in a kaiseki restaurant, where he was allowed only to wash dishes at first and where he lived off fish heads and daikon tops.

And that's the core kitchen staff at what may be the most expensive restaurant in the United States.

✥

I put on a kitchen jacket and brought knives, should I need them, but this was obviously a kitchen where I'd be allowed to wash dishes, maybe. I was, however, welcome to hang out and watch. Jacob Silver, a banquet chef in Honolulu and a friend of Nick's, had asked to trail, or stage, for a few days while he was in town. I asked Jacob if he was learning a lot and he said, "I'm not learning a lot—I'm *seeing* a lot." There was so much to see and to observe.

Fortunately, Nick and Kei were forthcoming and helpful in describing verbally everything they did, even as they were continually moving and working. Nick opens the long, narrow kitchen around nine, works steadily till opening, then participates in service, then cleans, and can usually leave shortly after midnight, six days a week. He says, "I try not to take a break, otherwise I might not get up."

There were several other cooks in the kitchen who worked for Bar Masa, on the other side, an informal Japanese restaurant that Masa also runs. (The Masa space is U-shaped, the kitchen being the bottom of the U.) But it was Kei and Nick who did the majority of butchering fish, peeling wasabi root, preparing the sauces, and making the rice for Masa.

Nick cooked the rice every night. He has a gentle, thoughtful disposition, and physically is like a smaller version of Masa himself. It was instructive simply to watch Nick scrubbing the rice, in a large steel bowl, using a gentle circular motion. He washed the rice and changed the water, washed it and washed it again, strained it into a colander. Finally, he submerged the colander in a large bowl of water and agitated it so that chunks and shards of broken rice fell through the mesh. These, he explained, could make the rice pasty. Cooking the rice is his daily job, and it's both an honor and a source of anxiety.

"Until Taisho puts his hand in the rice warmer, I'm not comfortable," he says, calling Masa by the Japanese word for "boss" (in the time of the samurai, *taisho* was the term for the leader of the samurai going in to fight, so the nuance of the term is apt). They've been getting in a different crop of sushi rice, and it hasn't behaved the same. Also, he ran out of Evian water and so had to use their filtered tap water to cook the rice.

Nick's been with Masa for less than two years, and even he thinks he's too young and too green to be doing what he's doing. "I shouldn't be making sushi rice, I shouldn't be cutting fish," he says, adding, "Masa's a great teacher and he's been pushing me."

When they cut fish, they typically do it on large oblong boards, single pieces of wood with rough edges cut straight from the ginkgo tree. They set this board over a sink, start a stream of cold water running over it, and begin cutting.

Often little needs to be done to a fish, but other times subtle manipulations are made. For the *aji* mackerel, which has a strong flavor, Nick removed the upper layer of skin but left the silver-blue sheen on the flesh. He removed the pinbones and laid the fillets, six of them, on a circular rack. He salted the fillets evenly and put them in the walk-in cooler, setting his timer. After twenty minutes, he retrieved the mackerel, rinsed and patted dry each fillet, all very delicately. He then dipped the fillets in rice vinegar, which will flavor the meat. "I find that after an hour or so," he said, "it becomes more rounded, and when you cut it, it looks more natural."

Nick next showed his friend Jacob how they prep the live lobster for the lobster risotto at Bar Masa, quickly removing the tail and claws from the body, halving the head, taking out the gills, wasting almost nothing. Nick moved the green tomalley, or liver, to a section of the board and quickly chopped the liquidy gland to a smooth paste, reserving this too. He'll add a little salt ("to get rid of the nasty flavor"), then add some soy to season it. This would be used as the sauce for lobster sashimi.

Meanwhile, Kei prepped the *hamo*, a pike eel, Masa called it, shaped like an eel but different in taste and texture, then *kawahagi*, "like a triggerfish," Kei said, wincing to think of an adequate translation. Most fish here is flown in from Japan. He then scraped the skin off a dozen wasabi roots, as Nick trimmed what he called a flounder. Kei said, "Fluke," made the shape of the fish with his towel on the cutting board, and pointed to where the eyes were on a flounder versus a fluke.

Nick nodded and Kei moved on to the orange clams, opening a dozen, cleaning and trimming them, then putting them into a steel bowl. He brought some sake to a simmer and dumped it over the clams, sloshed them around to get the strong ocean taste out of them, then transferred them to an ice bath. He cut a piece for me, washed it in a sweet vinegar, gave it a drop of soy, and put it on a bit of rice. It was sweet and tasted of fresh ocean, and it made me smile.

Sauces truly were often as simple as that. Masa did make a few sauces based on soy, sake, and mirin. *Nikiri* soy might be reduced with sake or mirin and seaweed. White soy would be used in summer, as would a sauce flavored by red *shiso* leaf. Another sauce was vinegar flavored with *tade,* a spicy green leaf. In winter, he would use sauces based on dark soy. The eel got a special sauce called *tsume*—eel bones were grilled and cooked in sake, mirin, and soy. The sauce was never made from scratch but instead was continually replenished. Nick said the *tsume* sauce had been used for twenty years at the previous restaurants but was lost in transit to New York when the container broke.

Lunch service at Bar Masa, a conventional restaurant serving a broader Japanese menu, bustled around Nick and Kei as they moved through their day. To their right a couple of chefs cut and sent out sushi for the lunch crowd. To their left, two cooks worked a hot line.

Masa occasionally does some of the prep but mainly sticks to service and running the business. He'll prepare the *toro,* spending twenty minutes scraping it from the membrane (he'll save the membrane to grill and eat for family meal later), transforming it into a kind of rich tuna mush that he'll serve with a huge heap of osetra caviar before he begins the sushi service.

Recently he's been getting the caviar from Per Se. Jonathan Benno, chef de cuisine there, had dinner at Masa the other night and had brought three 500-gram tins of Iranian osetra to the Masa kitchen himself.

Masa was at work at a board, removing the meat from the legs of a hairy crab by rolling them with a wood pestle, squeezing the flesh out through either end. Benno thanked Masa for the meal the other night.

"Did you enjoy?" Masa asked.

"It was a real inspiration to watch you," Benno said.

To which Masa more or less grunted. Benno thanked him again, promised two more tins of caviar on Friday, then departed.

Other chefs accord Masa extraordinary respect of the kind Benno showed, every bit as much as they do Keller. So it was perhaps the only way to get Masa to move across the country and into a mall—a request from Keller.

❖

According to Masa, he was working a chef's event in Atlanta and so was Keller. The two got to talking. Keller told Masa what he was doing, opening a restaurant in New York in a building to be called the AOL Time Warner Center. Masa should open a restaurant there, too, Keller said. How about it?

In fact, Masa had long thought of opening in New York, but he couldn't envision having two restaurants, and he didn't want to leave Los Angeles. He'd had children and had been married. Now his kids were grown and he was divorced. Maybe it was the time to think about New York—the timing was right.

As part of the agreement for opening a restaurant in the Time Warner Center, Adam Block had asked for Keller to have the right to veto any potential restaurants in the building. In the beginning, Ken Himmel, CEO of Related Urban Development, had not foreseen a gathering of the country's most elite chefs. Block said Related was considering a range of restaurants, including chains. Himmel agreed to Block's request. Neither side thought much about this part of the agreement at the time. Related was more concerned about preventing Keller from opening a Bouchon or another new restaurant in Manhattan. But this condition turned out to be pivotal. Since Keller could veto any restaurant, he also now felt invested in the process. Certainly he didn't want a chain restaurant next to his, and so it was up to him to find the chefs or restaurateurs he'd like in there.

Block said, "Who do you want?"

Keller said, "Masa." Keller had eaten at Ginza Sushiko, and it had been one of the best meals of his life. ("A total involvement with the process and flavors," Keller said, recalling what he'd liked so much. "You were engaged at every level.")

Block went to see Masa. Masa had no business counsel or agent or anything, really—just his staff and his restaurant. Block would soon be representing Masa.

Himmel flew to Los Angeles to eat at Ginza Sushiko, to talk with Masa and to show him the plans of the building.

Today Masa says, "I didn't think long about it."

With arguably the best American chef and the best Japanese sushi chef in the country in agreement to open restaurants next to each other in the Time Warner Center, restaurant space without street access suddenly seemed enticing. Vongerichten signed on. Block now felt that this was a good opportunity for his client Gray Kunz, who'd had four *New York Times* stars at Lespinasse, to make his return to Manhattan. Several people were considered for the fifth space, but ultimately Keller asked Charlie Trotter to join the group, and, after some grumbling about being the last asked to dance, Trotter, also represented by Block, said yes.

＊＊

Of all these chefs, the most intriguing and curious was Masa Takayama. He would be one of only two chefs who would actually be at the restaurant full-time. Keller, Trotter, and Vongerichten all had multiple restaurants that would divide their time.* Masa would earn four stars by cutting raw fish, serving it with rice, and charging more money than any restaurant in New York. Masa was a curiosity in the chef world.

"I am nothing," he would say. And, "I am naked." And, "I don't do anything. Eighty percent of the work is just ordering the ingredients." He means it, and it is true, if you include in that 80 percent, the *knowing*—knowing which ingredients to order and exactly what to do with them when they arrived. If so, then the other 20 percent comes from his hands.

Masa has no shortage of critics who can't believe anyone has the gall to charge what was now, in truffle-and-blowfish season, $350 per person, to which a 20 percent gratuity was automatically added, for a total of $420 per person, before you even ordered bottled water, let alone dipped into the sake list.

His response can be seen as either equally arrogant or straightforward and logical: "If it's too expensive, don't come," he says.

His business adviser, Block, says, "He is so uncaring about what the

---

*Trotter would back out of the deal in the fall of 2005. By the end of the year the space remained unspoken for.

public thinks. He's somebody who ignores the brand. He just knows, This is it, this is me, this is what I do."

And so Masa is completely inflexible as far as what he will and will not do in terms of catering to the New York market, more so than any of the other Time Warner chefs. "But the good news," Block says, "is that New Yorkers don't have the same awareness of what he's doing as they do with French food. So they're gonna flock, because he's got few seats, and because anyone who's ever experienced Masa would agree it's an amazing experience. It's amazing, he's amazing."

⇒∙⇐

Masayoshi Takayama was born on May 1, 1954, in Tochigi, Japan, an hour north of Tokyo. His family owned a fish shop and a catering business. Masa, the second of five children, worked at the shop while in high school. At eighteen, he says, he tried to go to the university, but didn't last long. "Suddenly, I realized I was not interested," he says, a couple of hours before service, seated at the $60,000 slab of *hinoki,* now completely covered with broken-down cardboard boxes. His accent is thick, his voice deep and rough, his cadence brusque. "To learn, to study, to be what? Businessman? I hated that."

His older brother was working as an apprentice chef in Tokyo, and so, given that Masa didn't have a better idea, he began working with his brother. His brother suggested he work in a sushi restaurant. *Why not?* Masa thought.

But the restaurant where he found work, a highly regarded 150-year-old restaurant called Ginza Sushi-ko, was run by a strict old man. Masa began by cleaning the bathroom and washing dishes—the way most apprentices started. Cleaning the bathroom was a serious job. When he moved into the kitchen, the work became only more difficult. "Very hard job," Masa says. "Every day, every night, I tried to quit." For two years, he wanted to quit. In his third year, he says, he started to learn things. And after five years he understood a new thing: He holds his hands up to me and says, "Here is my money." He touches his chest, and says, "Here is my money." But he knew, he says, "I had to polish myself, too. I worked hard, I studied."

Finally, he thought that sushi chef might be the right job for him.

In addition to having become a sushi chef (in all it would take eight years of training), he also drew and painted. He drew many landscapes of his country, vistas filled with hills and trees, which was all that he saw. He'd heard that landscapes by Americans his age were of big, flat, wide-open spaces. He wanted to see this. A customer at Ginza Sushi-ko had a business residence in Los Angeles and urged Masa to use it. Masa did. Masa wanted to see the big, flat land, and so he was told to go to Las Vegas. He did and he saw the desert.

Masa moved to the United States for the landscape. And for golf. He loves golf, and it was cheaper to golf in L.A. than it was in Tokyo. In L.A., he worked for a few restaurants before opening a small restaurant of his own in a strip mall on Wilshire Boulevard, which he named after the Japanese restaurant where he trained.

When he opened, there was not much fine fresh fish. Where he had trained, they used only very good fish from the waters surrounding Japan. But in Los Angeles, he couldn't get the same quality. So he told his fish purveyor, "Hey, buy from Japan." The purveyor shook his head and said, "Too expensive." Masa responded. "No, *I buy*." He developed good customers, many of them Japanese businessmen who knew how good this fish was and were willing to pay for it. He didn't need many, relatively speaking. He only had ten seats at the bar. And so he worked quietly and well, in relative obscurity, for several years.

"Then Ruth came," he says.

He was in the car on the way to the golf course when he saw the small restaurant item, just two hundred words, in the *Los Angeles Times*.

"When I first walked into this sushi bar," wrote Ruth Reichl, the paper's restaurant critic, "hidden in an unprepossessing strip mall in the mid–Wilshire District, I didn't know I was about to order the most expensive meal I had ever eaten in Los Angeles."

She pronounced the food sublime. "But what fish it turned out to be!

Perfect slices of pink abalone. The richest tuna I'd ever tasted. An orange-and-purple clam that looked like a painting by Georgia O'Keeffe. Sea urchins that were bigger, fatter than any I'd ever encountered. The meal went on and on, ending with two giant strawberries. And a bill for $100."

Wow! he thought, amazed. *That my restaurant!*

At the time, the early 1990s, the fanciest, most expensive sushi dinner you could buy was about forty dollars. At two and a half times this, Reichl said, Masa was a bargain. She would return to give the restaurant a full review, but the first piece seems to be what began Masa's notoriety regarding his expensive fish and rice dinners.

Even Reichl had made the point that Masa had in a way created a dream—"to own a restaurant where he can feed perfect food made with the best ingredients money can buy to a few discerning diners"—one that no other chef in Los Angeles had been able to achieve quite that way.

"What made you think you could get away with it?" I asked.

"I didn't care," he said. "I just charged them. . . . Very small restaurant. People come. People get it, they come; people don't get it, don't come.

"Some people accumulate the money a little bit all year," he continued, recalling a specific customer who would save and save for her annual meal. "Old woman. 'Masa, I come here once a year.' Herself. Not fancy." The thought of this woman, who saved all year each year for one of his meals, here in the dimly lit, quiet restaurant, moves him, and I see he is about to cry. He rubs his eyes to stop himself. "That's all we can do, you know. A hundred percent. That kind of face, when I see, *I love*. I'm *soooo* happy what I did. I spend a long time working. This is my best customer. Even no money. They understand. That's why I can do."

❧

It is an indication of his refinement as a sushi chef, perhaps, that he will not eat sushi in New York. He has gotten sick twice from eating sushi in this sushi-adoring city, and that's enough for him. There is no consistent training here, he says. In Japan, a chef must train for at least three years before he could even think of getting licensed, and then the chef takes his blowfish exam in order to serve this delicacy that can be fatal if not properly prepared. So Masa sticks to Korean restaurants and places that serve simple food. He can't stand the kind of food served by his fellow four-stars. It's confusing to him. It's too salty. There's too much butter. A dish that requires the work of five people doesn't make sense.

Krispy Kremes, though, they're another matter. "I *love* Krispy Kremes," he says, almost woozy with lust. He brings them in himself on Saturday mornings.

Japanese cuisine has two main branches: the samurai branch, rustic, farmer cuisine; and the Zen branch, which is the branch Masa works. Both forms are about simplicity rather than complexity. He tries to teach his staff, "my kids," he calls them, what this food is all about: "Very delicate," he says. He wants them to appreciate the beauty of the cherry blossom. This is what his food is all about. If you can understand this, the attributes of a cherry blossom, then you can understand his food.

In L.A., Nick planned to prepare a special meal for his family at the restaurant during its day off. He wanted the table adorned with cherry blossoms. He slaved all day in preparation for this meal, which was to be a gift. As the hour of their arrival approached, he saw that the cherry blossoms were fading and becoming old-looking and brown. He had too much work and not enough time, but more important he had to find beautiful flowers; he drove into downtown Los Angeles from Rodeo Drive to make sure the cherry blossoms were right. "Very delicate."

What Masa eats at his own restaurant is another example of what he appreciates—samurai food. As his staff leaned against counters in the kitchen eating family meal, Masa usually took his lunch on the cardboard-covered *hinoki*, where I joined him twice. On one day, we ate a broth flavored by the dark seaweed *kombu*, with soba noodles and a fried vegetable pancake floating on top. The other lunch was something I'd never had. A variety of fish tails, scraps from butchering, grilled or deep fired, and a bowl of marinated squid guts. The guts looked in my bowl like soupy pink spaghetti, and they had a tangy, fermented flavor. I'm pretty adventurous as far as what I'll eat, but fish entrails, fermented or not, would not ordinarily be something I'd be excited about. Masa ate them and wanted to serve them to me, though, and so I looked forward to it. Everything to that point I'd tasted had been excellent at least, if not quite a bit beyond excellent. Every single thing I'd ever had there. The squid guts were no different—they tasted really good, the texture and flavor fascinating, like tasting a new form of blue cheese. This was the nature of food at Masa.

When a fish order arrived from Japan, everyone got quickly to work breaking down eels and flat fish and round fish and shrimp to get them properly prepped and stored. Masa took the octopus leg to work on. The three-foot-long appendage was speckled brown and fat as a baseball bat at its severed end. It was so fresh its big suckers on the pale underside were still contracting gently and the muscle still twitched. Masa skinned it quickly and expertly cut a couple of pieces and gave me one. It had a strange, sweet, sea flavor, but more, its texture was new and surprising as well, chewy on the outside and gelatinous on the inside. He would serve this as sashimi or sushi, sometimes lightly grilled for a little flavor and with a few drops of *sudachi*. Again, I'd tasted something that was wonderfully new.

After Masa ate, usually by himself, he would smoke a cigar in his dark restaurant and draw food and dishes and think about food. ("Think about food all day long—it's fun!" he says.) He continues to enjoy drawing, as he has throughout his life. Many of the ceramic plates, dishes, and bowls he designed himself. In the spotlight above the bar, his bald head glowing, the blue smoke rising from a fat cigar, he looks like an Asian Mafia don perusing a stack of notes and betting slips, but he's really thinking about new dishes and new ways to serve his food.

The *shabu-shabu* dish is one such piece he designed: a dark brown roughly glazed orblike bowl on a small platform in which he serves piping hot *kombu* broth. Beside this is a small tray with a few thin slices of raw lobster and raw foie gras. You dip the lobster and foie in the broth using chopsticks, swish-swish for a few seconds to cook them, and then eat them. When I had this dish, I remember thinking that I never wanted to eat foie gras again any other way—what was the point?

Masa conceived of serving foie gras this way after a customer brought him from Scotland a fresh monkfish liver, which is a lot like the fattened duck liver. It was so fresh and good that he puzzled over how best to cook it. As delicately as possible, he thought. The *shabu* idea worked so well, it's become a staple dish.

The next course will simply be the *kombu* broth, which now has been flavored by the lobster and has drops of gold fat from the foie gras floating on its surface. It's beautiful to look at and delicious to eat, a work of great simplicity and efficiency. All hallmarks of Masa's food.

◆·◆

The previous spring, I'd traveled to Baltimore to be part of a three-person writers' panel at the annual International Association of Culinary Professionals (IACP) conference. Bourdain was also on this panel, and he made some tongue-in-cheek remarks about him and me touring as a kind of culinary Martin and Lewis—something that would be very bad for my health. It's part of his evil nature that he is enormously charming in person and somehow convinces you that it's not only OK but, in fact, a great opportunity to take up smoking again, and to stay out till dawn pounding beers with grizzled Vietnam vets who insist on buying the celebrity yet another round, the night before our eight A.M. panel discussion. Just when you're certain the guy's a deceptive scoundrel who cannot be trusted, is bad for your physical health and Midwestern integrity, he undoes you with an incredibly generous blurb for your cookbook.

So, early in the evening in Baltimore, well before I began to see double, he mentioned he was writing an article on Masa and had a rez in a couple weeks. He'd already been once but had been so seduced by the food that he had no idea what had happened; in fact, he'd become so enraptured by the experience that he had no notes whatsoever and thus could not write his story. So he was returning with our mutual friend Eric Ripert, arguably the most knowledgeable fish cook in the city.

I was by chance going to be in the city on that date, preparing to watch the reopening of Per Se. I begged to be able to join them. He said he'd see what he could do.

I truly wanted to be wary of Bourdain, but how, when it was he who first delivered me to the *hinoki* altar, and more: He picked up the tab for all three of us, which would be $1,300 (that's without the three bottles of wine sent to us as a gift from a friend).

Eating at Masa was one of the most original and extraordinary dining experiences I'd had. It was second in power only to my experience at the French Laundry, which had been, because of its timing in my life, right up there with losing my virginity, if not actually divine in some small way.

That said, I believe Masa is the most exciting fine-dining experience in Manhattan, period. By far. Maybe in the world.

The room is peaceful and refined, and when you sit at the bar you cannot help but rub your palms over it, it feels so sensual—you've never felt wood like this before. Masa simply walks out (the night we were there, he wore a loose blue shirt and an apron over loose trousers, wood clogs), nods, and starts serving. He mixes some cucumber salad and serves it with crayfish and the meal is begun. Next comes the signature *toro* with caviar, served with rectangles of toast, followed by bonito sashimi wrapped in daikon radish, soft-shell crab tempura, the lobster-and-foie *shabu* dish. And then the sushi begins, served by hand, eaten by hand. Two couples were seated on either side of us. Masa fed them as well, assisted by Kei on his right and Nick on his left.

He uses a long, slender knife with a carved handle made from the horn of a water buffalo, a beautiful object in itself. Before service he has sharpened it on a ceramic stone using lots of water, and rubbing it back and forth hard as if he were scrubbing the stone. He then washes his hands and thoroughly scrubs his nails with a brush. His movements are clean and fine, the apotheosis of grace and craftsmanship. When he cut the *aji,* he left on a thin swath of silver-blue skin. The skin remaining on the board had an artful pattern cut out of it—even his garbage looked beautiful. He then folded the mackerel over a pillow of rice with some fresh wasabi. Mackerel is something I've always associated with cat food and was not something I thought you wanted to eat raw. But Bourdain beside me was already making low-moan ecstasy noises. Indeed, the fish was smooth and sweet and buttery. Mackerel? This was not the world I knew.

The sushi also included the saltwater and ocean eel called *anago,* a sushi roll packed with a massive mouthful of *o-toro,* the fattiest part of this fatty part of the tuna. (Masa's tuna, the *toro* and the *akami,* the leaner part of the tuna, arrive frozen and are kept in a Thermo freezer, a serious piece of equipment Masa keeps at –87 degrees Fahrenheit.) We had grilled *toro* as well. A grilled shiitake, served on sushi rice like fish, whose texture ingeniously mirrored the fish. Sea urchin, a scallop that he tenderized by crosshatching it with his knife, sweet clam, calamari, shrimp, Kobe beef grilled so that when you bit into it, fat felt like it was pouring out of the meat. And it concluded with some sweet eel, freshwater *unagi.*

There was more to the genius I realized only after he asked if we would like something else. Greedily, I wanted to taste the *shima aji,* which had come early in the sushi service. It had been my favorite of the sushi courses. But when I tasted it at the end of the meal, it wasn't the same, it had lost its shine somehow. Masa had known not only exactly how but also when to serve this fish. It was critical to submit absolutely to Masa.

Masa is at ease and casual at his station, talking every now and then or answering a question in his broken English or grunting like a parody of a Japanese wrestler. He joined us with a glass of each of the wines we drank. He was working, but he conveyed that he was enjoying the work.

Midway through the meal, Bourdain, in *o-toro* ecstasy, said, "Put a gun to my head and shoot me right now. I'd be fine with that. I'd die a happy man. You know that at this moment no one on earth is eating better than we are."

And it was, I believed, actually true.

"Have you had enough?" he asked finally. We accepted that we had. He said, "Thank you very much."

❧

Reentering the mall after such otherworldly refinement jarred the senses. We made it to a relaxed hangout of Eric's and talked about the meal, and it was interesting to hear what other chefs thought of this guy.

Ripert had been to Per Se the night before and had, before we'd begun our meal at Masa, exclaimed in a rapturous whisper, "I think Per Se might be the best restaurant in the world." He'd had a good meal evidently, but what he had just experienced at Masa was unquestionably new.

"It is the antithesis of what Thomas is doing next door," he said. "Thomas gives you extraordinary sophistication and luxury, and Masa, he has a piece of wood and some chopsticks and a bucket of steamed rice, some china he made himself." Eric shook his head. "I think it's genius." Masa was a master, and the culture he was bringing to New York was extraordinary, Eric said.

Bourdain, too, remained reverential: "That's what he does—he turns everything we do, everything we know, on its head. What he is saying is, You know nothing."

❧

Masa is very much in control, not just of the food but of the entire environment in his restaurant. Arriving guests are asked to turn off their cell phones. He doesn't want to hear them or hear people talking on them. "That make me pissed off very much," he says. He will actually get angry during service if it happens. "Hey," he'll say. "Shut up with telephone, otherwise I smash your telephone. Another person in the private room— 'Hey, what you do? Get out of here! Make your phone call outside.'" Usually people apologize, he says. "I want people to enjoy this environment, this world. No telephone, forget it. Like Disneyland, you step into a different world, see?"

Anything that cuts into this environment makes his performance more difficult. It is just that, a performance. Chef Benno had remarked on this more than the food. When Masa asked if he enjoyed the meal, he had replied, "It was a real inspiration to watch you."

"It's part of the show," Masa says of his presence. "That's why I can charge three-fifty. If sit in some private dining room, they just see the dish, I cannot charge three-fifty."

"Everyday it's a fight," he says later. "If they like, I win; if they don't like, I lose. If they don't like, I get very pissed off."

And this: "I want to see the people eat. Joy. I want hear them say, 'Wow!'"

If Masa cannot make it into the restaurant, his assistant will call their reservations and cancel them all. "When I catch cold, I close the restaurant," he says.

I asked how he stayed healthy and maintained the energy to cook and perform six days a week, often twice a day.

"Don't eat too much!" he says, and then laughs his deep, long, exuberant laugh. "*HaHaHaHaHaHaHaHaHaHa!* Go to sleep! *HaHaHaHa-HaHaHaHaHaHaHa!*"

Masa is easy and funny when he's not working. When I was commenting on some of the dishes he served, he said, "Simple right? *HaHa-HaHaHa!* Thomas works *so hard.*" He makes an expression of mock pity. "I'm lazy!"

Every now and then he'll compose a complex dish with multiple components. The current *fugu* dish is an example. Fugu, or blowfish, is in season in the fall. The liver of the wild blowfish can contain toxins that are lethal, and the entire fish must be carefully prepared by licensed chefs. The blowfish Masa uses are not wild but rather are grown in their environment in large pens and are not dangerous. The toxin, Masa explained, originates in the shellfish that blowfish eat. The pen they're raised in keeps the shellfish out. But as they remain in their natural habitat, and are farmed seasonally, the penned blowfish have the same flavor as wild.

For the *fugu* dish, he serves the flesh as sushi, three different parts of its skin (each has a different texture), its intestine cleaned and cooked and stuffed with green onion, and a piece of its liver. Later in the meal he will serve chunks of the head deep-fried—Kei says, "It's *so* good. It's like fried chicken"—served with a ponzu-like vinaigrette.

With all those components and the heavily worked-over fish, I say, "That's kind of like a Thomas dish." He nods gravely and says, "I copied."

Masa doesn't use only Japanese ingredients. Many of the clams come from around here, the scallops too. And the ginkgo nuts come from a tree in Central Park. Masa smelled them during a walk. Their thick, soft shell has an intensely funky, unpleasant odor, but shelled, cooked, and skinned, the inner nut is delicious, sweet, and nutty tasting. He serves them as they are, the way you'd serve olives or cashews before the meal. I'd never had anything like them. His grill chef Ryan Becze goes out and gathers them from the park after lunch service.

Ginkgo nuts Masa knew from Japan, but the origins of any ingredient are less important than that they fit into a Japanese style. "It doesn't matter, Western ingredients, Japanese ingredients," he says, "only matter good ingredient—good stuff." He will batter and deep-fry an entire golf ball–sized white truffle, wrap it in rice paper, and serve it as a single course.

And this is partly the reason for the high cost. Not only does he make abundant use of the very expensive ingredients common in pricey restaurants, such as foie, truffle, and caviar, almost all of the ingredients are very expensive. The shrimp he uses, for instance, arrive live, packed in damp wood chips, and cost twenty dollars apiece, a high food cost for one item. "Even in Japan they can't do this way," he says. "So expensive."

I think I'm getting a handle on Masa, and I say, "You have the most expensive restaurant in the biggest restaurant city in the world, and you say the most important thing you do, the *most* important thing, is ordering the food."

Masa takes a sip of his tea and nods. "Very easy job."

"Really, you're just a crafty old cook. You figured out a way to charge the most money of any chef in the country, maybe the *world*, and you don't even cook."

He grins wide. "Nice, right?" he says, nodding vigorously and smiling. "Nice huh? *HaHaHaHaHaHa! HaHaHaHaHaHa!*"

⇥⇤

I asked Masa the art-versus-craft question. I used to think that only in the rarest of circumstances did the chef rise above being a craftsman into the realm of the artist. Most chefs who claimed to be *artistes* were full of it as far as I was concerned. Only when a chef changed the way you saw the world, through cooking, did food truly become art, and that was rare, indeed. But also I was softening on the subject—the restaurant world was so diverse and food was changing so fast, I was willing to concede some ground on the artist issue, especially having spent so much time with Achatz at Trio.

So I asked Masa, whom I knew to be, at the very least, a performing artist, and a very good one—tickets to his show started now at $350 a seat, and there would be, could be, no understudies—what he thought.

"Yeah, I think it's art," he said. "What I do, I'm showing the people, I'm going to work clean, nicely, fast, each piece of sushi, more artistic, nice shape. Art is not always seen." He placed an index finger below each eye. "When you taste it, part of the art. Each piece of fish. Rice. Fish. Good combination. Taste, texture, colorwise. Eat it. Beautiful. Melt. Flavor, nice flavor. Is a wonderful art. This is what I believe. Not only to see the art, not only the painting. The food is not the art. . . . Mostly it's taste. Our job is taste. Eat. Beautiful. Wow. This is art I think.

"If you don't have a good personality," he continued, "you can't make good food. If you are not a good person, forget it. You have to be honest. . . . More honest, more open, think more straight. Otherwise, you'll never get it, what's good food. We serve direct to customer. We don't say any lie to the customer. Nothing hide, just straight. We don't cook anything, mostly the raw fish. If the ingredients are not good, but still OK, people won't notice? They serve it for the money, people get used to it? They lower quality. That's the personality. The person has to be the right judge. This is no good, no good no, no good, don't do that. I tell them, you have to be a nice person, otherwise you cannot make good food. You show the customer face, try to make more entertaining. This kind of personality from your inside, from here. I don't care, it's just for money, I don't care the food, just serve? Those kind of chef cannot stand over here." He points to his station. "They can see our face. Every single dish has to be perfect.

"This is me," he concludes. "This is what I am."

⇥⇤

The enduring image I have from my short time in Masa's kitchen was from watching a lunch service.

At this particular lunch service, there was a single customer, an older woman, seated centrally at the *hinoki* bar. Masa stood before her unsmiling but looking comfortable in his loose clothing, his round shaved head glowing in the carefully lighted space. He bowed in plying his trade, in cutting fish on his board with his gorgeous knife. He first served the series of nonsushi dishes, ginkgo nuts, the *uni* risotto for which he's famous, the lobster-and-foie *shabu-shabu* for which he should be famous, the elaborate blowfish dish, before moving into the sushi performance that included a dozen different carefully prepared bites of *toro*, mackerel, grouper, *shima aji, tai, hirame, ken ika, tako, kanpachi, anago, ebi*, eel. He cuts each piece before the woman, forms a small ball of rice and seasons it with a bit of fresh wasabi or one of a few simple sauces, folds the fish over the pillow of rice, and sets it on a dark stone disk in front of her. The woman lifts it with her hand and, with a small dip of her head, like a bow, eats it in a bite.

The meal lasted more than two hours. Occasionally, Masa would take a break in the kitchen, talk on his cell phone, have some tea, who knows—maybe check in with his bookie or reserve a Sunday tee time, or just relax for a moment. But when his customer, the old woman, had been alone for the right amount of time, he would return and resume his work.

The entire restaurant was empty but for these two people, with fine spots lighting them both up vividly against the black walls of the restaurant, Masa slicing and serving exotic fish and the woman eating what he placed before her, all of it in perfect silence. I stood and stared transfixed from my hideout in the kitchen. They were beautiful to behold. A monk serving a monk.

CHAPTER 3

❧

Thomas and Masa

It wasn't until after I'd spoken with Keller in Per Se that I realized fully how unusual Masa Takayama was in this country. Keller was dressed for work in a dark jacket and white shirt open at the collar, and we talked about the changing role of the restaurant chef, the changing composition of the daily work, and the dramatic transformation of his own life in the wake of the international success of the French Laundry and his subsequent fame.

"What's a chef?" he asked. "The brigade system has chef de cuisine, chef de partie, chef garde manger. Does the 'chef' now become 'chef-restaurateur,' head of the restaurant? I don't know.

"The media are the ones who set the image for who we are. It's hard for us to set that image ourselves. The image began, you know, that whole romantic process of the chef going to the market, buying the freshest produce and the freshest fish and coming back to the restaurant and processing it and serving it that night. That's an image that was out there for such a long time—which is not true. Maybe Gilbert [Le Coze, original chef-owner of Le Bernardin] did go to the market in the beginning to learn about the fish and what was available in America, but after a while he wasn't up at four o'clock in the morning going to the market and then working all day. That's an impossible task for anybody.

"So what is the perception of what a chef does? That's really interesting. Because we don't cook everything. People say, 'Well the food is better when you're there, Thomas.' In some cases, I've just arrived. I'm coming in the back door, I put my jacket on, I go out to say hello to a guest, and they say, 'Oh my God, thank goodness you're here, because the food is so much better when you're here.' It's not, it's the perception that it is, which is important. Don't get me wrong. Perception is about everything. So if the guest *thinks* the food is better because I'm in the dining room or in the kitchen, then the food *is* better. And that's an important thing to realize even though sometimes I believe it's not legitimate. Sometimes I feel like a fraud."

The chef had moved out of the kitchen permanently. Or could, if he or she wanted to, and ultimately would have to, even if he or she didn't want to, simply from physical limitations in a physically grueling job. You couldn't cook forever. If you wanted to continue to strive, it had to be outside the kitchen, it had to be in multiple businesses, it had to be in providing opportunities to a few devoted and talented staff. Thomas earned a management fee for his work at Bouchon Las Vegas, and he was also a 50 percent owner of it, but money was not the same concern it had been ten years earlier when his office staff had to use milk crates for chairs. He no longer agonized over making payroll. Now he could say with real pride, "Mark Hopper." I'd met Mark when he was on meat station at the French Laundry, across from Grant on fish, had been watching the night he'd let a string go out on a piece of meat, and, humiliatingly and maddeningly, got it tossed back to him when Keller, at the pass and inspecting returning plates on their way to be washed, spotted it. "Mark Hopper is the chef of a twelve-million-dollar restaurant," Keller said with pride and gratification.

He looked back on his trajectory from when the French Laundry was young and not known, now no longer in chef's whites but on a plush couch in a four-star restaurant overlooking Central Park. That first kitchen, in what is now the vestibule of the French Laundry, where they'd cooked with secondhand pots and the oven doors wouldn't stay closed and they prepped each day to the sound track of *Reservoir Dogs,* hanging out after work and playing softball on days off. Those days were gone and could never return.

"I miss the people," he said. "I'm sad. I miss being in the kitchen with them." He smiled. "I want to go back to the sandbox to play but nobody's there!"

Gregory Short is gone to San Francisco. Grant Achatz is in Chicago. Eric Ziebold is in D.C. None of them work for him anymore. Nor do Ron Siegel and Stephen Durfee, who were part of the opening French Laundry brigade. And those who do remain with the company— Jonathan Benno and Corey Lee and Mark Hopper and Jeffrey Cerciello and many others, front and back of the house—well, his dealings with them are now sporadic rather than routine.

"I'm not a chef anymore and it breaks my heart," he said. But he knew this had been inevitable, and of course he felt incredibly lucky for the course of his career. Moreover, he knew that the best way to create a legacy was not to cook till he was in his sixties, like Soltner or Giradet, but rather to pass down his standards to others who *are* cooking now, his kids, who will create the next restaurants and books and train their own staffs, on and on.

"I'm in transition," he said, at ease but busy, soon off to Vegas, then to Yountville. "I'm trying to establish a new role for myself."

⋙⋘

All of this put his four-star colleague across the marble mall floor, Masa, in sharp relief for me. Masa, I realized, was something unique in this age of the chef-CEO; he was unique perhaps to any age of the chef. He had created the most extraordinary restaurant experience in New York. *"Here is my money,"* he'd said, holding up his hands. *"Here is my money,"* he'd said, touching his chest. He'd realized this as a young man, and he would do something none of the greats had done, not Keller or Soltner or Ducasse—none of them. He'd created a single restaurant that was wholly dependent on his presence. A restaurant that without him couldn't even open. *"When I catch cold, I close the restaurant."* The goal of most chefs was to train their staffs so well that they, the chefs, didn't have to be there—when the staff could replicate a chef's goals without his being there, that was an extraordinary achievement. The chefs' goal was to make themselves completely dispensable—they considered that their ultimate success.

Masa had done the opposite. In an age of the branded chef and TV chefs and Vegas outposts and Olive Gardens and P.F. Chang's, Masa had created a restaurant so personal, so dependent on his skills and spirit and personality, that it had no meaning when he was not inside it. Masa was the artist.

EPILOGUE

The Reach of a Chef

I'd left Keller at Per Se that day and headed immediately to the airport for one last stop, a return to Chicago to see Grant Achatz. I had to know what he'd come to, where his choices had led—from dishwashing at the family restaurant, standing on a milk crate, to high school line cook, to the CIA, to chopping his own shallots at the French Laundry, to the agar and alginates and a relentless quest for innovation at Trio, to Grant now opening his own restaurant.

When I showed up the morning of May 4, 2005, opening day, Grant was positively cool; the biggest worries were an AWOL fish delivery and a broken paint gun on the patisserie station—in other words, this promised to be a smooth opening. The offices in the basement weren't finished, the sommelier was still unboxing crates of wine in the cellar to inventory, guys with tool belts strode purposefully through the restaurant adjusting light fixtures and screwing tabletops onto bases, and the brigade de cuisine worked steadily through their mise en place, in their large, long, spanking new kitchen, game day at last.

"I've been gone from Trio for nine months," Grant said. "Me and John and Curtis, we've been in the kitchen working on the menu but . . . I just want to turn an artichoke."

And so he did. He had put an artichoke dish on the menu, listed by this description: *fonds d'artichauts Cussy #3970*. That was all. I had no idea what *Cussy* designated, but Grant wondered if I'd be able to figure out the significance of the number.

The whole menu was odd like this—you couldn't possibly know what was coming based on the descriptions. Martin Kastner, the sculptor who had designed some of the funky serving pieces for Trio—"the antenna" for the bobbing salmon dish, "the squid" for the tempura shrimp—was now the full-time designer for the restaurant and had created a clean and simple menu design in which a drawing of bubbles, beneath the translucent menu page, wound up between the main ingredients column and the dish description, indicating by their diameter the intensity and size of any given dish. A tiny bubble meant the dish was a small one-biter, a large circle predicted, say, the bison dish. You could at a glance get a feel for the emotional trajectory of a meal here, like reading a musical score (as Grant had wanted long ago), a meal that consisted of anywhere between eight and twenty-eight courses.

The bison dish—five separate preparations of bison, a bite each— was described this way: *beets, blueberries, smoking cinnamon.* What to make of that? Dungeness crab was described as *raw parsnip, young coconut, cashews.*

This was the new ultramodern edge cuisine in America—you couldn't describe it adequately in words, and it didn't have, at least by name, any reference point.*

But Grant liked this style of menu and these oblique descriptions. "It's exciting, that's what I think," he said, boning three dozen pair of frogs' legs *(FROG LEGS [medium-large bubble]: spring lettuces, paprika,*

---

*Pictures of these dishes, the menu, and the restaurant can be seen on the Web site of the eGullet Society for Culinary Arts & Letters (egullet.org), in a forum devoted to discussion of the restaurant: http://forums.egullet.org/index.php?showtopic=66997&st=0.

morels). "It's romantic, like a foreigner's interaction with service, when you don't understand everything on the menu. It adds a layer of good service and excitement." Servers here have to explain a lot, he noted: "They have to coddle, there's a lot of pressure on them."

But what about the artichokes and the number? Something at the edge of my mind recognized it, I knew, but nothing came to me.

Grant said, "Escoffier."

Damn. Of course.

In his book *Le Guide Culinaire,* published in 1907, Auguste Escoffier numbers every recipe, from 1 (*Estouffade,* or brown stock: equal parts beef and veal bones; a fresh ham knuckle and fresh pork rind, both blanched; carrots; celery; and bouquet garni) to number 5012 (*Vin à la française,* claret or Burgundy with sugar and lemon).

Grant had put Escoffier recipe number 3970 on his menu—artichokes Cussy. (Louis, Marquis de Cussy, was "one of the wittiest gastronomes" of the early nineteenth century, a food writer, and prefect of the palace of Napoleon I, according to *Larousse Gastronomique.* The French were big on naming dishes after people—a shame we no longer do that.) This, too, was part of the new ultramodern cuisine, a dish straight out of Escoffier. Cooked baby artichoke hearts were stuffed with a foie gras–truffle farce, then coated in sauce Villeroi (number 160; this sauce is sauce allemande, or a velouté flavored by mushrooms, with the addition of ham and truffle essence—meant to be very thick to coat things). After it was dipped in the sauce, then placed on a rack in the freezer to set and become hard, it was breaded with panko and deep-fried for service.

Artichoke #3970 was served as a single bite on a spoon resting in a porcelain ring, a bottomless plate in effect, or "the anti-plate," as Kastner called it, and garnished with a piece of fried parsley.

"Foie gras, truffles, and artichoke—it's perfect for us," Grant says. "It's a reference point for diners, shows us how far, or not far, we've come—I don't know. It's more than a hundred years old and it's new. And"—he grins—"it's a personal F-U to all those people who say, 'Ah those guys just work with foam over there.' We know how to work with foie gras, we know how to turn a lot of baby artichokes."

❖

The sleek rectangular kitchen, with two islands running on each side of a wide central isle beneath sleek hanging light fixtures, bustled. All cooks had their own stations and, at their stations, lowboy coolers and refrigerated drawers. One of the smartest design decisions he realized they'd made, Grant says, was to eliminate from the design a walk-in cooler. There was one large reach-in cooler and freezer, but for the most part, everyone could store his own food at his station; this way you didn't have everyone running back and forth to the walk-in—a great time-saver. Each person could more or less arrive at his station, get set up, and stay there all day.

Alex Stupak, the young pastry chef, was out back with a new paint gun from Home Depot. He'd filled it with very fatty chocolate. He'd set liquid chocolate that had been frozen and cut into rectangles on racks over sheet trays and was spraying them with chocolate that would become a shell for the chocolate that would melt within (*LIQUID CHOC-OLATE [big bubble] milk, black licorice, banana*).

The errant fish delivery arrived, and Curtis was breaking down and portioning turbot. He, too, was very excited the restaurant was at last opening. The biggest surprise in building and opening a restaurant, he said, was, "All the trades that come through here don't work at the same level of urgency as we do."

For all the past talk of foams and encapsulated liquids, there was very little visual evidence of the out-there food Grant was known for. Cooks cutting vegetables, stirring sauces. Grant had gotten to work on a big container of fresh hearts of palms, slicing dozens for the tasting of stuffed hearts of palm. My friend Jeffrey Pikus, who'd run out of bacon months earlier, was on meat station, cooking beets sous-vide for the bison, cleaning morels for the frogs' legs, rolling sheets of potato for the "beef with A-1 Sauce," and cooking them in rendered beef fat. Mary Radigan was frying little pieces of dough that had to puff so that she could inject them with chocolate. John Peters cryovacked bison after he finished glazing the artichokes.

If you looked carefully, though, here and there you'd catch signs of the unconventional. One of the pastry cooks was using the sugar tuile technique to create ultra-delicate tubes that he was filling with nuts and puffed wild rice, bulgur, hazelnuts, oats, toasted with curry and honey, and freeze-dried apricots. The syringe at Mary Radigan's station wasn't an item you'd find on most cooks' stations. One of the cooks lifted skin off heated soy milk, called *yuba*. This skin would become the wrapper for snapper. A white boxlike appliance being set out for service at the rear end of the pastry station island was something I'd never seen. Grant had this built for him by a man who designs cooling devices for hospitals. It's kind of like a small reverse flattop. The steel surface doesn't get hot, it gets cold, −47 degrees Fahrenheit. It will freeze a small spoonful of a sour cream mixture dropped onto its surface into a mini-blini shape. The chef in charge of this dish would hold a sorrel leaf in the mixture till it set up, then lift the sour cream off the surface by holding the leaf and rest it in a small circular holder, then shave frozen smoked salmon over it.

※

By 5:10 most people were wiping down their stations, but not all—a few were scrambling even though they'd spent eight hours prepping yesterday. A few minutes later Grant called out, "Fifteen minutes!" and all called it back to him. Vacuums began to hum over the carpeted mats. Others swept the floor. Grant had found a rag and a can of stainless steel cleaner and buffed every counter and steel surface in sight. Huge bouquets of purple and pink hyacinth had been laid out at the fish station, fragrance for the turbo dish.

Nick Kokonas was in and out of the kitchen, helping to oversee front of the house for his first restaurant opening: later he would eat with his wife and some friends. The first reservations, which they'd limited to forty in the sixty-five-seat restaurant, arrived promptly at 5:30, and the service began. A new restaurant had opened.

❧

The night went smoothly, particularly given the complexity of the dishes and how long they take to pick up. This is a good thing because, unlike Per Se, which hosted a series of "friends and family" dinners, practice services to work out the kinks, Alinea opened cold. And already the pressure was on; in fact, it was shaking Grant's hand.

Melissa Clark, a regular freelancer for the dining pages of *The New York Times,* arrived in the kitchen shortly after six to say hello to Grant. Evidently, the only way to get a reservation was to say who she was—not exactly an ideal situation for her but the only resort. She had told Grant that she happened to be in town visiting an old friend and was dying to check out the restaurant—could he squeeze her and her friend in? This story, however, had been thrown slightly into question when a photographer called requesting an elaborate photo shoot for *The New York Times* a couple of days earlier.

Grant didn't know what to make of it. The *Times* doesn't do official restaurant reviews of out-of-town places. If the paper were planning to critique it in any way, they'd certainly wait, for fairness' sake, for the restaurant to establish itself and iron out any opening-day glitches, before judging it. If a profile were planned, surely Grant would have been told this and been interviewed. He hadn't been yet, and the elaborate photography seemed to signal more than just a note about its opening. He wasn't going to think about it—he'd do what needed to be done, which was to oversee and help expedite Alinea's first night of service.

Melissa has straight reddish hair and big blue eyes, a thin frame, and an intense, highly caffeinated manner. She knows the flowers at the pass are hyacinth before you know it, and she knows the name of the flowering tree out the window which you've never heard of before. She talks fast and friendly. Immediately, almost embarrassed, it seems, she expressed her gratitude for the reservation.

"Thanks for finessing this," she said to Grant.

"No problem," Grant said, smiling, apparently at ease.

After exchanging a few more words, Grant stepped away to work on some outgoing dishes, and I whispered to Melissa, whom I'd met once before, "*What* are you doing here?"

Seeming not to move her lips but looking me in the eyes, she said, "Don't ask, don't ask, don't ask."

"It's not a secret that photographers were already here."

She rolled her eyes while shaking her head and said, "I *know.*"

⇥⇤

About a half hour later Grant strolled through the rooms on both floors, descending the back stairs into the kitchen, shaking his head. He moved immediately to the pass, and I didn't ask him why he was shaking his head.

When I'd had enough of standing around watching the food, I asked Grant if he thought they might be able to seat me. He said whenever I wanted. In the basement—even this space containing the wine cellar, the unfinished offices, some dry storage, and a washing machine and a laundry press so they could count on fresh linen (Grant was unhappy with linen service in Chicago, so decided to do his own) had fresh concrete and a new-wood smell to it—I changed my shirt and put on a jacket. I left through a rear door, walked around to the front of the building on what was a fine, warm spring evening, and entered Alinea. The entrance was tunneled, a visual illusion of shrinking space, making one's first emotional response to the restaurant a down-the-rabbit-hole *whoa*. I was escorted up the central Escher-like staircase and seated one empty table away from Melissa and her "friend"—Frank Bruni. Bruni looked at me and gave me a long, slow speechless nod—clearly an instruction. I'm not sure what he expected I'd do or say. *"FRANK BRUNI! WHAT IN*

THE HAM SANDWICH IS THE MOST INFLUENTIAL RESTAURANT REVIEWER IN THE COUNTRY DOING IN CHICAGO!?" He really does try to maintain as much anonymity as possible, so I kept my big mouth shut.

Grant already suspected it was Bruni, obviously. That's what he'd been shaking his head about when he trotted down the back steps. But then, there wasn't anything more he could do at this point. Just stay focused and keep the plates coming out as perfect as he and his brigade could make them.

⊰⋅⊱

The rooms are elegant, handsome, understated. There was nothing on the dark mahogany table except for a metal disk, gold and silver against the black wood beneath the folded napkin. A hand of ginger, sliced in half lengthwise to expose its yellow flesh, recomposed as a small sculpture with three long needles, was set down as a table ornament and would be used later in the meal. The floral decorations in the restaurant were all related to gastronomy in some way. Some very funky-looking broad-stalked plants on a central buffet, for instance, were fancy manipulations of a rhubarb plant. The room was quiet and the service was slightly awkward, in an opening-night way, but easy and friendly, not uptight.

The first course was called PB&J, which came off of Mary Radigan's station. A peeled green grape, still attached to its stem, had been glazed with peanut butter, sprinkled with chopped peanuts, and rolled in a very thin slice of bread, then lightly toasted under a salamander and placed in the arms of the squid, its cylindrical base fitting snugly into the silver-gold disk on my table—a lovely first bite, which led to a series of good to extraordinary courses, always fascinating.

The standout for me was an early course composed of a custardlike bar of raw parsnip, young coconut, and cashew nut that had been frozen and whipped in a Pacojet (the coolest toy in many restaurant kitchens—it freezes, then purees into a delicate ice cream–like texture just about any food). On top of this bar—the mixture had been spread on a sheet pan, kept frozen, then cut—rested a big chunk of crab, long noodlelike curls of sweet young coconut, a dehydrated chip of the parsnip puree, tiny basil leaves, saffron threads, and toasted cashews, with a small spoonful of a saffron vinaigrette. Parsnip-cashew-crab-saffron. Strange and wonderful, a completely comfortable dish to eat and completely new.

Not everything worked. The least successful dish was the most surreal and vivid-looking—julienne of prosciutto were formed into disks, dehydrated, and used to sandwich a passion fruit sponge. Grant rested these constructions in a small patch of living green sprouts called zuta levana, a eucalyptusy-minty herb often used in tea. It was a miniature still life, old wheels abandoned in a suburban lawn. The wheels were really chewy, and I thought the sponge was odd. The food was cool to look at but the flavors weren't especially good, didn't seem to go together, and the textures were unpleasant. (I'd find out later where the error lay—Grant tested this in Kokonas's kitchen and everyone loved them, and the kids ate them like candy. But the requirement to prepare the prosciutto wheels in advance for the restaurant and the humid environment of the Alinea kitchen left them overly chewy by service. The dish didn't translate from the home kitchen to the restaurant kitchen, and it was taken off the menu.)

Two dishes in particular revealed to me what had happened to Grant since I'd eaten at Trio nearly a year earlier. The first was the turbot. I was glad the delivery had arrived—it's a great fish to eat. Grant served it in a kind of frothy liquid custard, along with mussels, geoduck clam, and water chestnuts. The fish was perfectly cooked, with great body and flavor, the chestnuts and clam slightly crunchy, the soup-sauce soothing and smelling of the sea, mingling with the spring aroma of the hyacinths floating in a liner bowl that had been filled with steaming-hot water by my server. New flavors and combinations, the unconventional hyacinth vapor, but enormously satisfying to eat. Warm. Comforting luxury.

The second was *HAZELNUT PUREE [medium bubble]: capsule of savory granola, curry.* This was a sweet-spicy-crunchy dish, a sauce and puree in a glass bowl over which was set an enclosed golden brown cylinder. With a tap of a spoon, I broke the cylinder, a pleasant crack, and the contents spilled into the puree. It was nutty and sweet and spicy from the curry, creamy and crunchy. A kind of marvel of textures and flavors that I enjoyed for the sake of themselves until it dawned on me that I was eating a granola and yogurt breakfast, and I smiled at the fun of it. The strangeness had come from within the dish, and from without it was a pleasure of flavors and textures. Unusual and unfamiliar but still sensual and comforting and luxurious, even humorous.

Gone were the bizarre creations like the "pizza" on a pin and the shrimp cocktail spritzer, all those experiments of an innovative chef extending himself that have a cold and distancing effect on the eater, no matter how intellectually intriguing or new. At Trio, Grant had traveled beyond what he ought to have been doing in order to know his right and comfortable mark. He had to reach beyond what he could actually grasp in order to know the true range of that grasp. He'd found it here in Alinea.

Clark and Bruni at the next table talked and chuckled, puzzled and *mmm*-ed (at the artichoke especially, the frogs' legs, and the foie gras with rhubarb, onion, and walnut), and also shrugged. No matter their response (they liked the meal), what was significant to me was that this thirty-one-year-old chef, opening his first restaurant—in the heartland, no less—had lured *The New York Times*. Bruni's article that appeared the following Wednesday, a kind of survey of those restaurants plying the edge cuisine that used Alinea's opening as the hook for the article—a picture of a prosciutto wheel stuck in the grass ran big and bold above the fold—had a slightly condescending tone relative to the seriousness of the intent of the restaurant, but nevertheless claimed that the opening of Alinea "marks a milestone and invites an examination of how meaningfully this kind of cooking, born in Europe and pioneered in large part by the chef Ferran Adrià in Spain, has taken root in the United States."

Before the summer was out, even Ferran Adrià's brother Albert had come to eat. ("It was a great dinner and, as I said to you, one of the best of my life," Albert wrote after returning to Spain. "I have spoken with a lot of people about the quality and precision of your kitchen. You will be well known in Spain in a short time." His brother Ferran would be coming to the States and to Alinea later in the year.)

More members of the press and chefs were on their way. Ruth Reichl, editor of *Gourmet,* reserved a table. Amanda Hesser was in the same night Jeffrey Steingarten ate there. Steingarten, the lawyer turned eminent and highly respected food author, would write about Grant in his column in *Vogue.* Hesser later called Grant about doing an article for the Sunday *New York Times Magazine* supplement "T-Living." The *Chicago Tribune* and the *Chicago Sun-Times* were in, of course, as were the *Washington Post* and the *Boston Globe.* And *CBS News Sunday Morning* had called to ask to tape a segment there.

It was hard to imagine a more auspicious opening, with so many of the food elite traveling to Chicago to eat at Alinea. Moreover, business was brisk with reservations holding at seventy to eighty-five each night through the summer (normally a slow season), and the $185 check average was higher than they'd predicted.

I'd become a great admirer of Grant. I'd first watched him as a twenty-something line cook when I myself was just entering this bizarre, intense world, and look what he'd done. Impressive by any standards, even if he used to serve shrimp out of a mouth spritzer. He had arrived on the scene when the culinary climate in America was ripe, and he could cook for a more involved and savvy dining public eager to pay to try new food. Charlie Trotter and Thomas Keller had opened the doors to a kind of new landscape of fine dining in America, offering tasting menus of rarefied ingredients and elaborate technique to a country that knew only the protein-starch-veg meal, and big portions at that.

Grant had fully adopted the standards of these seminal kitchens to the point that their innovations seemed no longer innovations but rather the standard. Perfection doesn't exist, his mentor had said, because once you reach it, it means something else. So it is, too, with innovation: once meaningful innovation has been achieved, it quickly ceases to be innovative because others imitate it. His new menu, served three months after opening, contained items like *"crispy sheet of foam"* and *"pillow of lavender air."*

Who could say where this would lead? Grant had absorbed his chefs' innovations in fine dining in America, then found a source of extraordinary inspiration, a spark that would ignite this volatile creative fuel, in Ferran Adrià outside Barcelona, and propel those Charlie Trotter/Thomas Keller standards into new territory. Grant had extended the reach of the chef in America and upped the ante with his intent to make innovation itself the driving force in his kitchen, in work that was an ongoing evolution of creativity in food and cooking.

⌖

But he was just one chef cooking in a country bursting with talent and energy. Grant had pursued cooking with uncommon focus and efficiency. He had not only worked in great kitchens under greats from the previous generation but had learned faster and better than any of his contemporaries what that generation had to teach, and with Alinea, Grant was off like a rocket.

Melissa Kelly, a workhorse of a chef serving casual food in the best possible way in her old Victorian on a hill in Maine, not only thrived there but had opened Primos in distant parts of the country—Orlando and Tucson—restaurants that underscored her own convictions about working with farmers, cooking simply with the best ingredients. She'd even bent a giant corporation, Marriott, to agree to plant gardens and initiate a recycling program in those cities.

That previous generation, which trained the Grants and Melissas, were at or approaching age fifty, but weren't out to pasture. These chefs were using their thirty-plus years of experience to drive this profession forward as well. Keller's work as an innovator was less visible now. His influence was more in a continual raising of standards, raising the expectations of his staff, his customers, his fellow chefs, and his work was largely creating opportunities for his staff while growing his business.

Masa Takayama—he was the same generation as Keller, and he had been cooking as long, but his standards were learned, were grown into him, in Japan, in a 150-year-old sushi house. America had proved such a fertile culinary market that this solitary man could create not one of the country's most expensive restaurants but rather a restaurant that was unique, dependent on him alone, and expressing a culture of delicacy and artistry in a land famous for its love of meat and potatoes.

How far we'd come in America that enough people would pay $500 for a meal of raw fish and rice to support a restaurant in some of the most expensive real estate in the country. Indeed, in its first two years, Masa's space was the most profitable of the Time Warner food establishments.

Judy Rodgers, chef at one of the great American restaurants, Zuni Café, makes the point that if food is more expensive, that's not necessarily a bad thing—"We'd waste less food if it were more expensive," she says. And this is true, not so much by way of Masa's example, but of the food we eat on a daily basis. Artisanal food, hand-raised pork, free-range chickens, grass-fed beef, vegetables at the farmer's markets burgeoning throughout the country—this kind of food is often more expensive than what you can find wrapped in plastic at the grocery store. While some worry that this makes cooking with the best ingredients a form of elitism, Rodgers suggests that if we all had to pay more for our food, we'd take better care of it and better care of ourselves, and she's right. Expensive food in this fat, resource-rich country has great long-term benefits.

If there's a female counterpart to Keller, as rustic Melissa is to scientific Grant, it's Judy Rodgers in her funky San Francisco restaurant. She cooks in a corduroy skirt, stockings, and a sweater, and can't stand it when her cooks call her "Chef." She's also on the brink of fifty and has been a cook all her adult life. She has a powerful voice in the country, imploring us, by the example of her food and her restaurant and her excellent book, to pay attention. It's not necessarily a good thing to be able to have strawberries in January so we can garnish a deli plate in

New York or your Cheerios in a Kansas City Sheraton only to throw the strawberry out.

"That's what we're up against," she says, "that it's perceived as a *triumph* that you can get strawberries in January as opposed to a catastrophe. Not all choice is good. Even if the January strawberry tastes OK, even if you have a really good strawberry that's organic, I still know you turned down other things for that to happen.

"Part of not getting tired of food and cooking is not having every option every day, it's responding to your constraints. You don't have that much to work with, so you have to be more resourceful. If I were in St. Louis"—her hometown—"I'd have a different palate of flavors to play with, I'd have to be more resourceful, I'd probably be more aggressive about putting stuff up myself during the season, and guess what? *That's what culinary tradition is*—making the harvest season last all year long. My God, the most unique holiday we have is Thanksgiving. If you really ponder what Thanksgiving is all about, you would really understand *food*. But so many people think it's about gluttony, the beginning of the eating season—as opposed to truly revering this, your great harvest celebration, and now put stuff up so you don't starve over the winter."

This is Keller's colleague and contemporary with whom he can, through food and cooking, teach this country how to think about food, which of course is only a step or two away from teaching people how to think about life, which of course is the territory of the artist.

Some chefs argue with me for saying that chefs are craftsmen and not artists. Every chef is not an artist, but those chefs like Keller and Rodgers and Masa and Grant and Melissa, who try to tell us, through the example of their food, how we might live, they truly are the artists—artists who happen to be chefs.

≼▪≽

But Keller himself said he was not even cooking, that he wasn't a chef anymore in the old conception of it. What is "the chef" then? What kind of shoes does the chef wear today? What does a chef do? And have we lost something forever because of it?

The chef today is running a company, now composed of many separate businesses. The chef isn't in the kitchen, he's in the office. He wears a business jacket, not a chef's coat. He puts on a chef's coat for photo shoots and gives interviews to the press that he hopes will be good for his businesses. He meets with or conference-calls the general managers and chefs de cuisine of his various restaurants. Soon these chefs won't cook either, if they advance. Pretty soon, *they've* got on a business jacket. The chef puts on a Brooks Brothers no-iron shirt and a pair of casual slacks and moves into retail. The chef licenses his name to manufacturers, and he visits the factory in France or California to observe the quality of the product and meet with the company's directors. He puts on a hard hat to view the new restaurant under construction. Flying home he reviews the proofs of the manuscript for the next book, which has been created by another faction of his team.

"The chef is the one who's setting the standard," Keller says. "The chef expresses a vision. The chef motivates people. The chef gives his staff the tools they need to excel. Is that being a CEO? Definitely."

This fact, the fact that the chef is a CEO, changes the whole restaurant culture, forces the people working in it to reevaluate their skills and their ambitions, a reevaluation that begins now all the way back in cooking school, where so many young culinarians begin their careers. The changing nature of the work of a chef is shaping the schools that are shaping the kids. And the best of them will open restaurants like Primo and Alinea, they'll move into food corporations and hospitality institutions and raise the standards there. Some of them will find their way onto television and perhaps have the most influence of any of their colleagues because of the vast numbers of people they can reach through this medium, provided they remember food television is about personality and entertainment and only incidentally about food.

The chef is now a powerful force, and with that power the chef can start businesses, develop products, and change people's minds. Is this a good thing? If the business is a good one, it is; if the product is good, yes. But only if.

⊰▪⊱

Within all this complexity—chefs traveling around the globe, everywhere but in their own restaurants it sometimes seems—all this product development, entertainment, rollouts, buyouts, licensing, and merchandising, where is the romance of professional cooking? The chef in his kitchen, the romantic life of the chef. Was it a lie, a kind of consumer-generated fantasy that made it more fun to eat out and made more respectable the slog of kitchen work? The best in the country scarcely cooked anymore *as a direct result of their success at cooking.* If it was inevitable that the best in this field ultimately selected themselves out, was the American restaurant in danger of a kind of reverse Darwinism? A thriving of the least fit? Somehow that doesn't seem outlandish in this crazy food-neurotic country, driven by agribusiness that eliminates the variety of our crops and debases our livestock. But is it true?

No, because Melissa is in the kitchen this very moment, and so is Grant, and Masa's restaurant can't open if he's not in his kitchen. Polcyn and Pardus and Turgeon are teaching scores of the next generation— they're in their whites and holding a student's chef's knife to begin a demo, and if that knife isn't sharp as a straight razor, I hope they keep that knife till the student learns that his or her knives are sacred. They are the tools of the trade—and it *is* a trade, a proud one when it's properly practiced, and also a trade that can become an art only if the cook chooses to stay in the kitchen. The kitchen is where the complexity of the professional cooking world is not muddled by business-school jargon and greedy ambition and ego. The product is good or it is not, it's cooked right or it's not, it's delicious or it is not. The end makes it clear.

When this whole chef world gets too complicated, when all this talk of branding is too much, and the head spins with notions of rollouts and management contracts and licensing deals and charitable foundations and television opportunities and Vegas, there's always this: the kitchen. We've all got to eat. A kitchen is a good place to be, almost always the best place in the house, whether that house is a home or a restaurant. A place where you can't lie to yourself. Go to the kitchen. Wipe down your counter till it shines. Set out a heavy cutting board. Steel a paring knife and a chef's knife. Gather your shallots, your parsley, your tomatoes, and the rest of your mise en place, and stand in one place and cook for a long time. That's the greatest thing about a kitchen— it's guaranteed always to be there, will always be only and exactly what it is. That's where the greatness begins. And it will be there for you when you come back in from the complex world that it opened up for you.

❧❧

ACKNOWLEDGMENTS

I'd like to thank all the chefs who participated in this book. They were unfailingly generous with their time, their knowledge, and their kitchens.

I'd also like to thank, as ever, my agent, Elizabeth Kaplan, and my editor, Ray Roberts. I'm grateful also to production editor Bruce Giffords at Viking. The copy editor of this book, John Jusino, deserves special thanks for saving me from innumerable embarrassments regarding name spellings and dangling clauses.

Two magazines, *Gourmet* and *Golf Connoisseur,* gave me assignments (and travel and expense money) to pursue information that is included in this book, material I'd have been unable to get otherwise.

Last, I'd like to thank my family for allowing me so much time away—and for being so fine when I got home.

❧·❧